LEGENDARY LOCALS

OF

NORTH RIDGEVILLE

OHIO

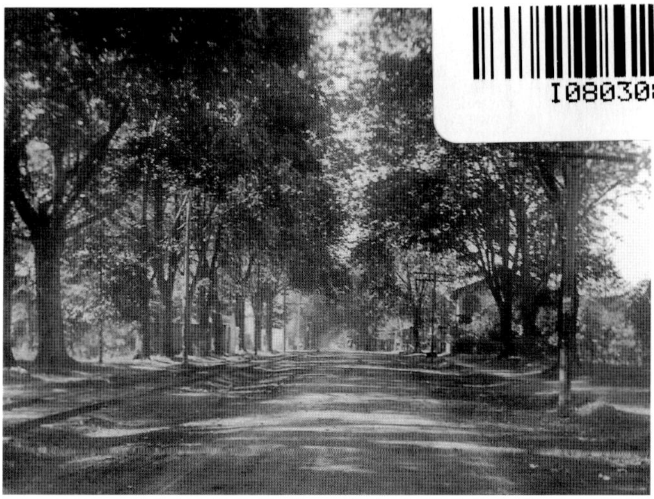

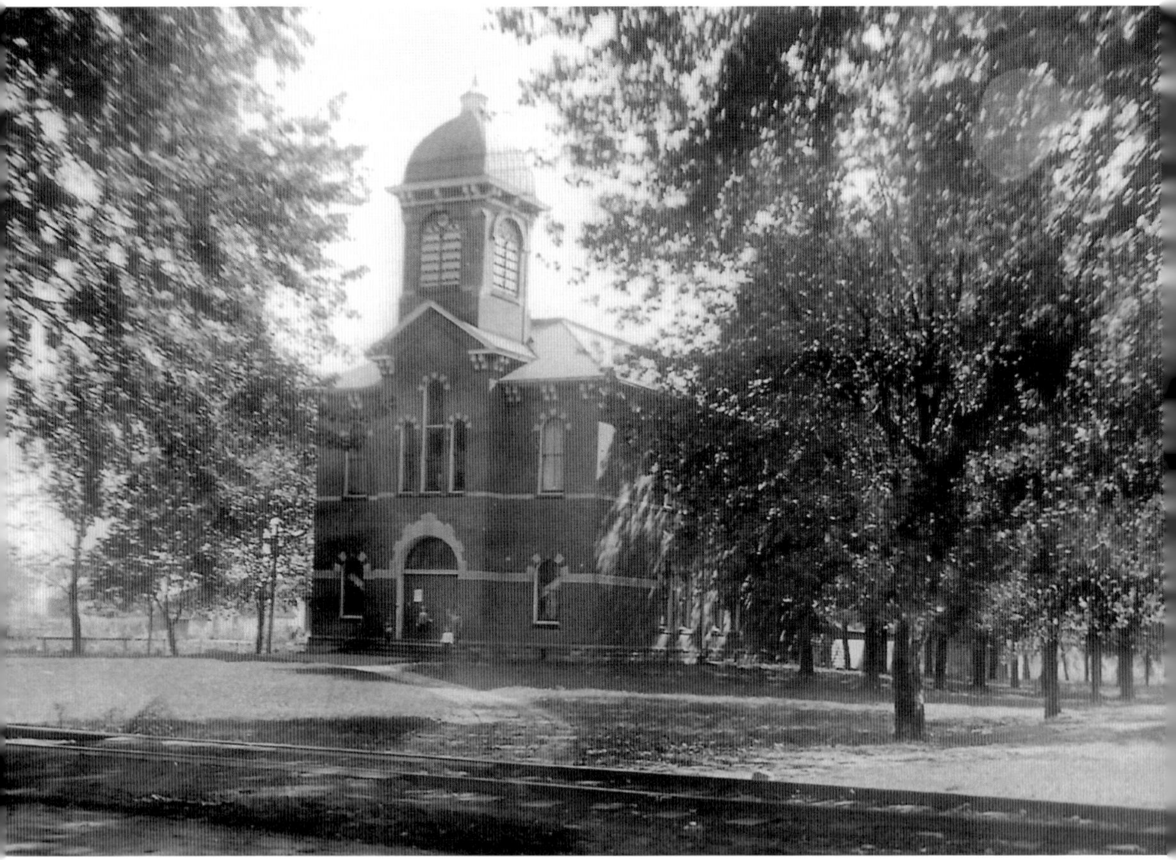

The Landmark
North Ridgeville's landmark, the Old Town Hall, was built in 1882–1883 on Center Ridge Road (Route 20), west of Avon Belden Road (Route 83). (Courtesy of the North Ridgeville Historical Society.)

Page 1: Center Ridge Road
Ridgeville Township's first settlers planted maple seedlings along both sides of Center Ridge Road (Route 20) in 1821. As they grew, the trees formed a canopy over much of the road. (Courtesy of the North Ridgeville Historical Society.)

LEGENDARY LOCALS

OF

NORTH RIDGEVILLE

OHIO

CAROL G. KLEAR

LEGENDARY LOCALS

ISBN 978-1-4671-0144-8

Legendary Locals is an imprint of Arcadia Publishing
Charleston, South Carolina

Printed in the United States of America

Library of Congress Control Number: 2013955110

For all general information, please contact Arcadia Publishing:
Telephone 843-853-2070
Fax 843-853-0044
E-mail sales@arcadiapublishing.com
For customer service and orders:
Toll-Free 1-888-313-2665

Visit us on the Internet at www.arcadiapublishing.com

Dedication
To the residents of North Ridgeville, past, present, and future, each of whom has a story to tell.

On the Front Cover: Clockwise from top left:
Urban Buescher, hardware store owner (courtesy of Nita Baker; see pages 40, 41), Dennis Boose, banker and actor (courtesy of the Rotary Club of North Ridgeville; see page 92), Spencer Myer, concert pianist (courtesy of Spencer Myer; see page 107), Deanna Hill and former mayors (courtesy of Eugene Kleinholz; see page 38), John Musson, retired judge and reenactor (courtesy of John Musson; see pages 98, 99), Sister Mary Patricia, SND, school principal (courtesy of Sister Mary Patricia Vovk; see page 108), Russell Sigsworth, World War II pilot (courtesy of Russell Sigsworth; see page 122), Edward Ratusz, restaurant owner (courtesy of Kathy Hepp; see pages 50, 51), Richard Monaco, antique-shop owner (courtesy of Carol Klear; see page 42).

On the Back Cover: From left to right:
Gary and Toni Krone, farm owners (courtesy of Toni Krone; see page 15), Dorothy and Harry Painter, June Yost, and the Corn Festival mascot (courtesy of the North Ridgeville Historical Society; see page 79).

CONTENTS

ACKNOWLEDGMENTS

The author thanks all who contributed to this book with their stories, as well as the following people, who shared their personal photographs: Jeffry Armbruster, Patricia Bahr, Nita Baker, Ronald Bauer, Georgann Blair, Jeanne and Leonard Boey, Kathleen and Harold Bogner, Nancy Bowman, Bernadine and John Butkowski, Brother Ray Carpenter, William and Regina Comerford, Paula Cope, Kevin Corcoran, Susan Crobaugh, Pastor Kevin and Robin Crow, William Davis III, Janet Devine, Eugene Diederich, Geraldine and Wayne Diederich, Loyola Diederich, Patricia Fallon, Robert Franks, the Gerhart family, Jean Gilder, G. David Gillock, Audrey Ginley, James Ginley, Patrick Ginley, Rev. Dr. Richard Gonser, Ronald Granneman, the Halagan family, Kathy Hepp, Scott Hosler, James Johnson, John Kapelka, Thomas Klear, Eugene Kleinholz, Toni and Gary Krone, Laurence Kuchenrither, Robert LeHoty, Marge Lesnick, Barb Mamrak, Gayle Manning, Garry Minute, Kerry Mueller, John Musson, Spencer Myer, Pamela Nolan, Dayle Noll, John T. O'Neill, Floyd Peaco, Rita Price, Norman Rak, Robert Schmittgen, Mary Ann Serazin, Karen and Jeff Sigsworth, the Sismour family, Joyce and Joseph Solomon, Michelle Stambaugh, St. Peter Parish, Barbara Sutton, Allen Swindig, Maria Sycz, Marcia Thibo, Sister Mary Patricia Vovk, Karen Ware, James White, and Alan Willoughby.

I also offer my appreciation to the *Chronicle-Telegram*, Lake Ridge Academy, North Ridgeville Chamber of Commerce, North Ridgeville Fire Department, North Ridgeville Historical Society, North Ridgeville Kiwanis Club, North Ridgeville Lions Club, *North Ridgeville Press*, Olde Towne Hall Theatre, and Rotary Club of North Ridgeville for allowing me to use their resources to compile the stories in this book.

I extend special thank-yous to St. Jude; to my editor, Amy Perryman, for her advice and patience; to my family, for their loving support; and to my husband, Thomas Klear, who again played the role of my courier and, even more, for always being the wind beneath my wings.

INTRODUCTION

It was the spring of 1810, and, though the idea seemed foolhardy to some, a group of men in Waterbury, Connecticut, were talking about leaving their home and heading west, to what they hoped would be a new life in a land of promise for them and their families.

As the days went on, they became increasingly restless and impatient to begin what might be a long and arduous journey. But their staunch New England determination overcame any doubts they might have had, and the band of men, many from the Terrell and Beebe families, packed belongings, including tools, food, clothing, and blankets, and, with horses and wagons, made their way to Ohio.

On May 10, 1810, the pioneers reached their destination and set about establishing the first community, which they called Rootstown. This would ultimately become North Ridgeville. When word traveled back to Waterbury, others followed the example of those who had gone before, and they, too, migrated from Connecticut to Ohio, including the first female settler, Electa Wilmot Terrell.

The initial priority was to clear land and construct shelters, but the need for food was vital as well, so some of the men tilled the soil and began planting, hoping that good weather would produce healthy crops of wheat, corn, and other foodstuffs. The conditions proved more difficult than the pioneers had anticipated, but they forged ahead with their plans, determined to stay the course they had set for themselves. As time went on, small farms sprang up. Over the years, the ever-expanding acres of land responded to the constant care of the farmers who tended to them.

With the basic needs of shelter, food, and water met, the settlers began considering ways of educating the children who joined the pathfinders in their quest for a better life. Initially, the youngsters were taught in a one-room cabin belonging to one of the pioneers. In the spring of 1814, the first log schoolhouse was constructed, on the northeast corner of Center Ridge Road and Center/Avon Belden Road, now Routes 20 and 83. It was 18 feet by 22 feet, with a fireplace at one end, where logs often caught fire. The first teacher was Lydia Terrell, age 16 or 17, who taught in the summer of 1814. She died before the term ended after contracting an illness. Betsy Shellhouse, 19, took her place, followed by John Reading Jr., 28, the first male teacher.

In 1821, the settlement divided into two school districts, east and west. People in the center of town were unhappy with the arrangement and built their own school. As the community grew, it was divided into 10 school districts, with one school in each district, including the one-room schoolhouse in District 9 on Snow Road (now Jaycox Road), located just south of Mills Road. The main subjects were reading and spelling, though older students were taught writing, and the older boys were instructed in arithmetic.

Through the years, the education system began to thrive, and much larger schools replaced the original one-room buildings. Children were separated by grades, and the older students were housed in the high school. The first graduating class from Ridgeville High School was in 1926, with 15 members. The following year, the number doubled. Subjects were added to the curriculum, including such courses as art and music. In 1963, Lake Ridge Academy joined the framework of the city's education system, and the private school was established for students from kindergarten through high school.

As the school system developed, so did the political situation. In 1813, adult males in the settlement approved the creation of Ridgeville Township, a designation that remained for 145 years. It was later learned that there was another community named Ridgeville, in the southern part of Ohio, near Dayton. This caused mix-ups and frustrations over mail delivery. To resolve the situation, the postmaster requested Ridgeville Township be renamed North Ridgeville. In 1958, with an ever-increasing population, the township became a village and, two years later, was deemed a city.

The early settlers had a strong faith, and they began holding prayer services in homes. In 1822, the First Congregational United Church of Christ was founded, and a frame building was constructed to house worshippers. In 1875, the present church, located on Center Ridge Road near Stoney Ridge Road, replaced the earlier building. The Reverend Joseph Trapp served the congregation at St. Peter Catholic Church in the early 1900s. Trapp not only was a devoted priest, but also enjoyed the hobby of photography. During his time in Ridgeville, he took many photographs of everyday life. These images are treasured today for the visual history they offer.

Farms continued to flourish, but they were not the only institutions that took root in Ridgeville. Small shops and other businesses were formed. Many of them that began in the 1900s have continued, some having been passed down to younger family members, such as Buescher's Hardware and Becker's Donuts. Police and fire departments took shape as well, to ensure that the community those first pioneers had worked so hard to establish would be protected. Some of the town's citizens also joined the military and went to war, putting themselves in harm's way to defend not only their town, but the nation as a whole.

CHAPTER ONE

Sowers and Growers

Tilling the soil was part of the daily lives of the early pioneers. As Rootstown grew into Ridgeville Township and later North Ridgeville, farms continued to be sources of livelihood for many people. There were years when Mother Nature did not smile on the farmers, and their crops were diminished or destroyed by heavy rains or below-freezing temperatures. However, when conditions were favorable, one of the main commodities in North Ridgeville was corn, grown on the Sweet family's farm. True to its name, the Sweets' corn had a fresh, succulent taste that was so appealing it became the basis for the city's annual Corn Festival, which began 40 years ago to honor Harold and Lorna Sweet.

As the years went on, the Corn Festival began attracting people from across Ohio and beyond. Members of the festival committee also began giving back to the community by donating a portion of the proceeds to such places as the Old Town Hall, which was in need of structural repairs. The Gerhart Farm on Avon Belden Road produced a variety of vegetables and shared them at farmers' markets. Acreage on the same road included the Solomons' strawberry farm. Although the Solomons raised other foods, their large, luscious strawberries took center stage.

While the produce farms were plentiful, other growers decided to raise flowers, and constructed greenhouses in which to do so. These growers, as well regarded as the farmers who sowed fields of grain and vegetables, included J.P. Diederich Sons, one of the oldest businesses in North Ridgeville; Minute Greenhouse; and Thibo Brothers Greenhouse.

One of the community's earliest farmers was Mathias Nuhn, who was born in Alsace Lorraine and whose family came to America and eventually to Ridgeville Township in the early 1800s. Nuhn's father bought land on Case Road and built a house for his family. The red clapboard house remains today, as stately as when it was constructed.

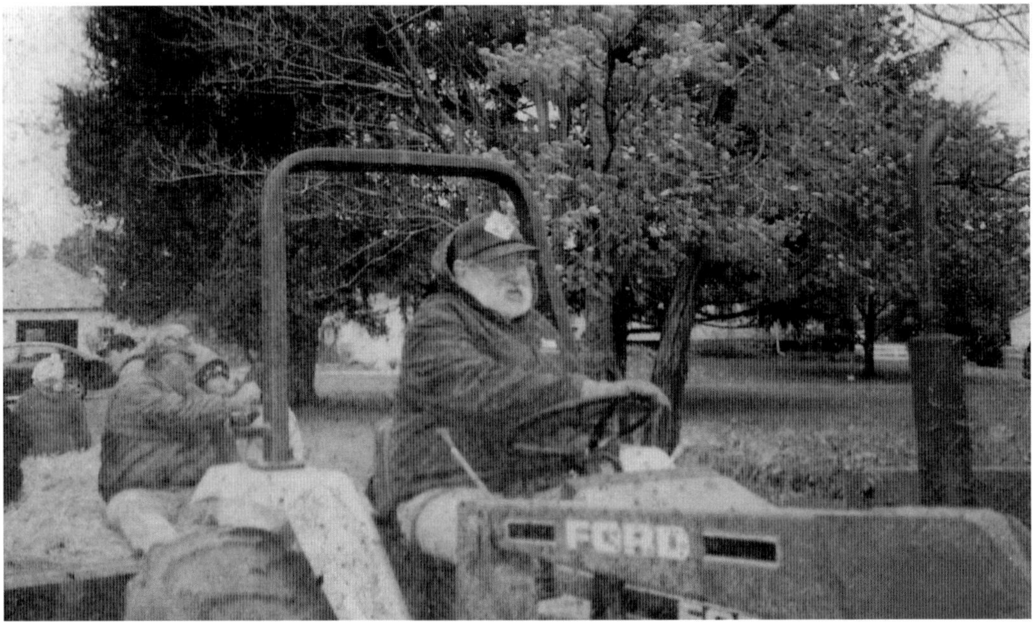

Joseph and Joyce Solomon

The Solomons' 20-acre farm was at one time known as Strawberry Farm for the tasty, red fruits raised there. Strawberries were not their only crop, but they were the highlight of the farm. Joyce Solomon's grandfather Frank Bommer built a house in the 1800s just north of where their house would later be and had 14 acres of grapes he used to make wine. Joseph Solomon (above) recalled weather that was so cold at times that he had to spray the strawberries to salvage them, sporting icicles on his whiskers in the process. At one time, the Solomons took their produce to a farmers' market in Oberlin to sell, but not long ago, they began scaling back the number of crops they grow and turning to raising beef. (Both, courtesy of Joyce Solomon.)

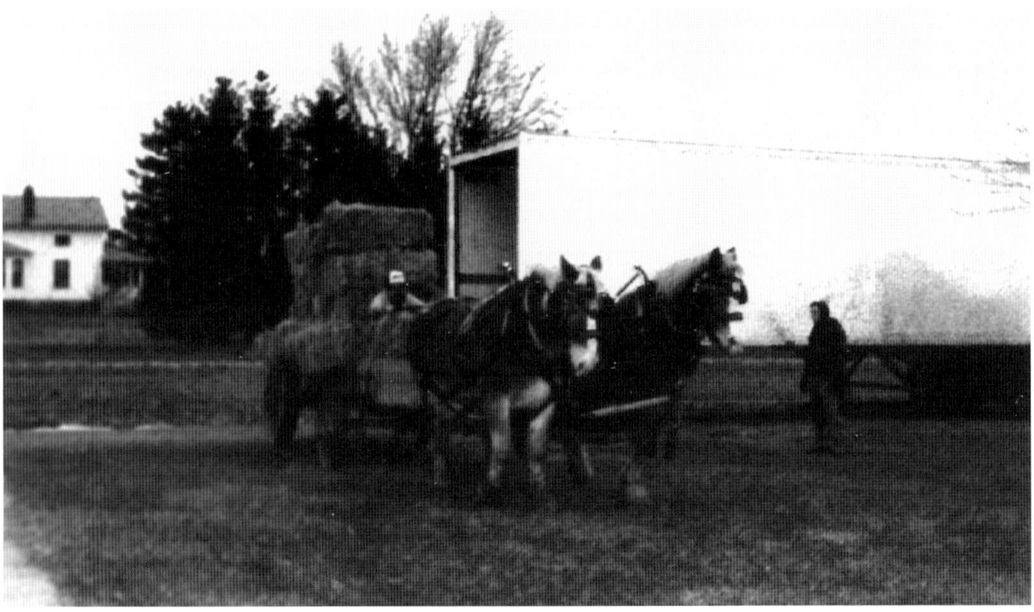

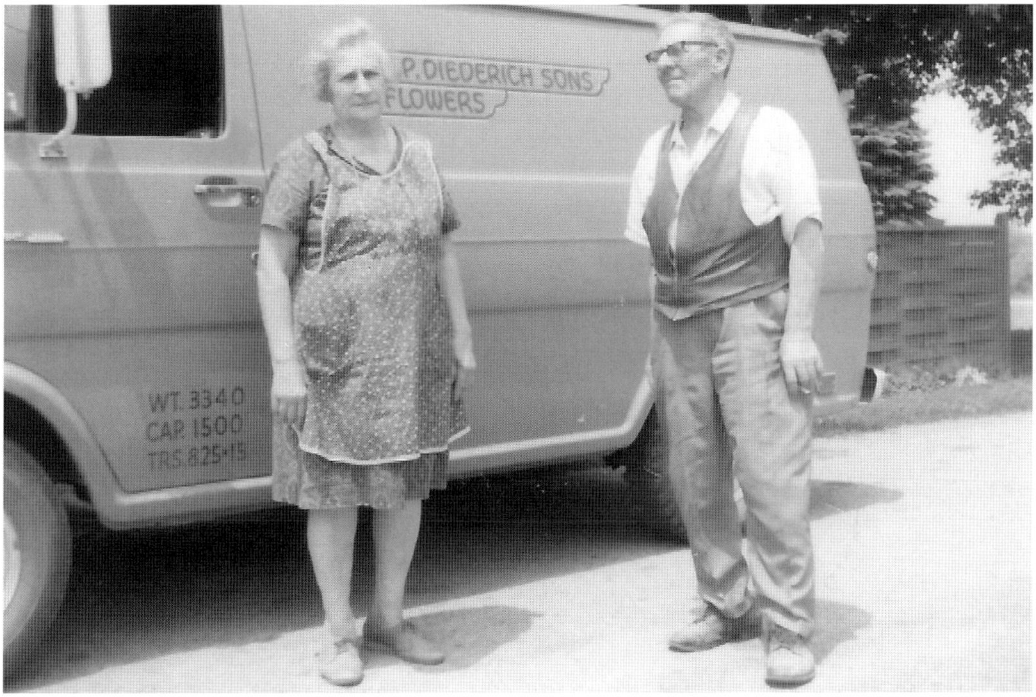

Aurelia and Audoen Diederich
John Peter Diederich and his sons, Audoen and Justin, built a greenhouse in 1924. In 1925, Audoen Diederich (right) married Aurelia Pitts (left) and founded J.P. Diederich Sons on Center Ridge Road. The couple lived in what is now the floral shop, but later built a large home and added greenhouses. The company is one of the oldest continuously run businesses in North Ridgeville. (Courtesy of Loyola Diederich.)

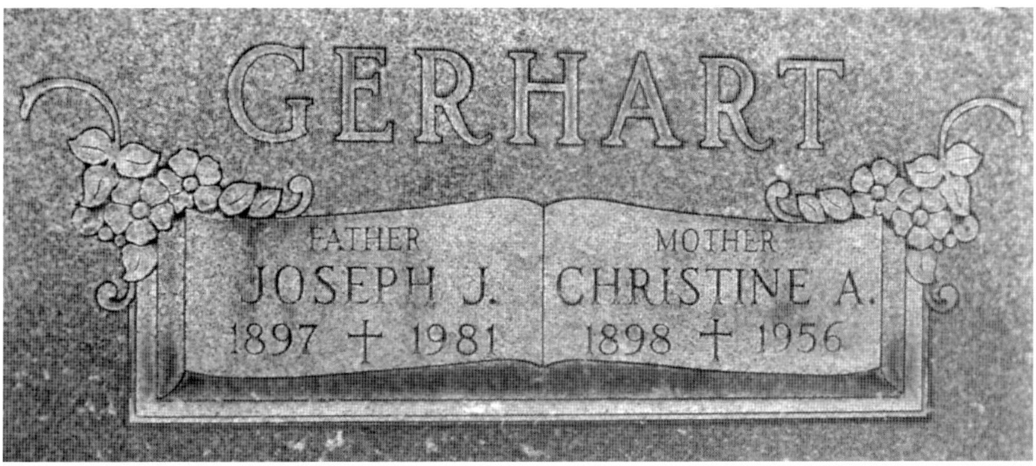

Joseph and Christine Gerhart
Gayle Gerhart Manning's grandparents Joseph and Christine Gerhart began the Gerhart Farm on Avon Belden Road. At that time, North Ridgeville was known as the "Greenhouse Capital of Ohio." The Gerharts grew their vegetables in greenhouses, then trucked them west to Cleveland. Manning's aunt, Sister Mary Celeste, and her friends sometimes visited the farm, where they enjoyed rides on the hay wagon. (Courtesy of Carol Klear.)

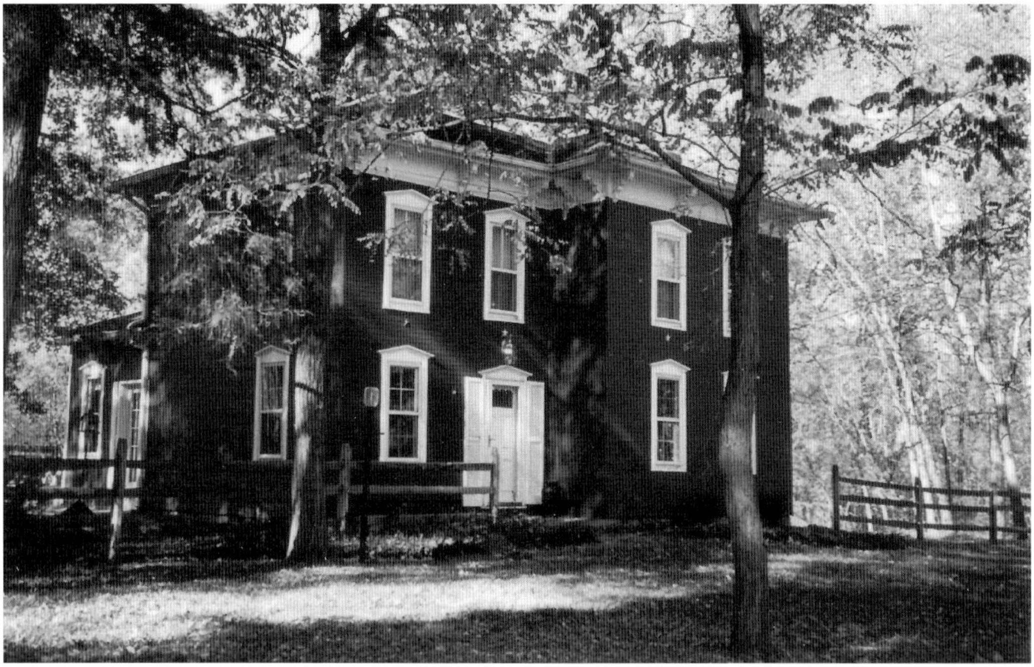

Mathias Nuhn

Nuhn was born in Alsace-Lorraine on September 8, 1838, to Peter and Anna Mary (Moss) Nuhn. When he was about seven years old, Mathias and his family left Antwerp aboard the ship *Emma*. Arriving in New York, they went to Ohio by way of the Hudson River, Erie Canal, and Lake Erie all the way to Cleveland. From there, they traveled by wagon to Ridgeville Township, where Peter Nuhn bought 25 acres of land and cleared it while working as a shoemaker, a trade he had learned in France. He subsequently purchased more acreage. He and his wife raised nine children on their farm. Peter Nuhn died on March 8, 1874; his wife passed away the following year.

Mathias Nuhn recalled living in a barn on Stoney Ridge Road the first summer he and his parents were in Ridgeville while a log house was being constructed for the family on Case Road. A frame house (shown here) was eventually built, completed in 1888. The log cabin remained part of the structure. Mathias lived in the house until he died. Even today, the house is occupied. He learned to be a carpenter and joiner and later successfully combined farming with his trade.

On February 7, 1860, Mathias Nuhn married Mary Kolb in Liverpool, Medina County. They had 13 children, one of which was Mary Nuhn, who, in 1892, married Charles Boey. The Boeys had eight children, including Leonard Frederick Boey, who married Jeanne Arlene Betts on July 13, 1963. They had five sons. Although Nuhn was a Democrat, in matters concerning the township he voted for whoever he considered best for the job. He was active in school and community matters and was a firm believer in education. He and his wife were among the founders of St. Peter Catholic Church in Ridgeville.

A member of the 107th Regiment, Company G from Ridgeville, Nuhn was mustered as a private on September 9, 1862, then rose to corporal. He was captured at the Battle of Chancellorsville on May 2, 1863, and held at Richmond, Virginia, until 1865. He was a member of the Wesley, Kirby Post Grand Army of the Republic Ridgeville, serving as assistant quartermaster for two terms. In the top photograph on the opposite page, Nuhn is standing at center right. When he died in 1928, Nuhn was thought to be one of the last three survivors of the original post. (All, courtesy of Jeanne and Leonard Boey.)

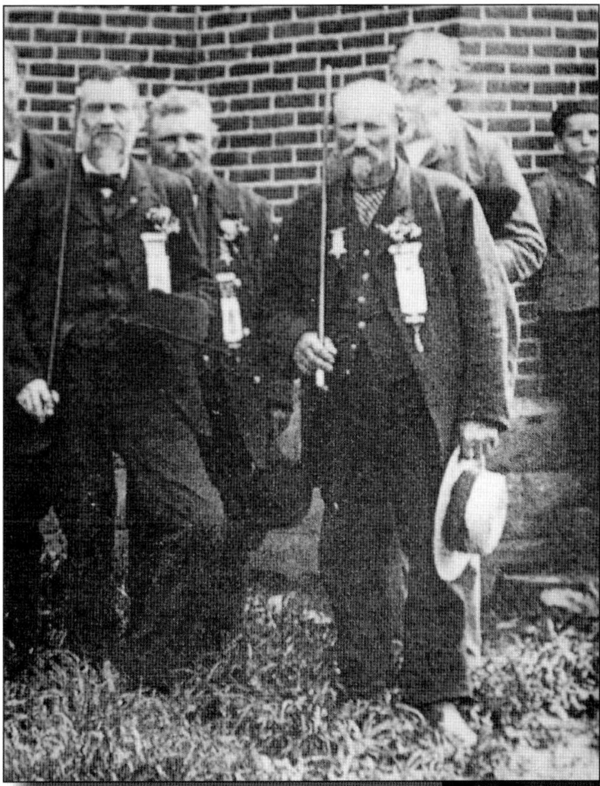

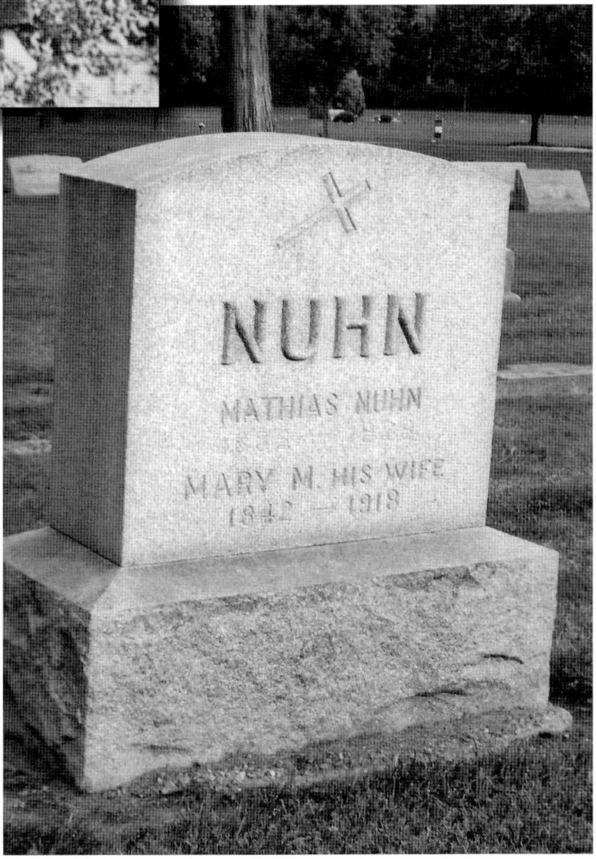
NUHN
MATHIAS NUHN
MARY M. HIS WIFE
1842 — 1918

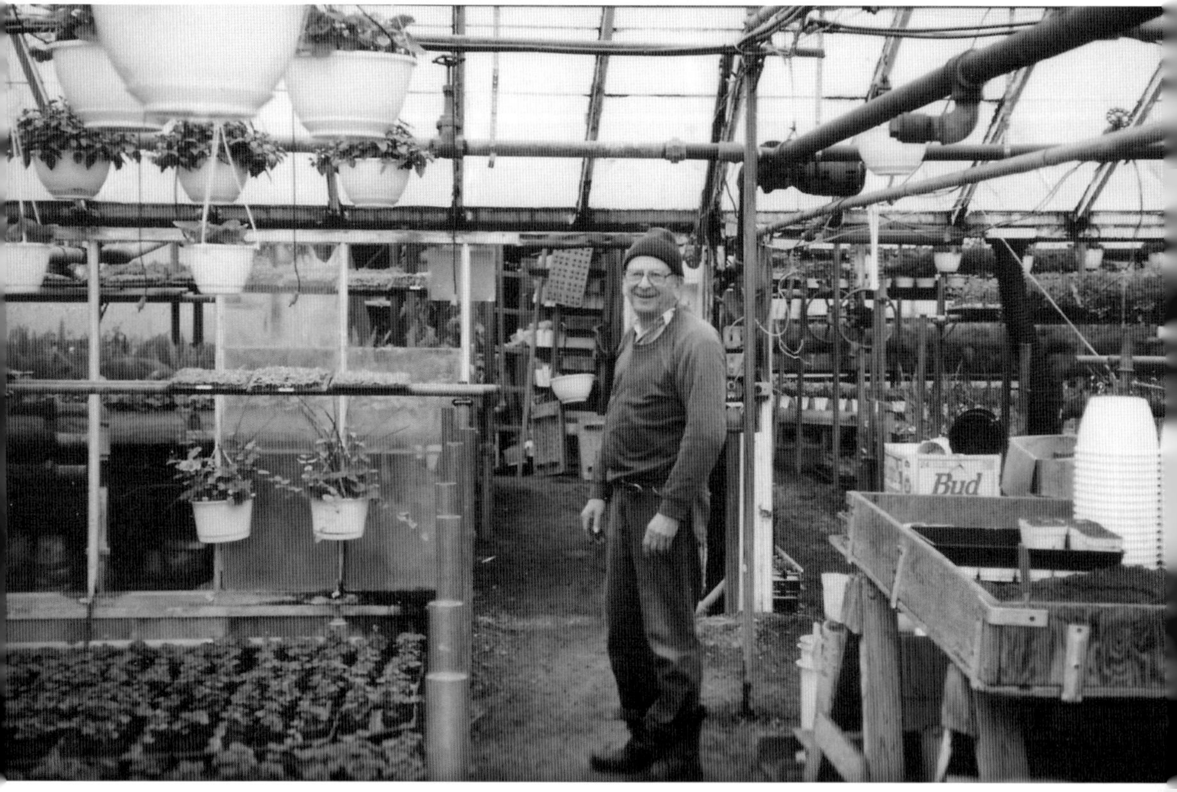

Robert Minute

Robert (pictured) and Neva Minute married in 1946 and began Minute's Greenhouse. They sold geraniums in Cleveland, and son Garry Minute often went with his dad. As he got older, Garry worked in the business, and worked hard. "I did not play baseball or anything, I just worked to save money to buy a new car," Minute said. But his new 1971 Firebird sat idle, he said, because he did not have money for insurance. "I always worked," he said. When the crops of flowers were up for the season, the family went on vacation, leaving employees to care for the plants. However, after Garry graduated from high school, the vacations stopped. His sister helped some, he said.

Garry Minute said he added mums to the geraniums in the mid-1970s, and in 1978, he opened a store. One of the best parts of the company was the work-family relationship. His parents loved the business and instilled the same passion in their son, who now owns Garden Village. "The guy worked his whole life, and so do I," Minute said. "Dad died in 2002; God, we miss him."

In the old days, farmers and greenhouse owners would analyze problems, but the big-box stores have affected the industry, Minute said. He feels that even customers' outlooks have changed, although he said he still likes to help people. Today, gas stations are selling mulch, he said, something that only greenhouses once did. Garden-center employees carry the bags to the car, but at gas stations, it is more of a do-it-yourself operation.

The price of gasoline affects the growing business, as well. It is not like when Minute's father started in business. When gasoline goes up, prices at the garden centers do, as well. "I used to charge $7.99 a flat [of flowers]," Garry said. "This year, they are $14.99." Customers tell Minute they are price shopping, but he feels they need to look at what they are getting for their money. "People will buy $200 in plants and cheap soil, then they come back and say the flowers did not bloom. I tell them to put some plants back and spend more on soil."

Although today's garden business is not like it was in his father's day, Garry Minute's greatest pleasure is helping people grow healthy and beautiful flowers. (Courtesy of Garry Minute.)

Toni and Gary Krone
October at the Krone farm on Root Road means pumpkins, but in 2013, the wet spring destroyed the pumpkins before they had a chance to grow. Gary Krone said there were 16 days of "just too wet." The Krones have lived in their Sears house on the 53-acre farm since 1979. They grow vegetables and flowers, while others farm a portion of their land. They also raise farm animals, including goats and sheep. For nearly 20 years, the Krones volunteered with the Ridge Kids, a local 4-H Club. "We ran a tight ship," said Toni Krone. The couple pushed community service and often visited nursing homes. They also encouraged health and safety through 4-H speech contests. But there was fun as well, as shown with the 4-H float below. (Both, courtesy of Toni Krone.)

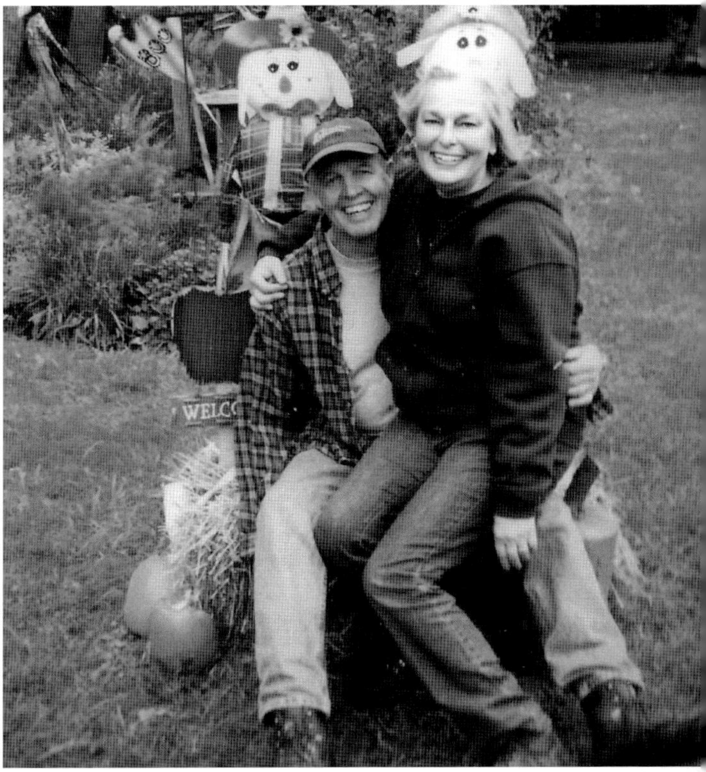

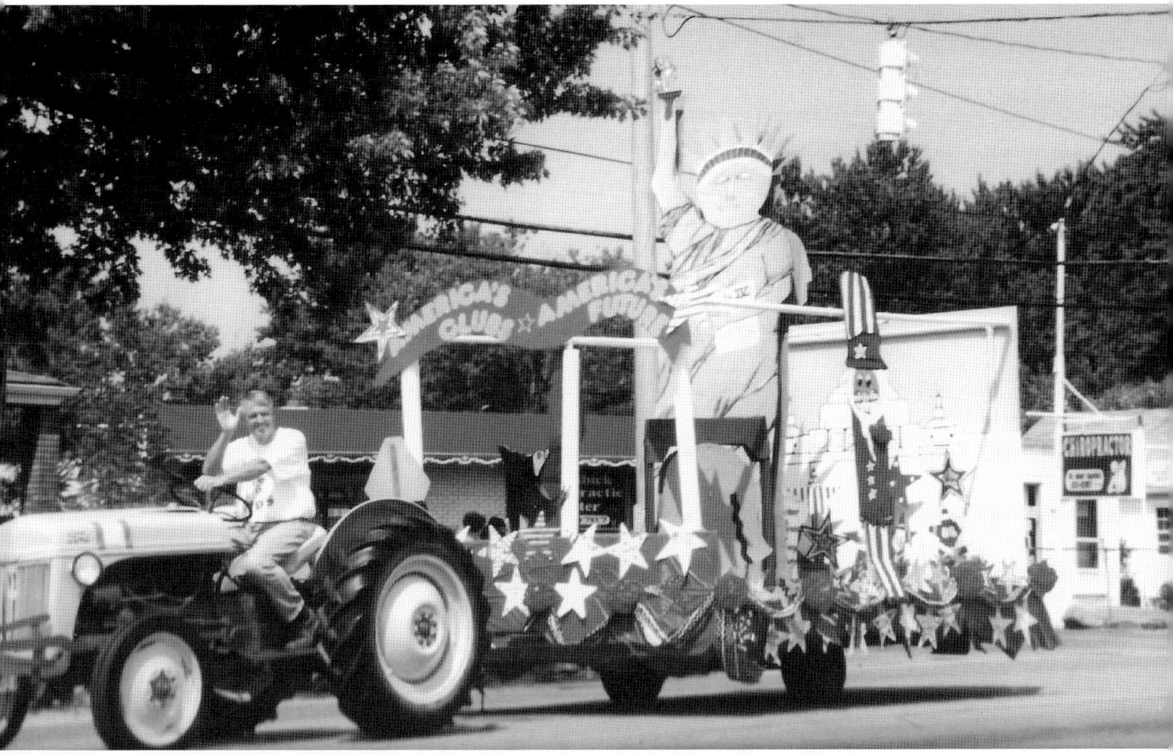

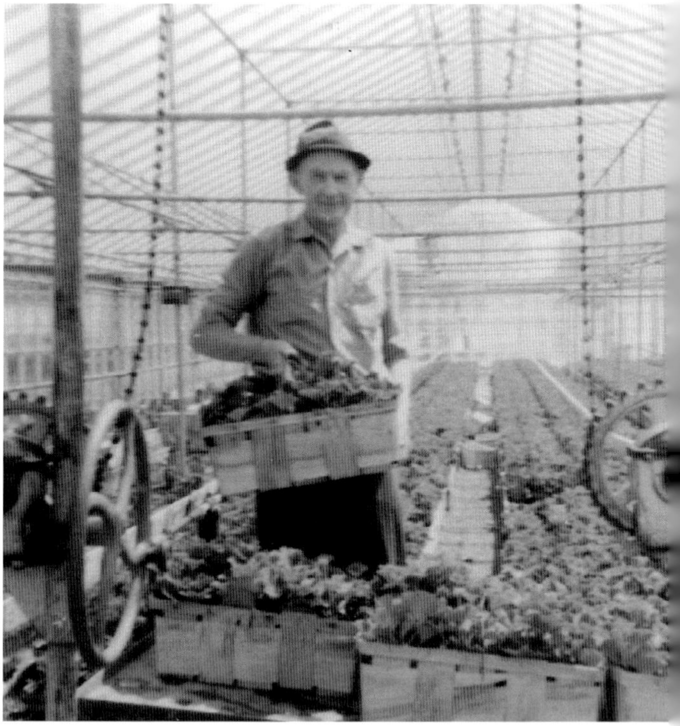

Martin Thibo
Thibo was born in Indiana in 1917 and lived in Fairview Park for 17 years. During the Depression, he ran a widow's greenhouse in Rocky River. He then served in the Army Air Force from 1942 to 1945. Returning from service, he bought property on Avon Belden Road and built his first greenhouses. In 1952 he married Veronica Kane, and they had five children. In the 1950s, geraniums became popular, which meant expanding the greenhouses. Bob Thibo joined his brother, and the company became Thibo Brothers. Over the years, high school students and adults have worked at Thibo's. Martin Thibo was a member of the volunteer fire department until it went full time in the mid-1970s. He liked to golf, fish, play cards, and pilot his ultralight plane. (Both, courtesy of Marcia Thibo and Karen Ware.)

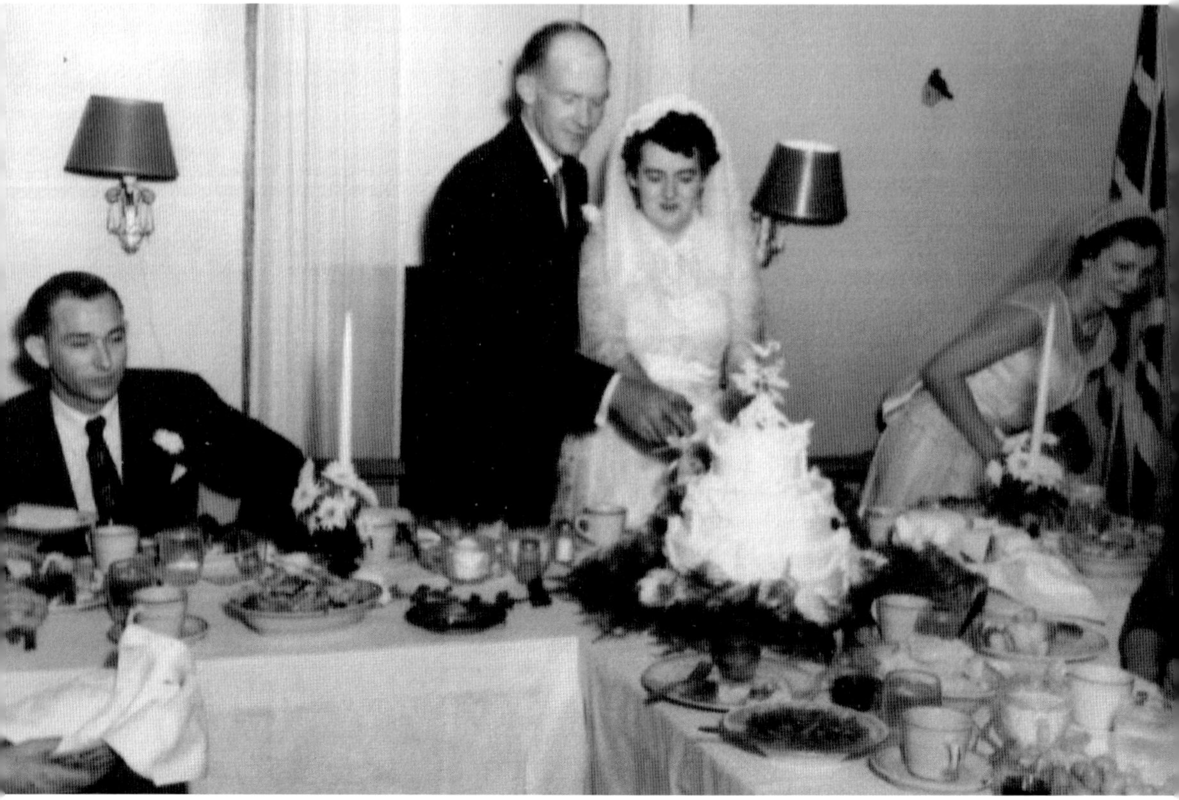

CHAPTER TWO

School Days, School Days

When the early settlers arrived at Ridgeville Township, there were no shelters, let alone schools. As more and more pioneers joined the original group from Connecticut, bringing with them children of varying ages, they set about trying to find ways of providing for the youngsters' education. There were no formal schools initially, as the construction of log cabins was reserved for residences. The boys and girls attended school in family homes. In the spring of 1814, the first log school was constructed, on the northeast corner of Center Ridge Road and Center/Avon Belden Road, presently Routes 20 and 83.

Young women began teaching in the school, including Lydia Terrell, who was not much beyond 17 when she stepped into the classroom. However, the daughter of Noah and Esther (Beebe) Terrell taught just one summer when she became ill and died. Terrell was followed by several other teachers, such as Betsy Shellhouse, 19; John Reading Jr., 28; Betsy Barnum (Reading), 18; Abigail Davis, 18; and Samuel Mills, 23. Mills taught from the summer of 1817 to late 1817, when the school was destroyed by fire.

Since those early days, several schools have been built in North Ridgeville, including elementary schools and a high school, which eventually became the middle school, located on Center Ridge Road. Following the success of the 2013 election, that building will be relocated in the near future. A schoolhouse remains from the 1800s: a one-room structure located on Jaycox Road that belongs to the North Ridgeville Historical Society and is open to the public during the spring and summer seasons. Julie Bajda and Barbara Sutton reenact the role of the teacher, to the delight of visitors.

Bus transportation was initiated for taking students to and from school. The role of education has expanded to include such subjects as physical education, art, and music. A panel of residents was established in the early 1900s to determine school policies, and members continue to be selected through a public voting process.

Julie Bajda

The District 9 one-room schoolhouse is located on the west side of Jaycox Road, south of Mills Road. When it was originally erected around 1859, it was on the east side of what was then Snow Road. According to the writings of the late Frances Smith, the schoolhouse was situated on John Muhling's farm. Smith wrote, "In 1865 Mr. Muhling sold his 46 acres to a Mr. Lehman for $2,000, i.e. $43.50 an acre." The structure remained on the corner until 1880 or 1881. On November 19, 1880, the school board paid $100, and the building was moved. Eventually, the John and Grace Sullivan family, owners of the adjacent farm, purchased it and used it for storage.

Around 1985, the Sullivans approached the North Ridgeville Historical Society about purchasing the schoolhouse, but the organization was in no financial position to do so. Then, in 1988, the living heirs of the family donated the building and the property to the organization, which the members gratefully accepted. Plans were made to renovate the clapboard structure; there was much to be done. The schoolhouse's dark and dank exterior required refurbishing, and the building suffered from a leaking roof, broken windows, and chipped paint. In addition, raccoons and skunks had begun nesting inside, and crops of poison ivy were thriving outside. By 2001, after nine years of hard work and fundraising, the schoolhouse was ready for visitors.

When people go to the schoolhouse, they are often greeted by Julie Bajda, who retired after 35 years of teaching in the North Ridgeville City Schools. She sometimes assumes the role of a pioneer teacher at the schoolhouse. As a teacher, Bajda always taught her students about the city's history and allowed them to reenact pioneer life. Her students also wrote for the Young Authors creative writing program and presented dramatic performances.

Beginning in the summer of 2003, Bajda began traveling to Poland to teach English summer school in Stary Sacz. She usually had a class of 25–30 students. When the three-week program ended, Bajda used the opportunity to visit relatives. (Courtesy of the North Ridgeville Historical Society.)

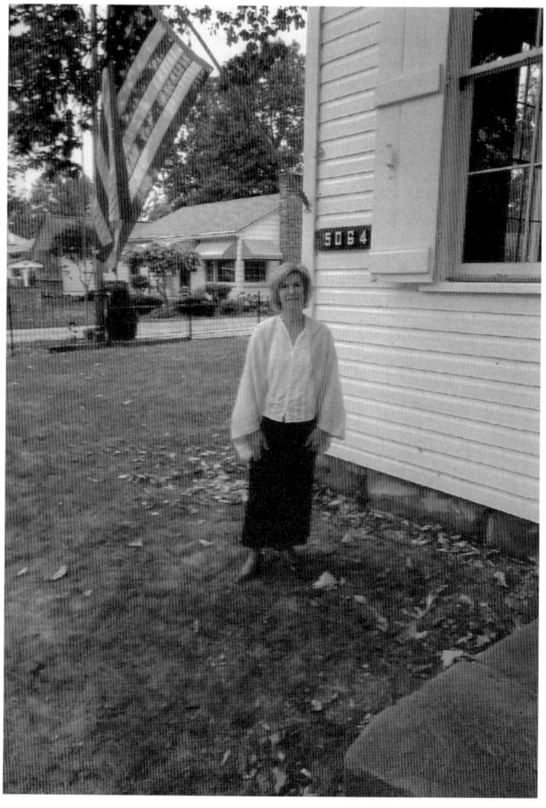

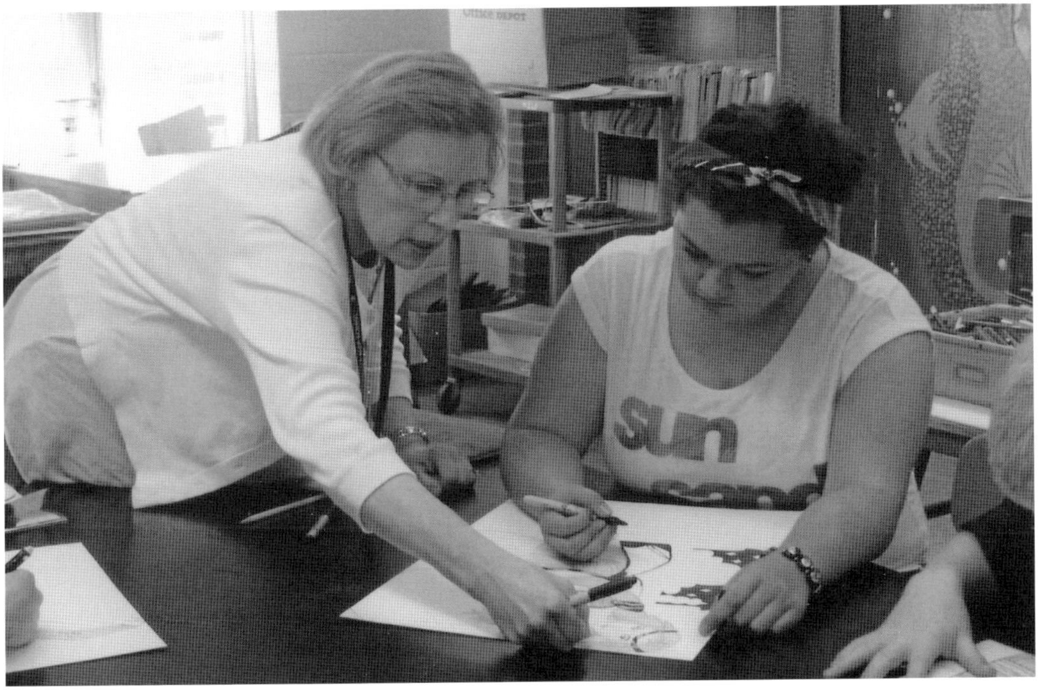

Georgann Blair
Georgann Blair has been a visual art educator in the North Ridgeville City Schools for 19 years. She holds a bachelor's degree and a master's degree, and her professional experience includes being an adjunct professor for Ashland, serving on Cleveland conference committees for the Ohio Art Education Association, and being named Ohio Art Educator of the Year in 2002. She is shown above giving individual attention to a student. "My teaching philosophy centers on communicating the importance of visual art education so it can be understood, appreciated, and supported by others," Blair said. Visual art becomes a "personal adventure." She encourages teachers to stay current in their profession and students to do their best. Below is a painting by Devin Garcia, a student in Blair's class. (Both, courtesy of Georgann Blair.)

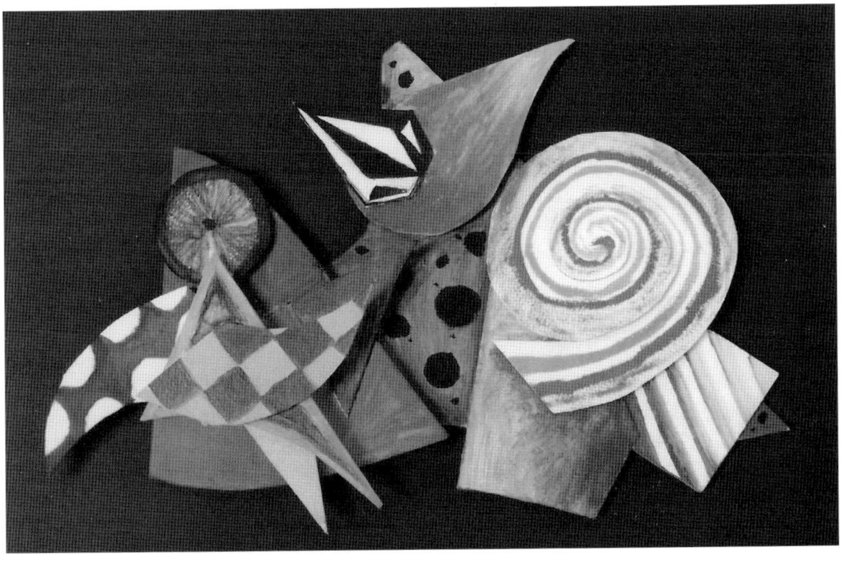

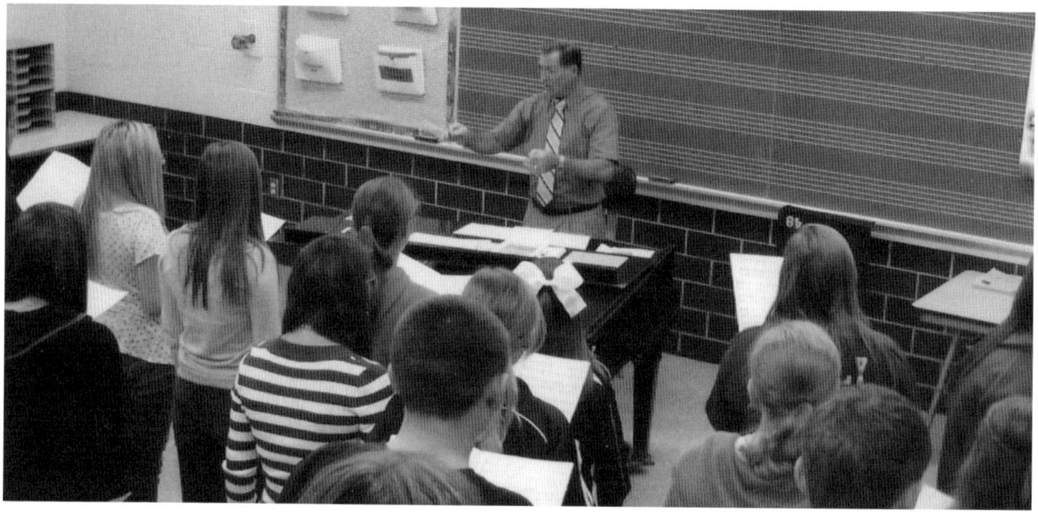

William E. Davis III

William Davis III, a native of New Jersey, received his bachelor's and master's degrees in music from Bowling Green State University through a four-year choral grant. He has done postgraduate work and has taught for 38 of his 43 years at North Ridgeville City Schools. Under Davis's direction, choirs have scored superior ratings at district, state, national, and international levels and have earned 33 Ohio Music Education Association (OMEA) State Superior Ratings. The vocal instructor has been active in directing musical theater as well as in productions at Lorain County Community College. In addition to high school and college choirs, Davis has directed church choirs for 38 years and is the Finney Choir director at First Church in Oberlin. He is past president of OMEA District IV. (Both, courtesy of William E. Davis III.)

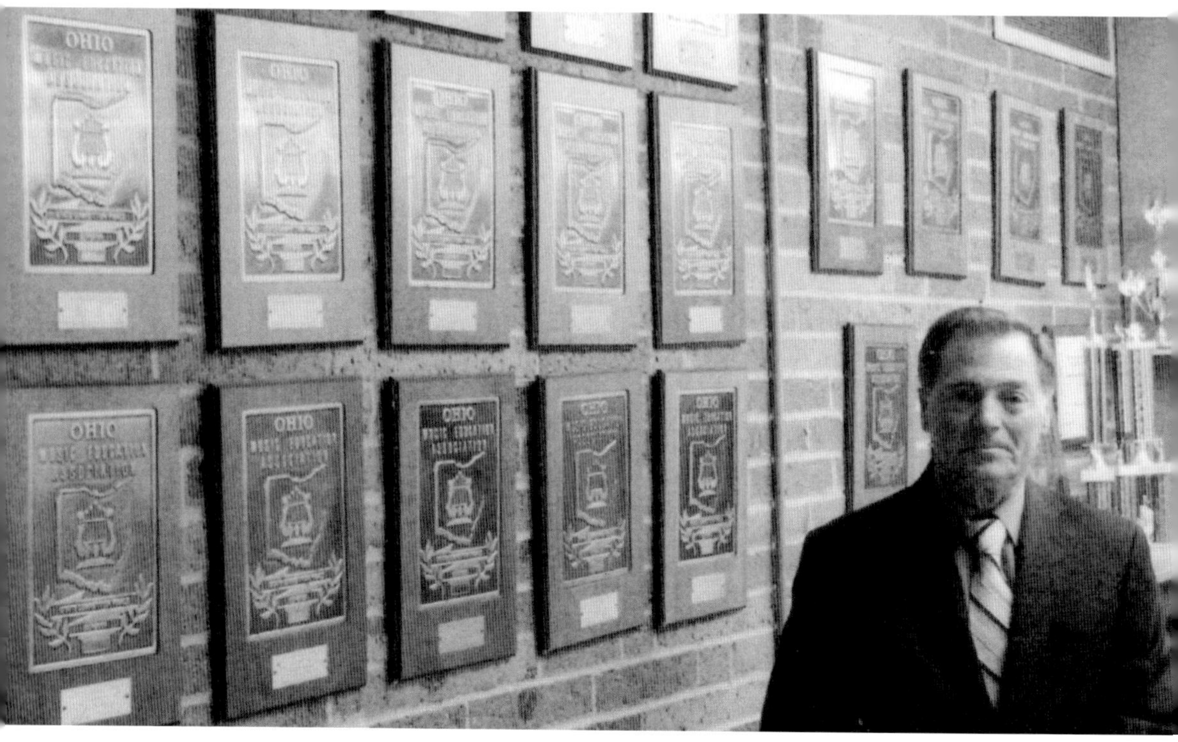

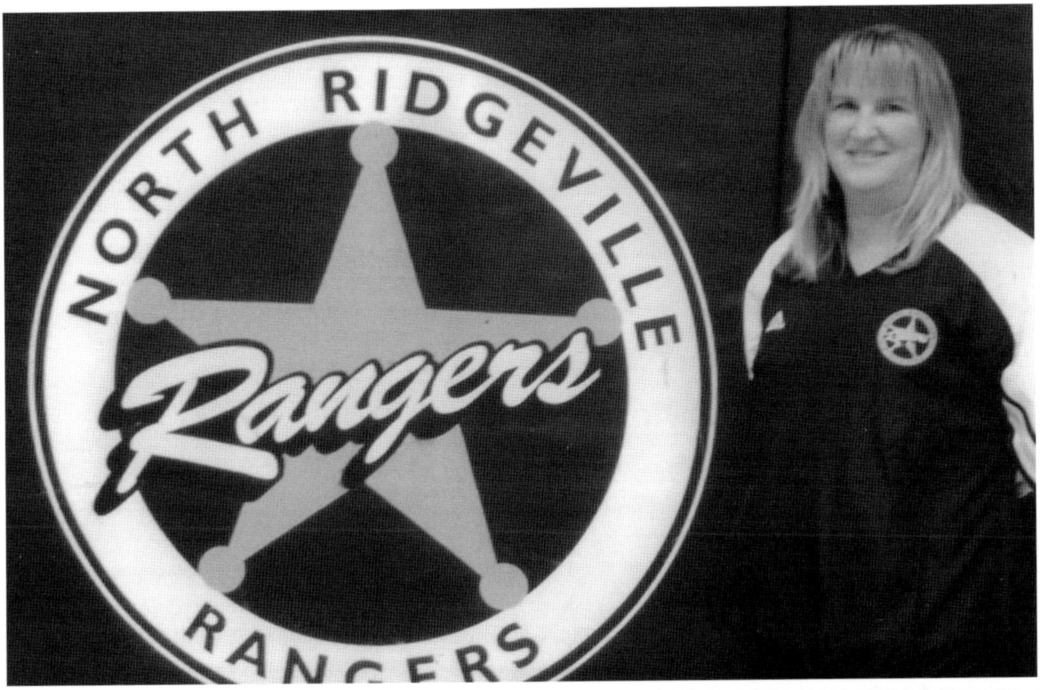

Maria Sycz
Sycz volunteered when her children were in school. Feeling that she could do more at the district level, she joined the school board. That was 10 years ago; for seven of those years, Sycz was president, and she loved it. Her philosophy was, "It is not the board's job to run the district, but to make sure the district runs well." However, she was not reelected in 2013. (Courtesy of Maria Sycz.)

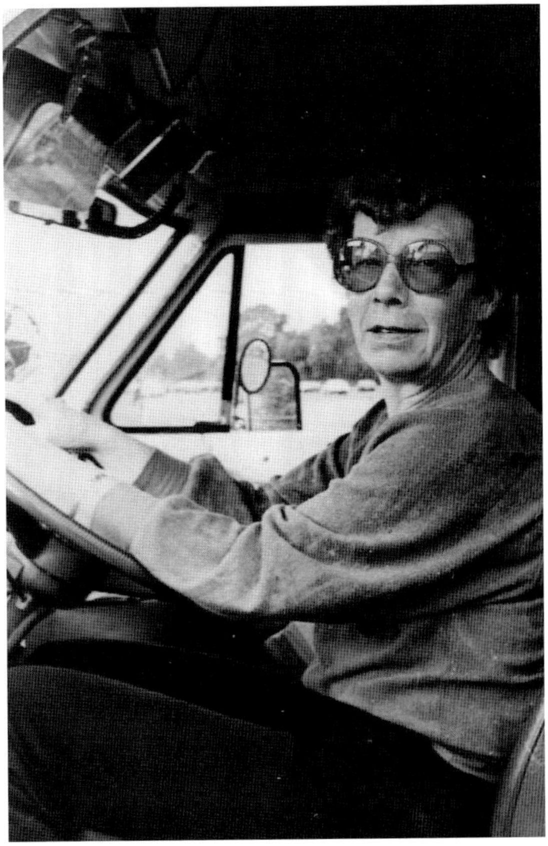

Jean Gilder
When the school board decided to hire women bus drivers, Jean Gilder and two friends took a course in 1955. "I was driving to get a dryer," she explained. She still had a child at home, but, two years later, Gilder climbed into the driver's seat, eventually spending 28 years transporting youngsters. At day's end, drivers took their buses home. (Courtesy of the North Ridgeville Historical Society.)

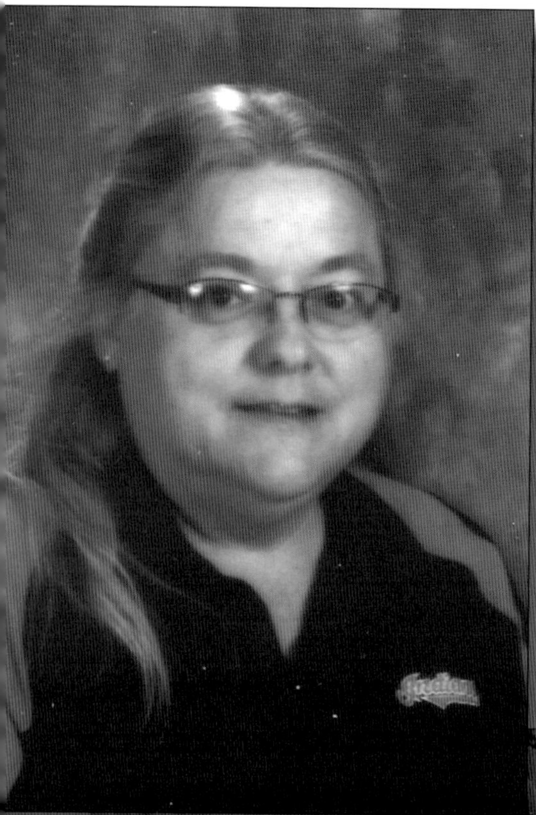

Pamela Nolan
Nolan has been a physical education teacher at St. Peter School for 34 years, teaching youngsters from preschool through eighth grade to keep fit, stay healthy, and have fun. The younger children love "snowball fights" with yarn balls, and the older ones enjoy volleyball, bowling, tennis, and discussions about life.

Nolan, a graduate of the University of Akron, has earned many honors, including the Bruce Yeager Memorial Award. She was enshrined in the Catholic Youth Organization Hall of Fame, was a member of the Athletic Advisory Board of the Diocese of Cleveland for 10 years, and a basketball commissioner for 10 years for the Western Region of Lorain. Nolan started several programs at St. Peter, including "Hoops and Jump Rope for the Heart." Nolan, 59, tells her students, "You guys make me feel young." (Both, courtesy of Pamela Nolan)

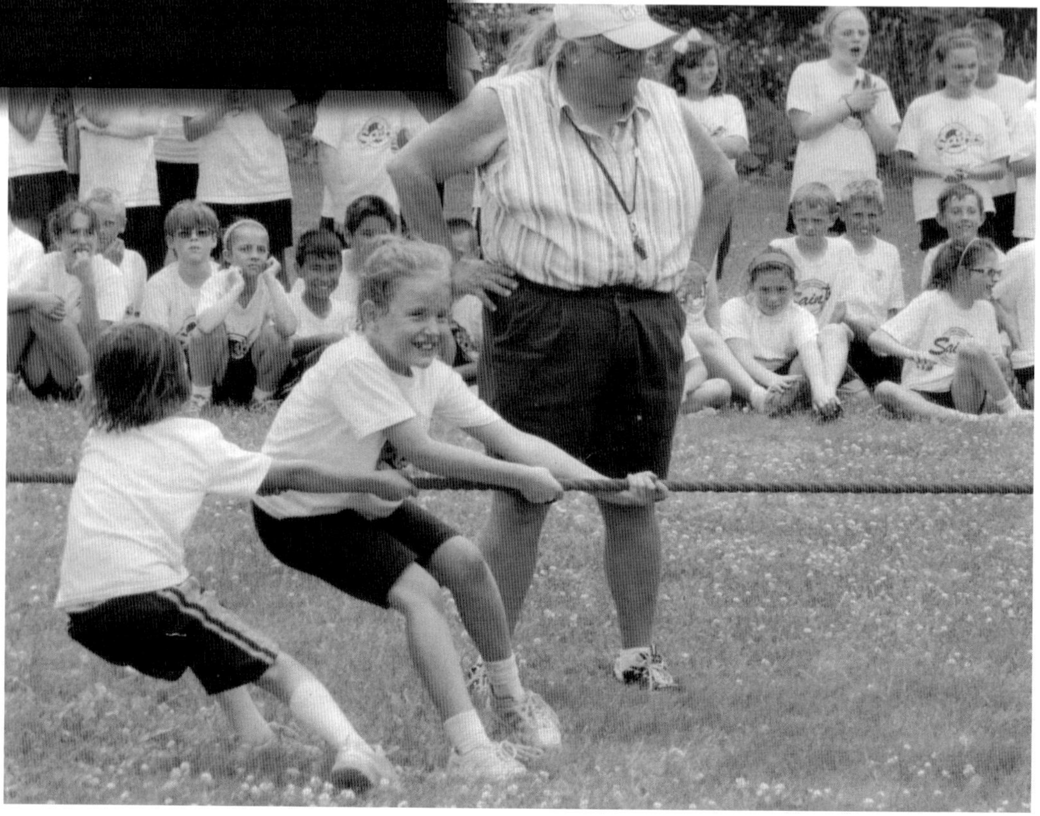

Patricia Bahr

Before retiring in 2013, Bahr was an educator for 35 years, 18 of them as principal of North Ridgeville High School (NRHS). She graduated from Bowling Green State University in 1978 with a bachelor's degree in education, and earned a master's in 1985. Although she began her career coaching volleyball, she said "I never had a good record." She also spent seven years as a business teacher, specializing in occupational work experience. Bahr served seven years as assistant principal. She has much to be proud of, including the student athletes honored on Sports Time Ohio, a regional sports television network serving Cleveland and northern Ohio. She said that while many schools do not have Parent Teacher Associations, NRHS has Ranger Parents, the Hall of Fame, and the Academic Recognition Committee. Bahr is shown below with Hall of Fame inductee and 1980 graduate astronaut Charles Hobaugh. The retired principal said, "I love, love teenagers." (Both, courtesy of Patricia Bahr.)

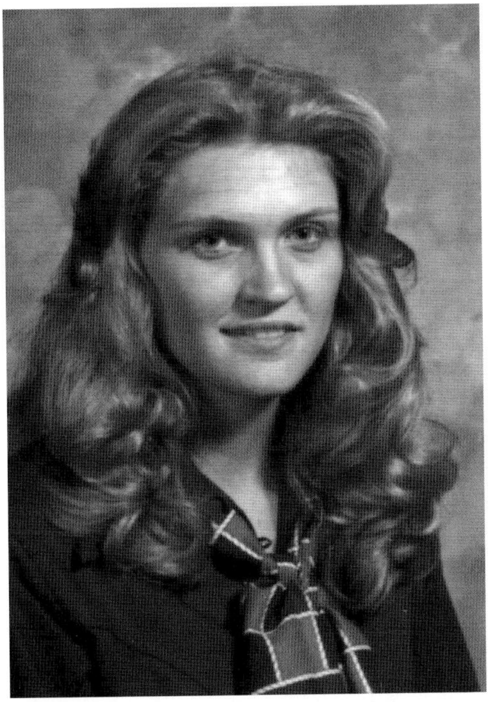

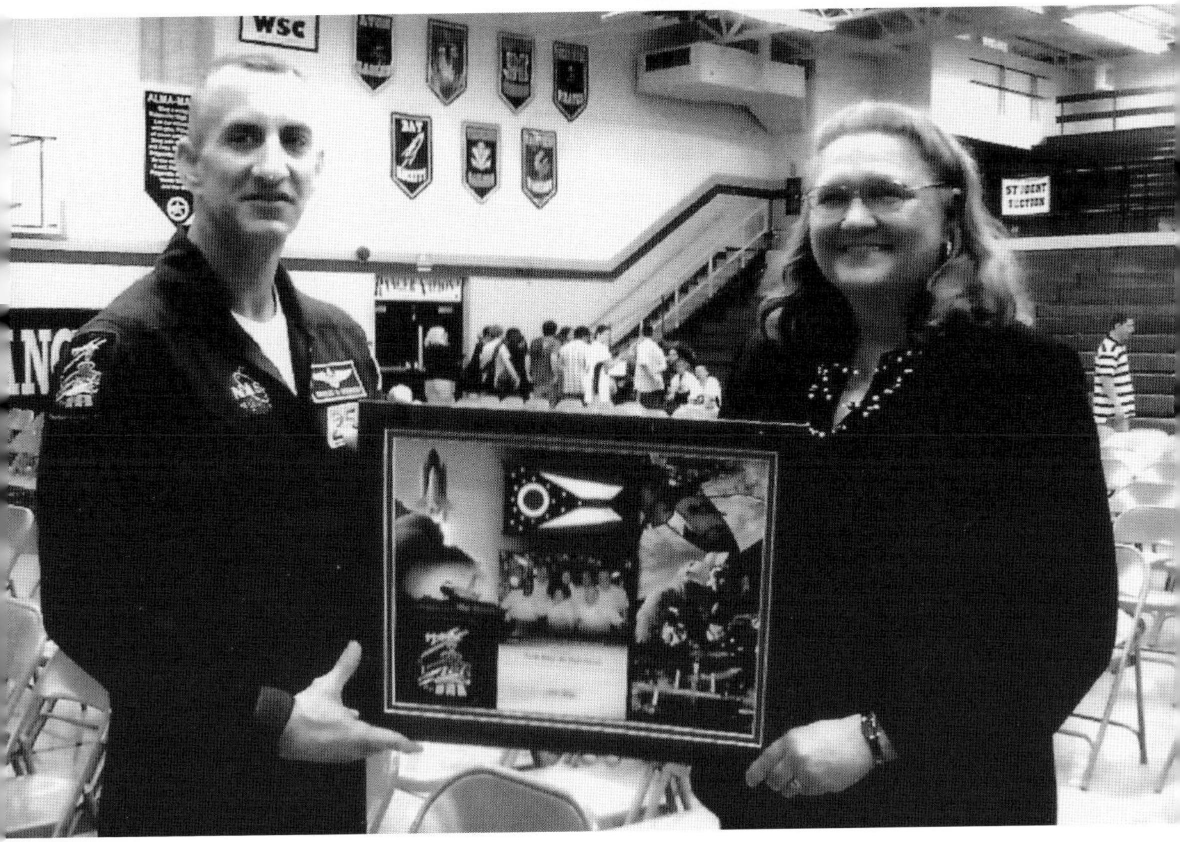

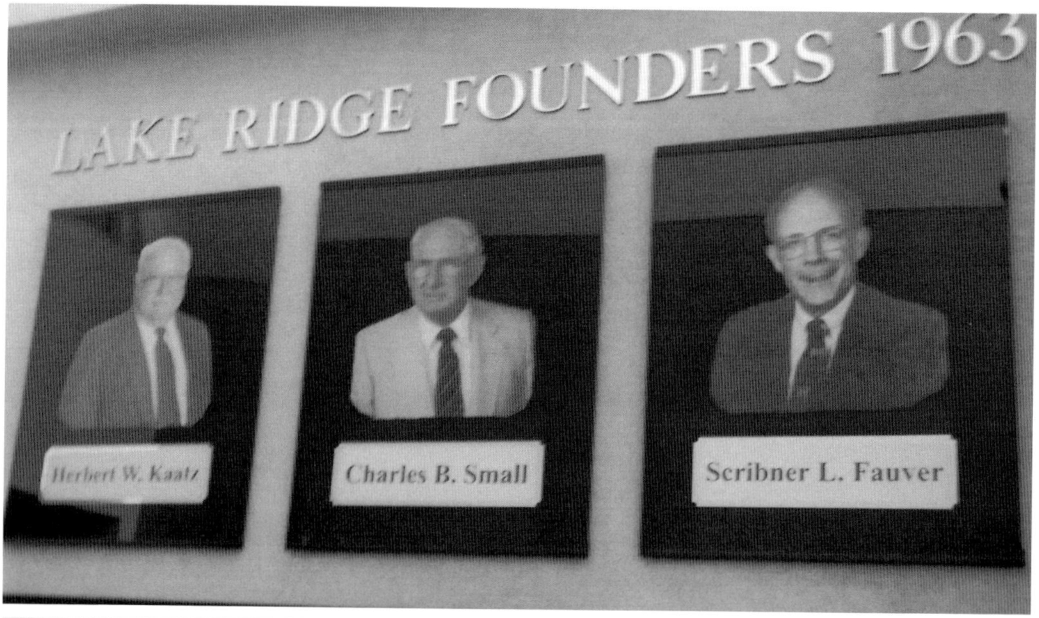

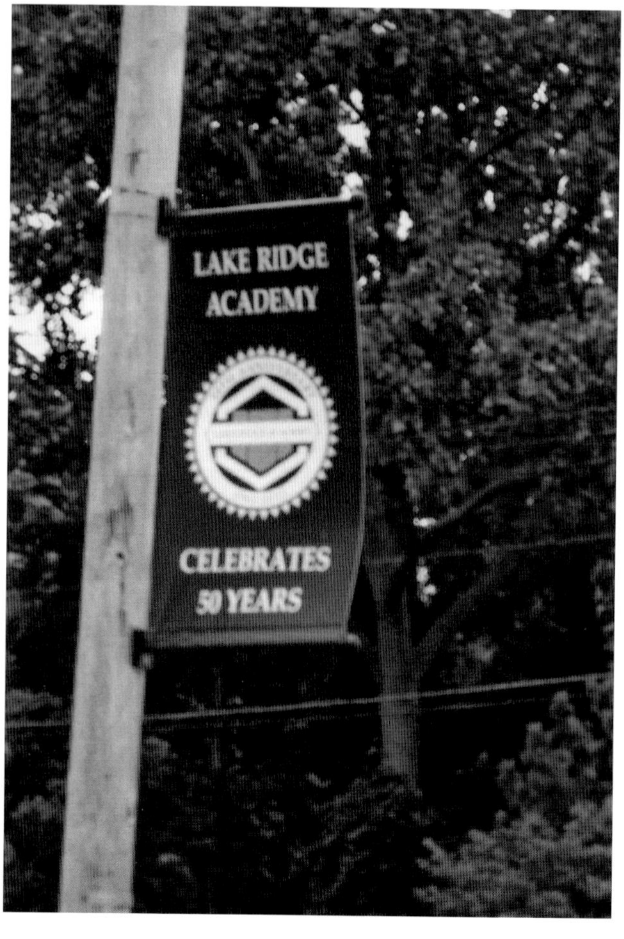

Lake Ridge Academy
Lake Ridge Academy, an independent, nonsectarian day school with classes from kindergarten through 12th grade, celebrated its 50th birthday in 2013. Located on 88 acres off of Center Ridge Road, it began with Charles B. Small's visit to Elyrian Herbert W. Kaatz in 1961. Small was moving to Elyria from Willoughby and heard that Kaatz, a successful businessman with 40 patented inventions and the founder of a manufacturing company, had more than a passing interest in education. Small was hoping to create a school with small classes and a college-bound population. Following a long conversation, Kaatz found himself interested in Small's ideas. The two then paid a visit to attorney Scribner L. Fauver, and the tradition that today is Lake Ridge Academy began to take root. (Both, courtesy of Carol Klear.)

CHAPTER THREE

Roots and Branches

Establishing a method of government has always been necessary to maintain order in a society. The government may be led by a tribal leader, a king, a township trustee, or a mayor. In a city the size of North Ridgeville, the flow chart is topped by a mayor, who administers the laws that city council members determine are needed for the community. The process may not always run smoothly, and tempers may flare from time to time due to political or personal differences, but that is the procedure.

There have been a number of mayors since North Ridgeville became a city in 1960. Some were more popular than others, but the selection was made through a vote of the people, and the successful candidate seemed to be the one whose political party—Democratic or Republican—got the most voters to the polls. From time to time, there have been efforts to eliminate political parties. According to some people, this would ease the in-house battles that sometimes erupt on the council floor and pave the way for smoother government. But the idea has never been totally accepted, so the Democrats and Republicans continue to vie for positions.

Some North Ridgeville politicos have earned respect at the local level through serving on committees or commissions, such as G. David Gillock, who continued to climb the governmental ladder and was eventually elected mayor. Others paid their dues through terms on council, all the while mulling the idea that one day they might step away from the local landscape and rise to a post at the state or federal level. Though politics was often thought to be solely a man's arena, Deanna Hill transitioned from a career in education to one in government, becoming the first woman to take the mayor's chair. She served two terms, carrying the torch for other women who feel they may be up to the challenge of being the city's top official.

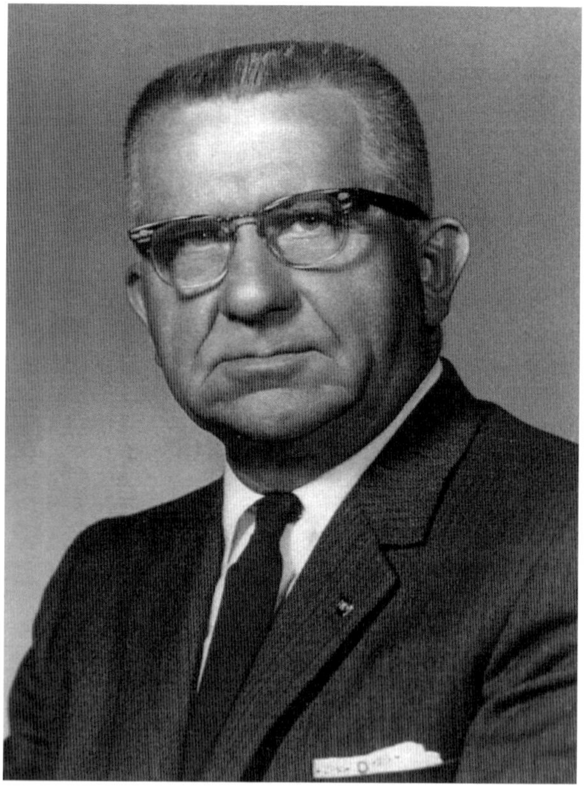

Marcellus Benedict Diederich

Diederich's roots can be traced to Prussia, but his heart belonged in North Ridgeville. Born on February 15, 1900, Marcellus was the youngest of eight children of Nicholas and Catherine (Schneider) Diederich. The family farmed and lived in Sheffield Village, not far from St. Theresa Church and school. Diederich trained to be a server, and he had a favorite saying, "Any problems can be solved with God's help and hard work." He did well in school, but did not go beyond the fifth grade because he was needed on the farm. When he was older, he worked at the Lorain steel mill but left after two years, determined he would work only for himself. In 1924, a tornado destroyed the family orchards, part of their house, and most of the farm buildings.

In 1927, Diederich married Kathryn Meyers and purchased the Lindsley Chemical Company. In 1929, the up-and-coming businessman built a house on Avon Belden Road, but he lost it in the Great Depression. The next year, he partnered with Frank S. Ewing to learn to make and install the Ewing Weight Protector, a device attached to beam-type scales. Marc and Kathryn Diederich had two children, Wayne, born in 1932, and Nancy, born two years later.

Diederich was sure his adopted community had great potential. He often said that all towns should have "a doctor, a bank, and a town newspaper," but North Ridgeville's most pressing need was city water, which did not arrive until 1957. In the late 1930s, he gathered some influential men and formed the Ridgeville Civic League, a forerunner of the Kiwanis organization.

Diederich and his wife joined the Young Democrats of Ridgeville and Lorain County. By the 1960s, he served as a Democratic precinct committeeman, and in February 1969, he announced his candidacy for mayor. Diederich won the election and became a hands-on mayor; working through city council or state and county agencies did not suit his style. Once, as city workers cleaned a ditch, Diederich pulled up in his Thunderbird. The workers saw him but didn't think he would wade through a swampy area to check on them. Diederich opened his trunk, pulled on his boots, and headed over to talk to them.

When his term ended, Diederich decided he would run again, but he lost to a Republican opponent. He died on January 12, 1974. (All, courtesy of Geraldine and Wayne Diederich.)

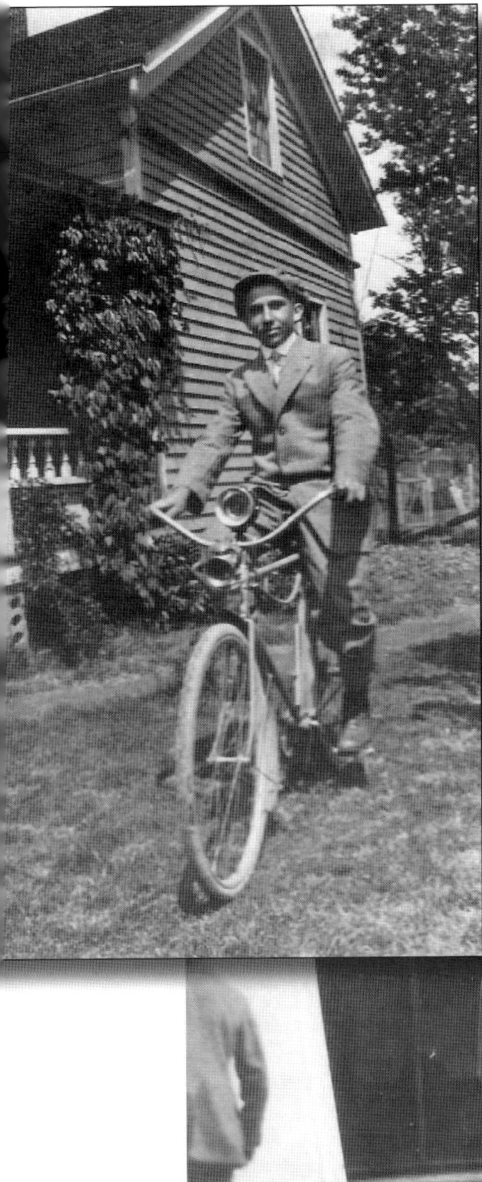

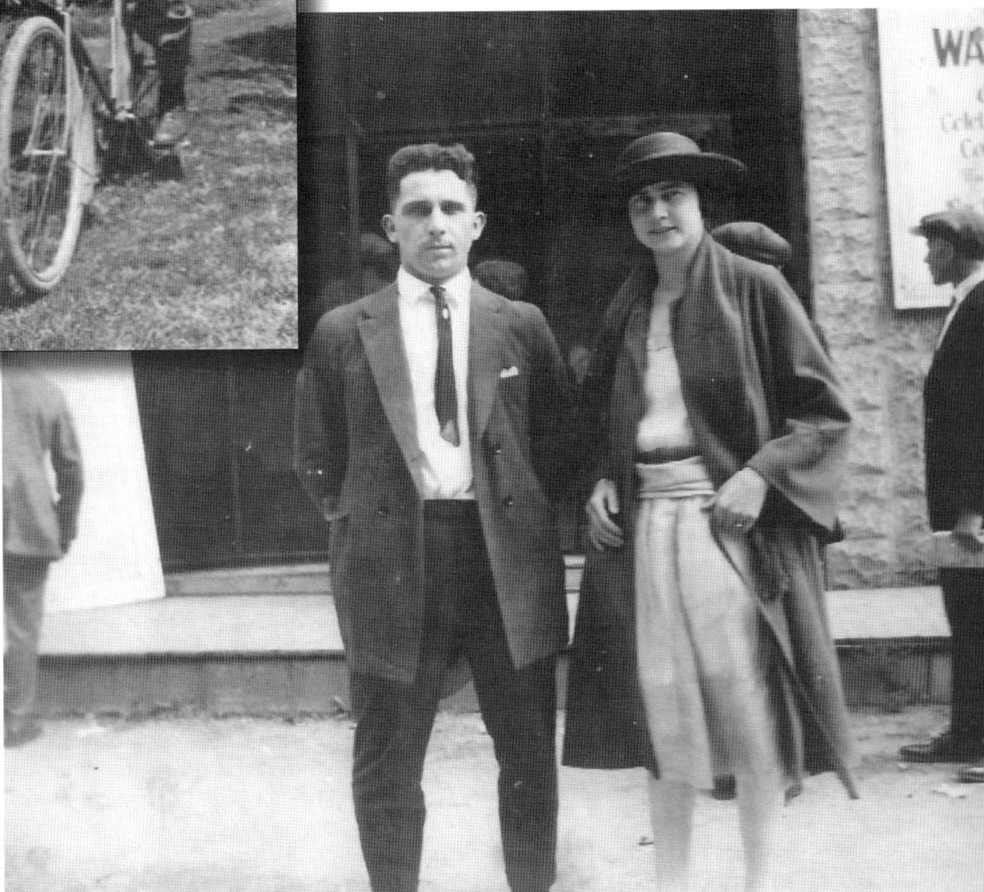

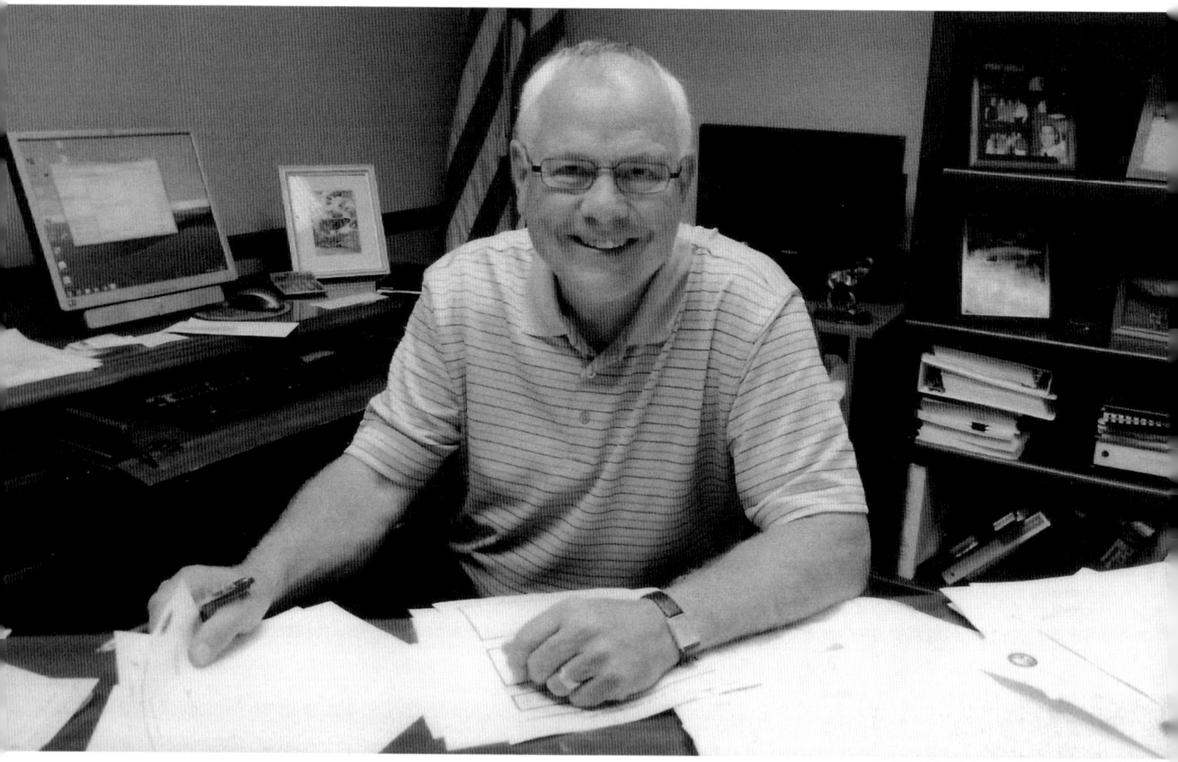

Jeffry Armbruster

Following his 1969 graduation from college, Armbruster began working for Shell Oil in St. Paul, Minnesota, until February 1970, when he headed to Toledo, Ohio. In 1971, Shell closed the Toledo office, and again Armbruster moved, this time to Middleburg Heights. Around that time he met Cono Pinzone, a successful dealer who owned the Crocker Shell and Clague Shell stations in Westlake. Pinzone told Armbruster he wanted him to move to Houston and be his partner.

Armbruster's wife, Susan, cautioned that he would not be happy sitting behind a desk. By that time Armbruster had two stations, one full-service and one offering some services. He then started his own business and increased the number of stations to six. "We got it all set up and Cono told me he was retiring," Armbruster said. The announcement was a shock, but he felt Pinzone had taught him valuable business ethics.

Armbruster then entered politics, serving three terms on the city council. But then, life handed him another blow. Susan became seriously ill with leukemia. She died in 1984, leaving him with their children, Heather and Jason. Armbruster ran for mayor three years later, losing to Floyd Peaco. He tried again, and won. In time, he married a widow with two children, trying to rebuild his life. But fate turned its back on Armbruster when his second wife, Judy, also became ill with leukemia and died. Following her death, he had four youngsters to raise. Judy's sister, Lee Schwirtz, lived in Texas, but she came to North Ridgeville to become the children's nanny. While caring for them, she and Armbruster found themselves attracted to each other, and the couple eventually married. They have two sons, Russell and Will. "Twenty-five years later, we are still married," Armbruster said.

Explaining his ability to cope, he said, "You look at the cards you are dealt and work through it." Armbruster also faced difficulties in his professional life. He was accused of gas gouging and ethics violations, but none of it was true, he said. He was elected state senator, but, due to term limits, he found himself without a job. Suddenly, the safety service director, Dennis Johnson, retired, and Mayor G. David Gillock asked Armbruster to step in. His job includes both desk duties and fieldwork. Opposite, Armbruster is pictured with heavy equipment employee Brian Ralich. (Both, courtesy of Jeffry Armbruster.)

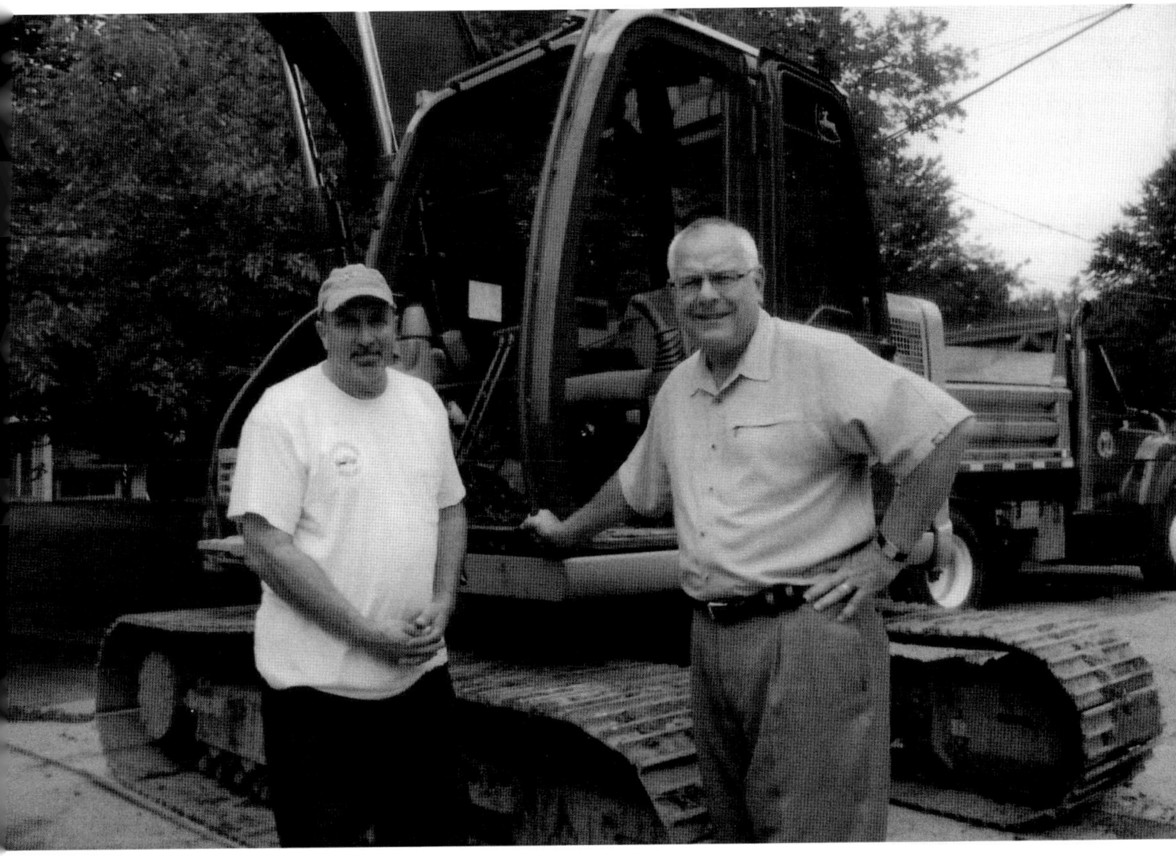

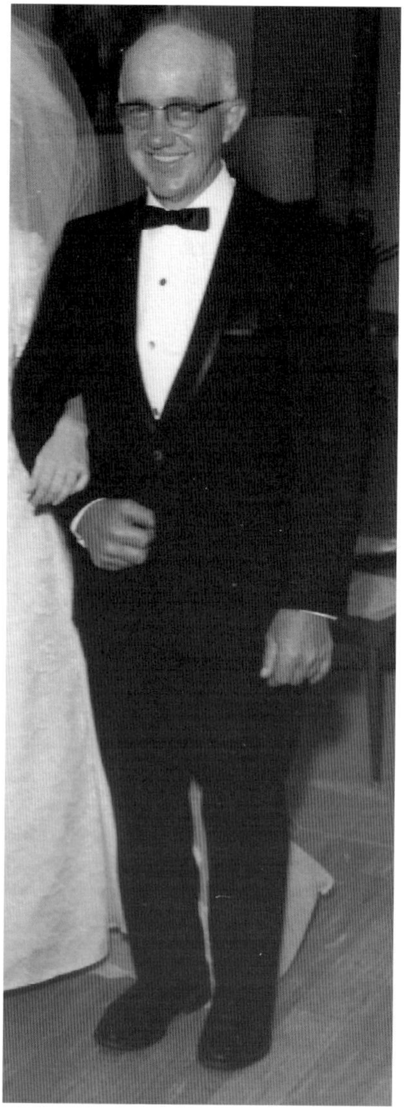

Bernard L. Noll

An involved resident of North Ridgeville, Noll served four terms on the council and six on the planning commission. In 1959, he became vice chairman of the city's incorporation committee. Noll organized the French Creek Council of Governments and chaired it for six years. He had hoped to be mayor, but it was not to be. Noll and his wife, Rita, had seven children. (Courtesy of Bernadine Butkowski.)

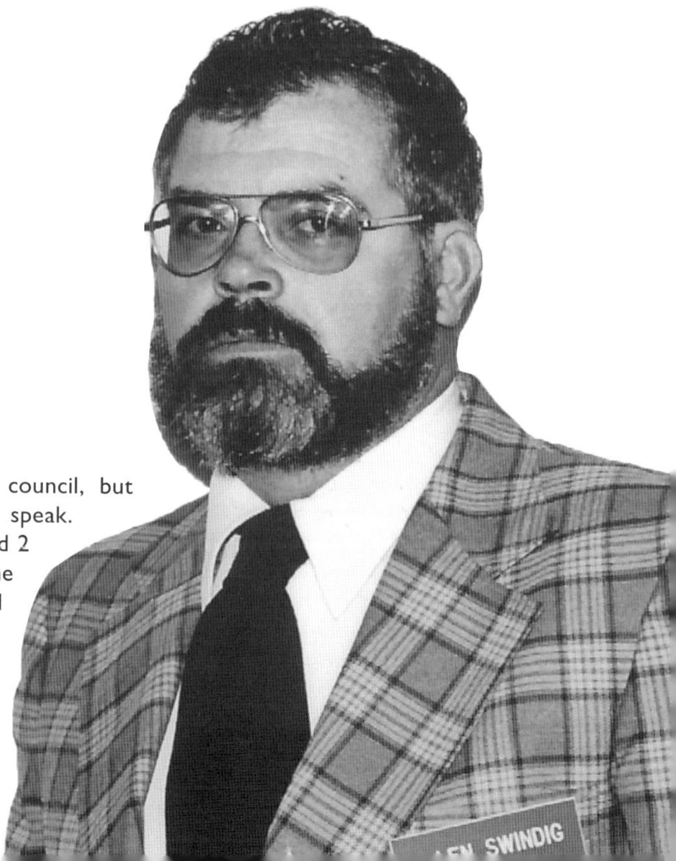

Allen Swindig

Swindig was the "quiet man" on the council, but when he had a question, he asked to speak. His personality served him well, as Ward 2 constituents allowed him to remain on the council for 24 years. He was once elected just after having open-heart surgery. Judge Mark Betleski went to his home to administer the oath of office. (Courtesy of Allen Swindig.)

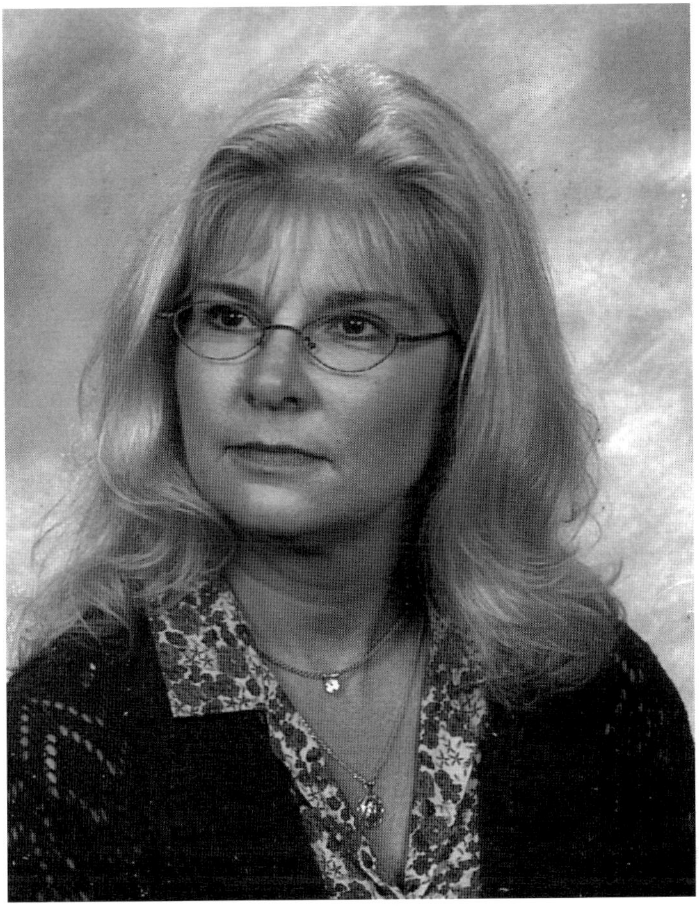

Paula Cope

Cope was barely out of high school when she began working at city hall as a typist-clerk. For the next three decades, she remained in the hub of local government. Some residents felt that, as government officials came and went, Cope was the only one who really understood what was going on. During her years in the hallowed halls, the city saw six mayors. Despite ruffled feathers from time to time, Cope said she loved her job.

Clerk of council Pat Dreger hired Cope in 1978, and Cope always remembered Dreger as being her mentor as she grew into her position of assistant council clerk. As the years went by, Cope gained experience in her job. Meanwhile, she continued to join organizations and take classes in anything that would make the council clerk's office more productive. She became a certified municipal clerk and also received the designation of master municipal clerk in 2005.

She enjoyed helping residents wade through the various ordinances to get the answers they needed. She also tried to make the council's job easier and lend a helping hand when possible. Cope encountered some special people from day to day, but there was one who she will never forget. Lois Sullivan "religiously attended council meetings during my employment and touched my life beyond words," she said. In addition to her post as assistant council clerk, Cope was secretary to the planning commission, the board of zoning and building appeals, and the civil service commission. She was also the recording secretary for the tax abatement review board and performed orientation programs for council members.

Looking back on her time with the city, Cope said her memories and stories could fill a book. "This has been the best city to live, work, cry, and play in, and I wouldn't choose any other life if given the opportunity." (Courtesy of Paula Cope.)

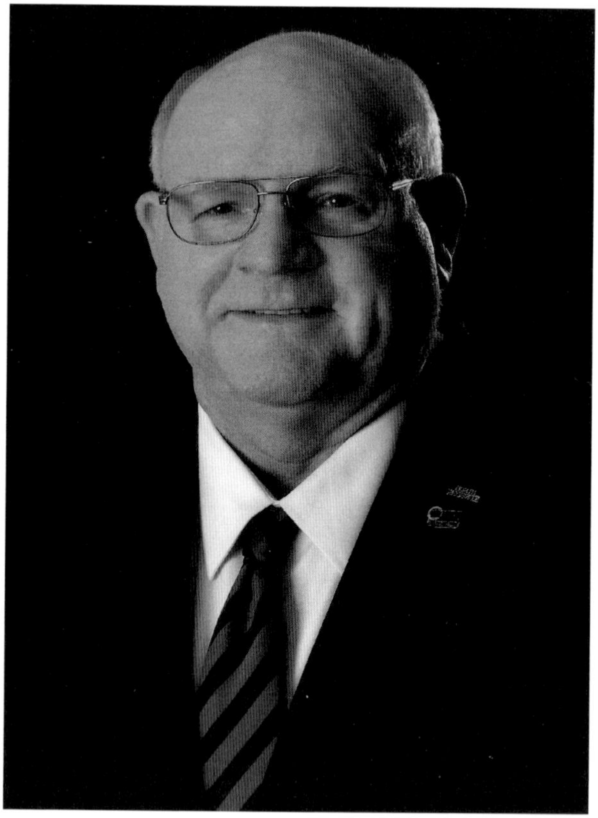

G. David Gillock

This North Ridgeville mayor was raised to be civic-minded, a philosophy he learned from his late father, George David Gillock Sr., who was on the village board and the volunteer fire department in his hometown. He was also a member of the Lions Club and the Masons.

When the younger Gillock moved to North Ridgeville, he began carving a political career for himself, spending four years on the city council. He ran for the Ward 2 seat, but lost by 17 votes to Democrat Allen Swindig, who was well known in his ward. Gillock then set his sights on the at-large race and eventually won. He served on the council when Jeffry Armbruster was mayor. By 2013, Gillock had been mayor of North Ridgeville for 10 years and was halfway through a third term.

Prior to running for council, Gillock gained experience by being on the fair housing board, the zoning board, and the planning commission. While keeping politically active, Gillock and his wife, Beverly, raised four daughters, then found themselves in a "second time around" situation, caring for three of their ten grandchildren. Gillock admitted that it was difficult juggling city business and the home front as well. He would leave the house in a suit, then try to catch a youngster's sporting event later in the day. If he was at a meeting and it was nearing 7:30 p.m., he would "zip out of there." Meals were sometimes forgotten in the flurry of making a softball, football, or soccer game, but he would always take the children to church. His free time is spent attending Rotary Club meetings and fishing, as shown here.

Gillock said he likes government, but not politics, and he admitted that North Ridgeville is a political city. On a day-to-day basis, it is important to get things done by working together, he said, but he also likes to see how things are done on the outside. To that end, he belonged to several organizations, such as the Ohio Municipal League and the Ohio Department of Transportation.

There are always issues, but Gillock said he does not micromanage. Flooding during storms is a problem, and the mayor accepts dealing with it as part of his job. "I enjoy being the mayor 110 percent," Gillock said, "not 95 percent." (All, courtesy of G. David Gillock.)

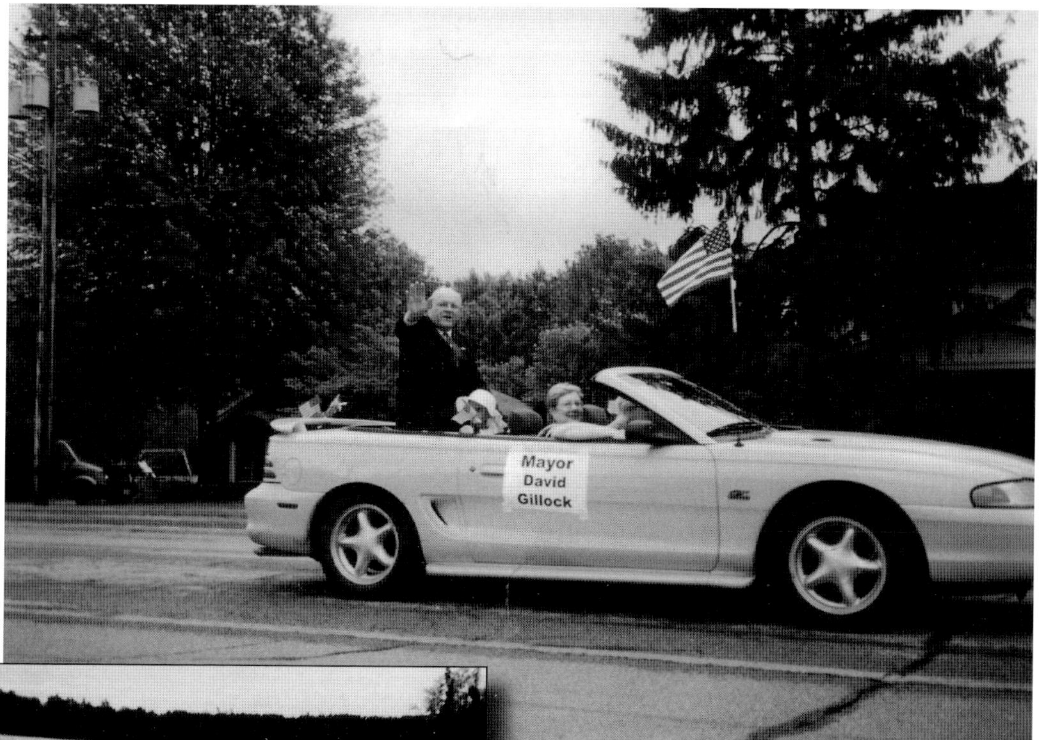
Mayor
David
Gillock

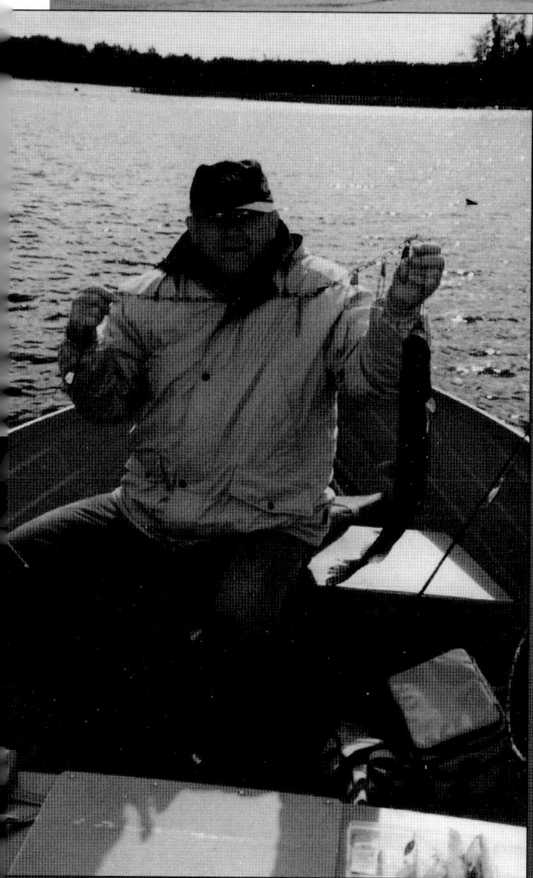

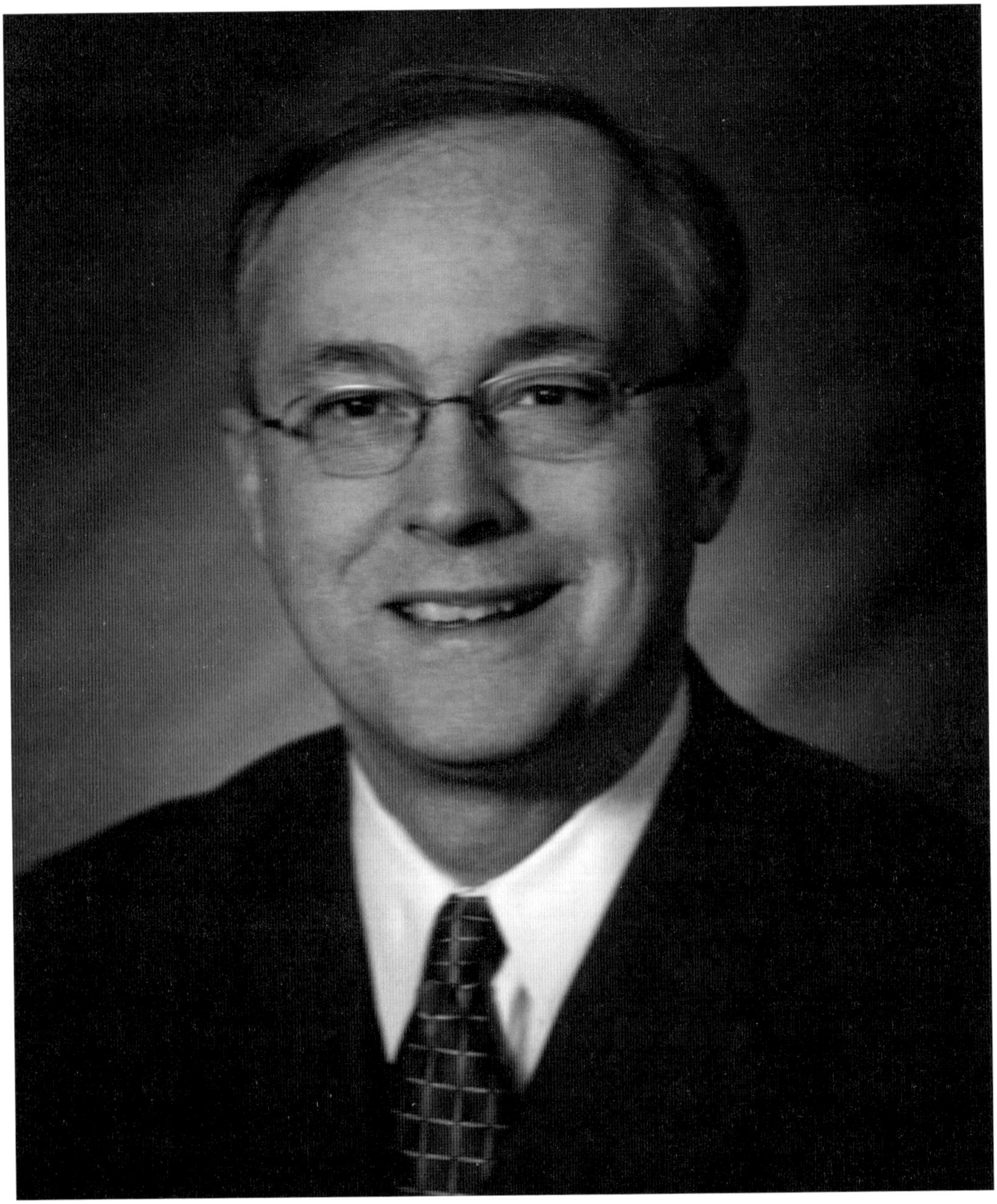

Jeffrey Manning
Manning graduated from Brookside High School and seemed destined to become a history professor or a lawyer. He lived in Medina and, after college, he and Gayle Gerhart married. Manning opened a law practice around 1977. Richard Noll, the mayor at the time, tapped Manning, just 29, to be his law director. When a new Democratic mayor took office, Manning lost the job. The city grew, and Manning became involved in Boy Scouts and the Jaycees, where he was voted 1978 Young Man of the Year. He won the Charles Stewart Memorial Award in 1999 and worked with boys' basketball. In 2000, he became a state representative. Manning and his wife had two children, and life was good. Then, on February 13, 2004, at just 54 years of age, Manning died unexpectedly. (Courtesy of Gayle Manning.)

Gayle Gerhart Manning
Manning and her future husband began dating at 17. After high school, they went to college, Jeffrey Manning to become a lawyer and Gayle Manning to become a teacher. When her husband began his law practice, she started teaching, and stayed for 35 years. The Mannings lived a 45-minute drive away in North Olmsted. Their schedules were difficult, but they tried to coordinate them to attend their children's sporting events. And Gayle and Jeffrey enjoyed their careers. But one day, Gayle Manning received a call that her husband was in the hospital. He died a few days later. Manning retired from teaching and was asked to run for state senate. Initially, she had no interest. But she had served on the city council and decided to give it a try. It proved a rewarding second career. (Courtesy of Gayle Manning.)

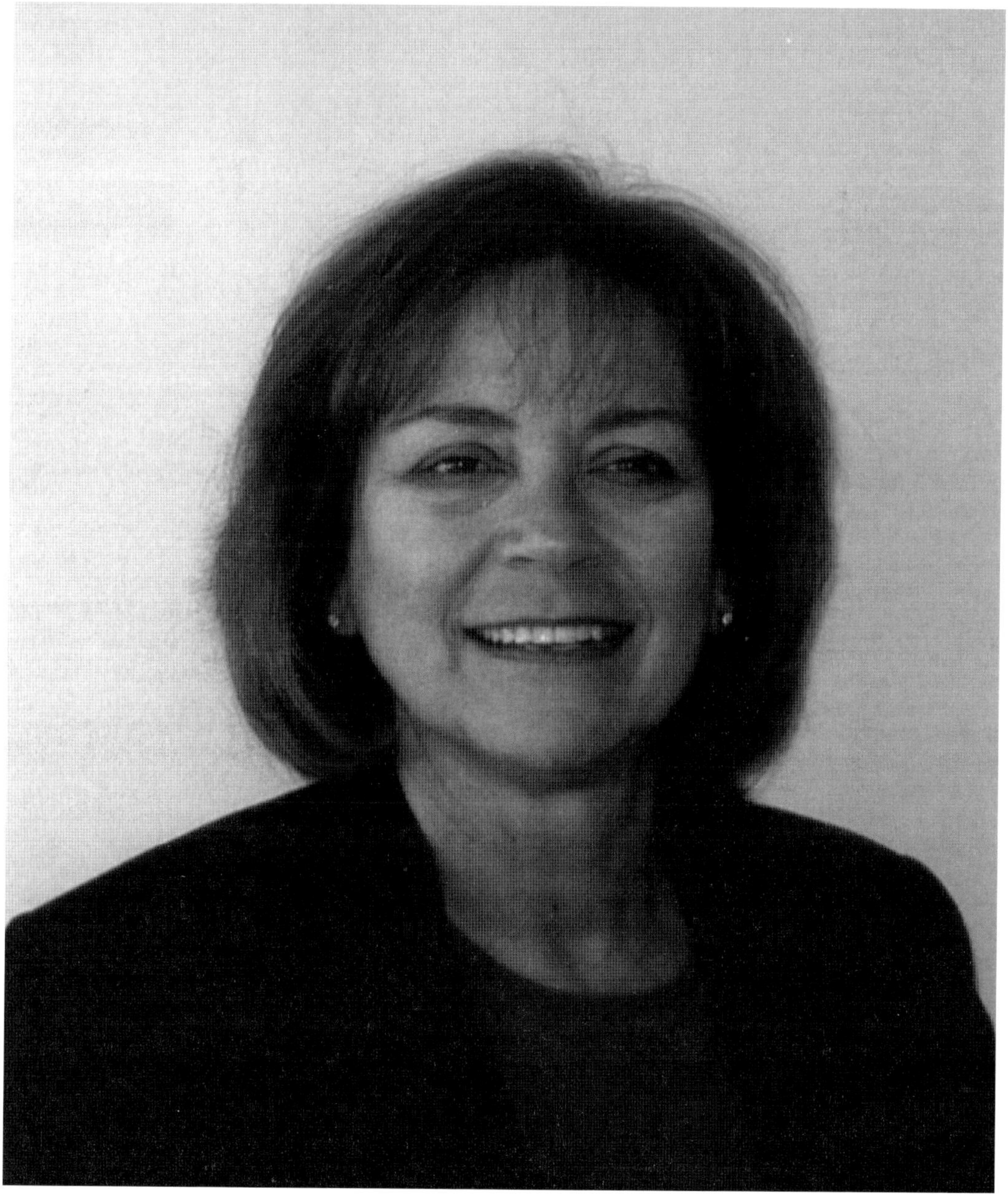

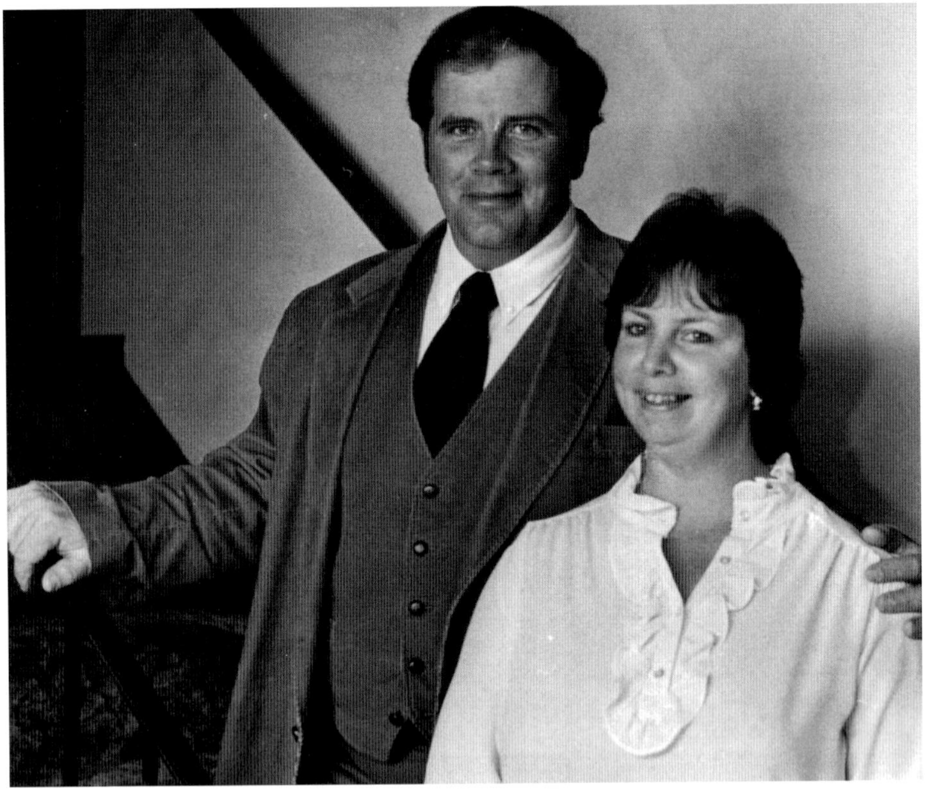

Floyd Peaco

Peaco worked as a millwright before winning a seat on the city council. He then toppled Republican mayor Richard Noll in 1983. When Noll challenged Peaco two years later, Peaco won again. Floyd and his wife, Mary Jane, are seen here on election night.

Peaco enjoyed running the city. On occasion, though, his longtime friend and safety service director, Ray McLaughlin, had to mend fences. A hands-on mayor, Peaco had no problem getting down and dirty to get a job done. Residents would often see him driving a snowplow to help clear roads.

By the time the 1987 election rolled around, Peaco was settled into a job he really liked. During the annual State of the City address, he touted successes, like the 625 new jobs that surfaced after his 1983 election. Not one to be satisfied, he was always looking for ways to improve the city. He sought another term, but rumors hinted that he intended to run for county commissioner. He quickly quashed that idea, saying that if he won again, he would not consider a run for commissioner.

Peaco wanted North Ridgeville to be a standout community. In 1986, Bart Wolstein, owner of the Cleveland Force soccer team, wanted to build an outdoor stadium complex. Just "for the heck of it," Peaco sent Wolstein a letter of interest with information about Ridgeville. In a push to show Wolstein the community at its best, a huge Party in the Park was held on August 24, 1986. In the end, Wolstein chose another location. In 1987, Peaco had another opportunity to show off the city, when comedian Martin Mull participated in the Corn Festival. A headline in the local newspaper read, "Mull'-titudes enjoyed the Corn Fest." As a youngster, Mull lived in the city for just a few years, though residents considered him a native son. Mull was in town to film an HBO special, and he and his crew got the royal treatment. Mull is seen with Peaco in the top photograph on the opposite page.

In 2004, Peaco and his wife moved out of Ridgeville, a situation dictated by health issues, but they continued to travel. The former mayor enjoyed car races and owned two racecars. He began announcing races in Norwalk, Ohio, and then became a national event announcer for the International Hot Rod Association, traveling to race locations. (All, courtesy of Floyd Peaco.)

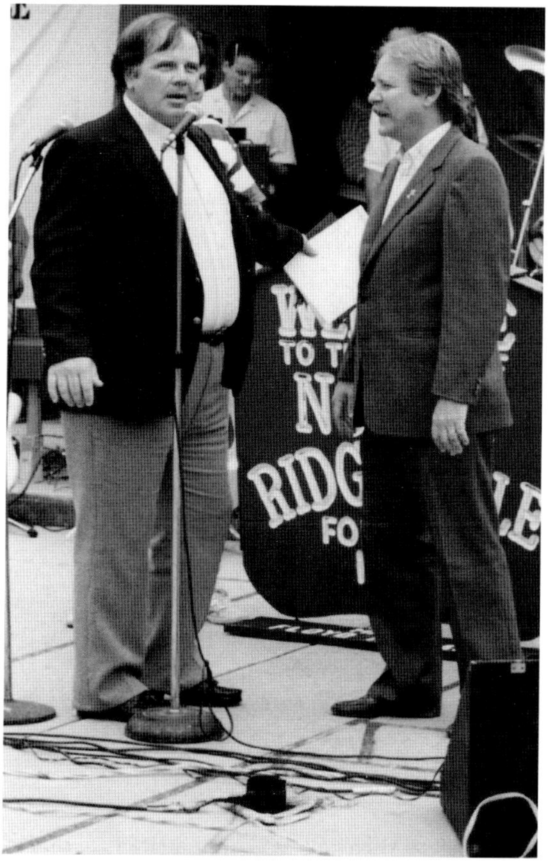

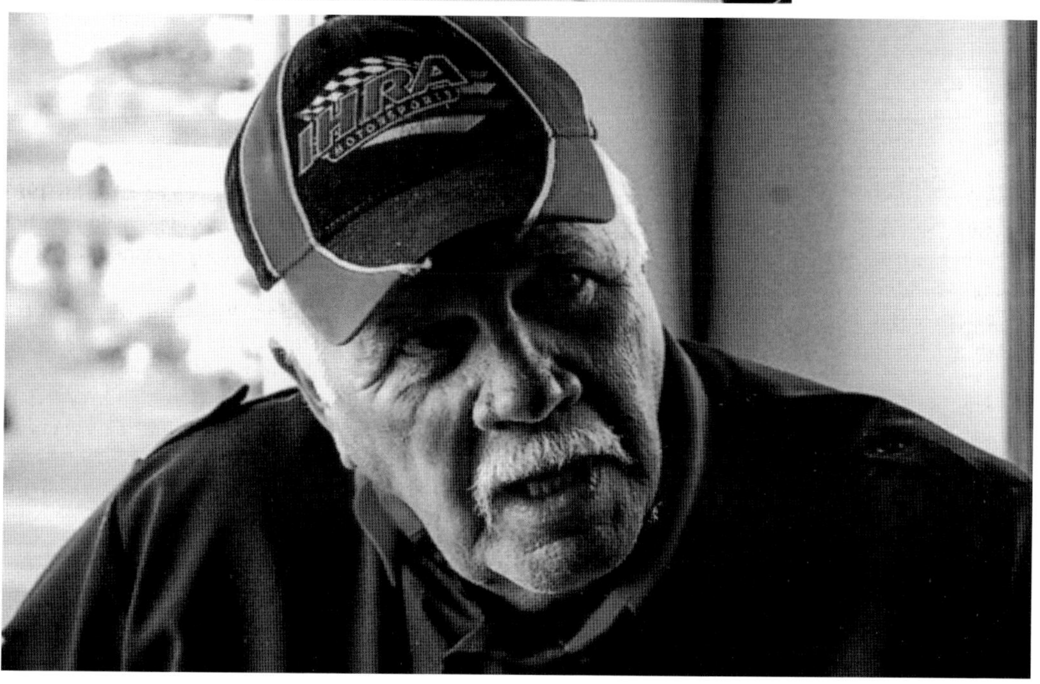
IHRA

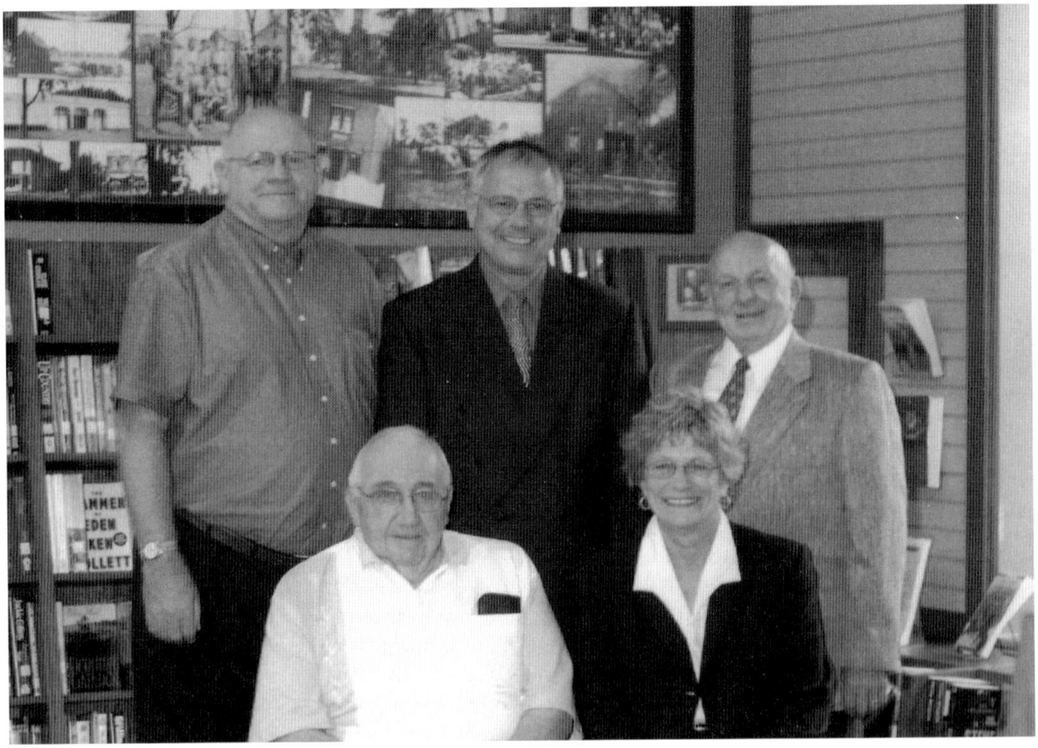

Deanna Hill

Hill was an educator, a former member of the state house of representatives, and the first woman to be elected mayor in North Ridgeville. She died on May 26, 2013, at the age of 69.

Hill was head of the teachers' union during a contentious strike, and, as a teacher and mayor, she was her own person and could be tough to deal with. She knew her mind and had no problem maintaining her position. An example of her standing firm took place in February 1996, when Hill informed the chamber of commerce that it would have to leave its longtime home in city hall and find a new location. The chamber is a private, dues-paying group that does not belong in a public, city-owned building, she said. Initially, the chamber officers took exception to the mayor's demand, but Gary Mould stepped up and offered office space rent-free at Mould's Plantation. The chamber moved into the office five months after being told to move, and the spat diminished.

Hill was not all work. She loved a good joke and had an infectious laugh that could turn a somber scene into a fun time.

During her 2002 State of the City address, Hill alluded to a lawsuit filed by attorney Gerald Phillips, who represented a group of residents. Hill told the audience that the supreme court had dismissed the three lawsuits filed by Phillips. However, when the ensuing applause subsided, the mayor said that Phillips, Christopher Crobaugh, and friends had filed another lawsuit to take the Waterbury Planned Community Development to voters. In her address, Hill reported the city's progress, noting that her "proudest accomplishment" was the Westerly Sewer. During that term, the city's bond rating went up, and the Issue 2 state grant allowed the city to do many things that had been put on hold.

In 2004, Hill joined former mayors to show support for the 2004 library levy. Shown here are, from left to right, (first row) Richard Noll and Hill; (second row) G. David Gillock, Jeffry Armbruster, and Paul Sweda. (Courtesy of Eugene Kleinholz.)

CHAPTER FOUR

Firmly Planted

Long before the 25 square miles of land that eventually became North Ridgeville evolved into the community it is today, farms dotted the landscape and men worked from dawn to dusk to provide for their families. Helping them to carry on the business of farming were sawmills and gristmills, located near rivers, streams, or creeks, and powered by waterwheels. Farms that grew wheat employed a number of men to help when threshing day rolled around. And in the early 1900s, gas wells were drilled with the help of a rig pulled by horses to drilling sites.

A building along the east side of Avon Belden Road, north of Butternut Ridge Road, was erected in 1871 as the Excelsior Cheese Factory. Since then, the structure has housed a number of other businesses. Gilder's Blacksmith Shop, owned by Charles Gilder, was started in the late 1800s. It was one of many businesses that began in the 1800s or early 1900s. Joseph Laubenthal's milk-hauling company began in the late 1920s, and J.P. Diederich Sons started its greenhouse operation in 1925. The latter business seemed to trigger the advent of other companies, some which are still in operation.

Stagecoach inns not only offered weary travelers a good night's sleep, but proved to be a boon to the North Ridgeville economy. One such inn was the Four-Chimneys on Center Ridge Road, a haven for those making their way from one place to another.

Some of the businesses begun years ago continue to be in operation, such as Buescher's Hardware, located on Center Ridge Road west of Avon Belden Road. The building was previously known by different names and owned by different individuals. Initially it was called Fisher's; it later became known as Loescher's General Store, and then Diederich's Grain and Feed. Another longtime firm is the Bogner Funeral Home, which opened in 1963 on Center Ridge Road at the intersection of Stoney Ridge Road. In 2013, it celebrated its 50th anniversary. Other businesses have withstood the test of time in North Ridgeville, in the process perhaps making modifications of some sort or adding more space, all in the name of progress.

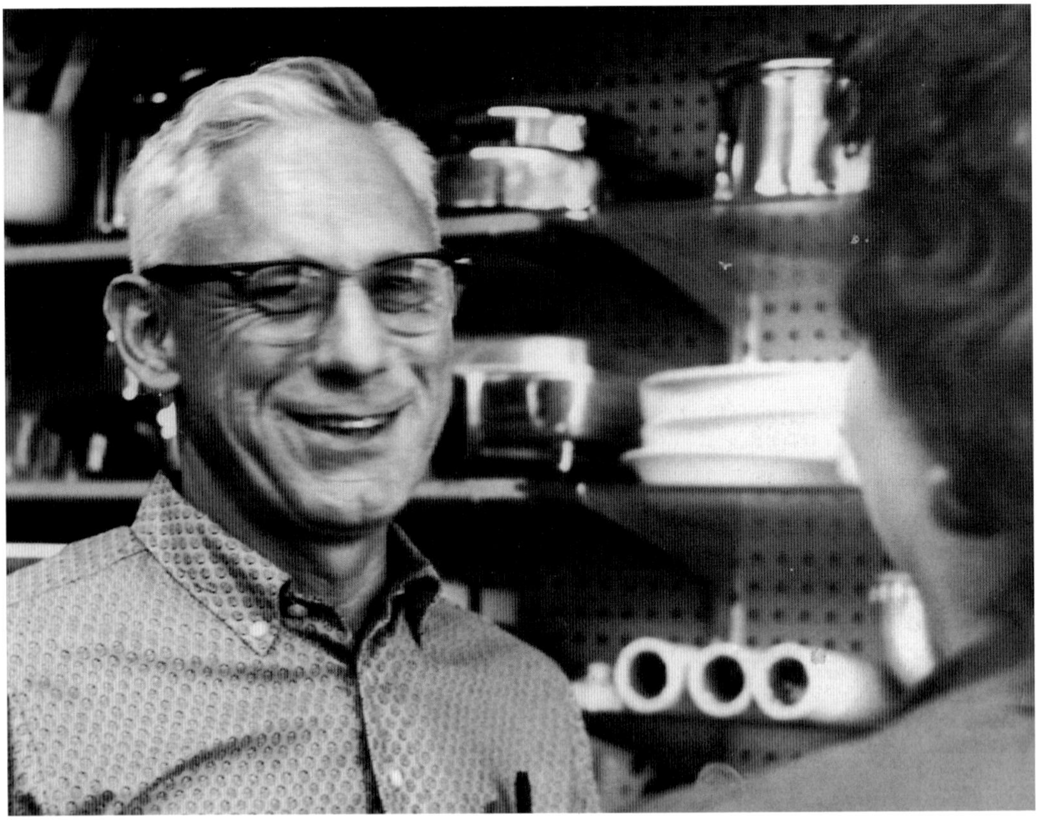

Urban Buescher

Urban Buescher was born in Cleveland in 1910 and began learning about hardware stores from his father, who owned one in Cleveland. Buescher moved to North Ridgeville during the Great Depression, hoping to make a good life for himself and his bride, Margaret. A farm community was something Buescher knew nothing about, so it took a bit of learning to fit into the lifestyle. He opened a farm supply store in the gas station that was located near what became Buescher's Hardware. In 1936, he purchased the building.

The family quickly outgrew the apartment that went with the building, and Buescher began constructing a home on Center Ridge Road in 1955. He completed it two years later. However, all seven Buescher children were born in the apartment.

As more customers began shopping at the hardware store, Buescher began expanding the space and adding more items, such as chicken feed, barbed wire, and poultry netting. Not much later, he began stocking stovepipe and plumbing supplies. The rear warehouse was converted into a feed storage area in 1942. In 1946, the west section was remodeled to house garden and electrical supplies.

Watching the passing residents along Center Ridge Road, Buescher began to get a feel for the town and the people who frequented his store. He also became active in the community, appearing in the annual shows put on by the local Kiwanis, an organization he helped found. He also became involved in the political scene. In 1961, Buescher announced that he was running for Ward 3 councilman on the Republican ticket. One of the improvements he talked of during his campaign was a swimming pool for residents.

Although his hopes of representing Ward 3 did not materialize, Buescher served three years on the planning commission and two terms as councilman at large. During his second term, he was council president. By the 1980s Buescher's son, J. Kenneth, had taken over the hardware store, giving his mom and dad time to travel. (Both, courtesy of Nita Baker.)

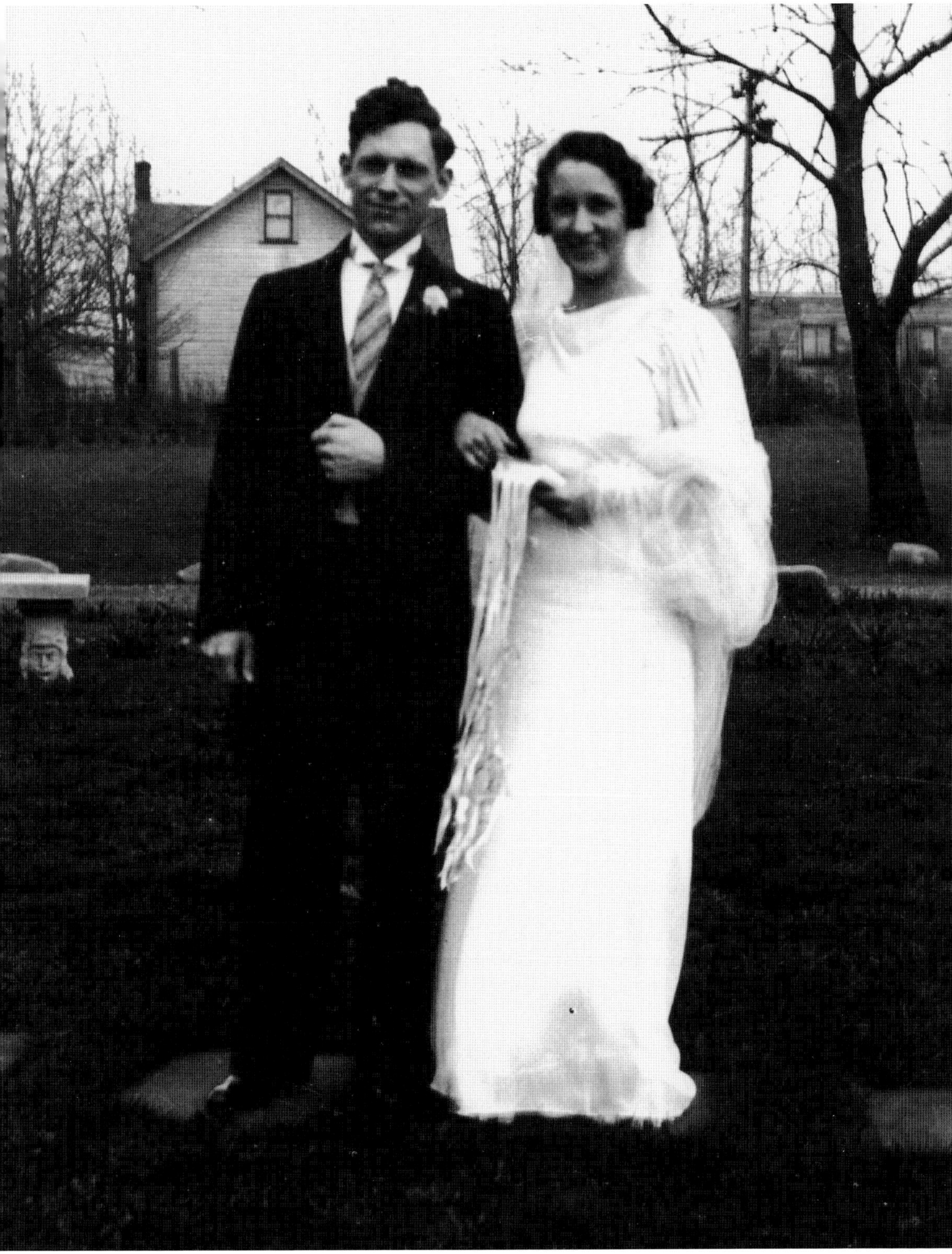

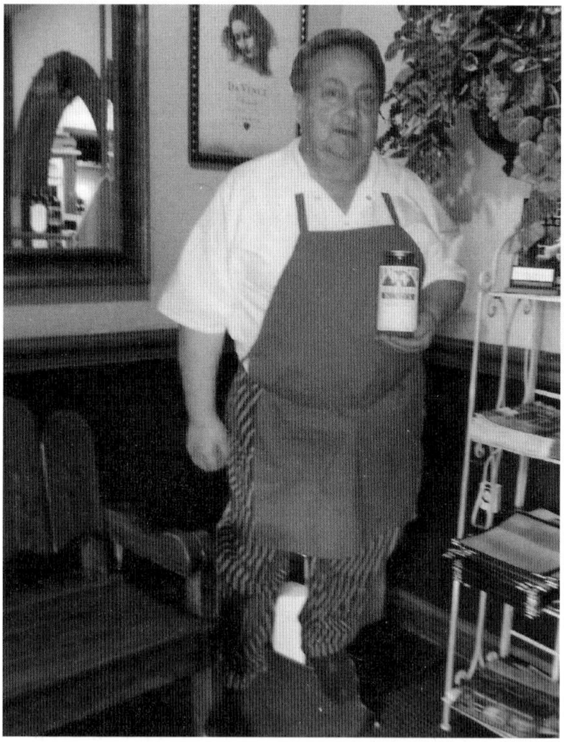

Thomas Barber
Tom Barber opened Nino's Italian Restaurant near Mills Creek Lane 23 years ago. He had worked in various restaurants and wanted his own place. Nino's gives diners the sense that they are in Italy. Some customers have been to Italy, and they like Nino's better. The highest praise is when another chef eats at his restaurant, Barber said. He added that there have been engagements, a wedding, and anniversary celebrations at Nino's. (Courtesy of Carol Klear.)

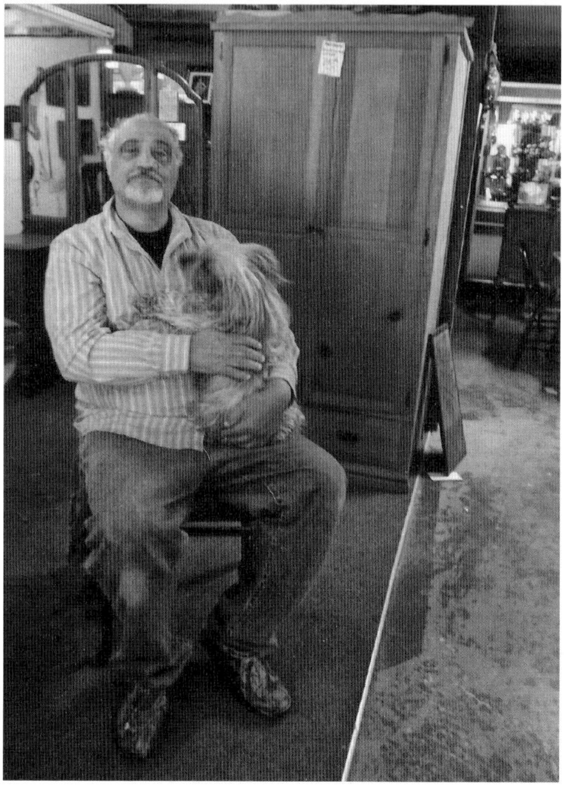

Richard Monaco
Louis Aurensen built the Hatchery on his farm in the 1920s. It closed in the 1950s and reopened as an antique mall in 1972. In 1989, Monaco bought the shop on Avon Belden Road, which has several rooms of antiques. He had chickens in pens in the front yard as an attraction, but neighbors complained, and the city made Monaco get rid of them. (Courtesy of Carol Klear.)

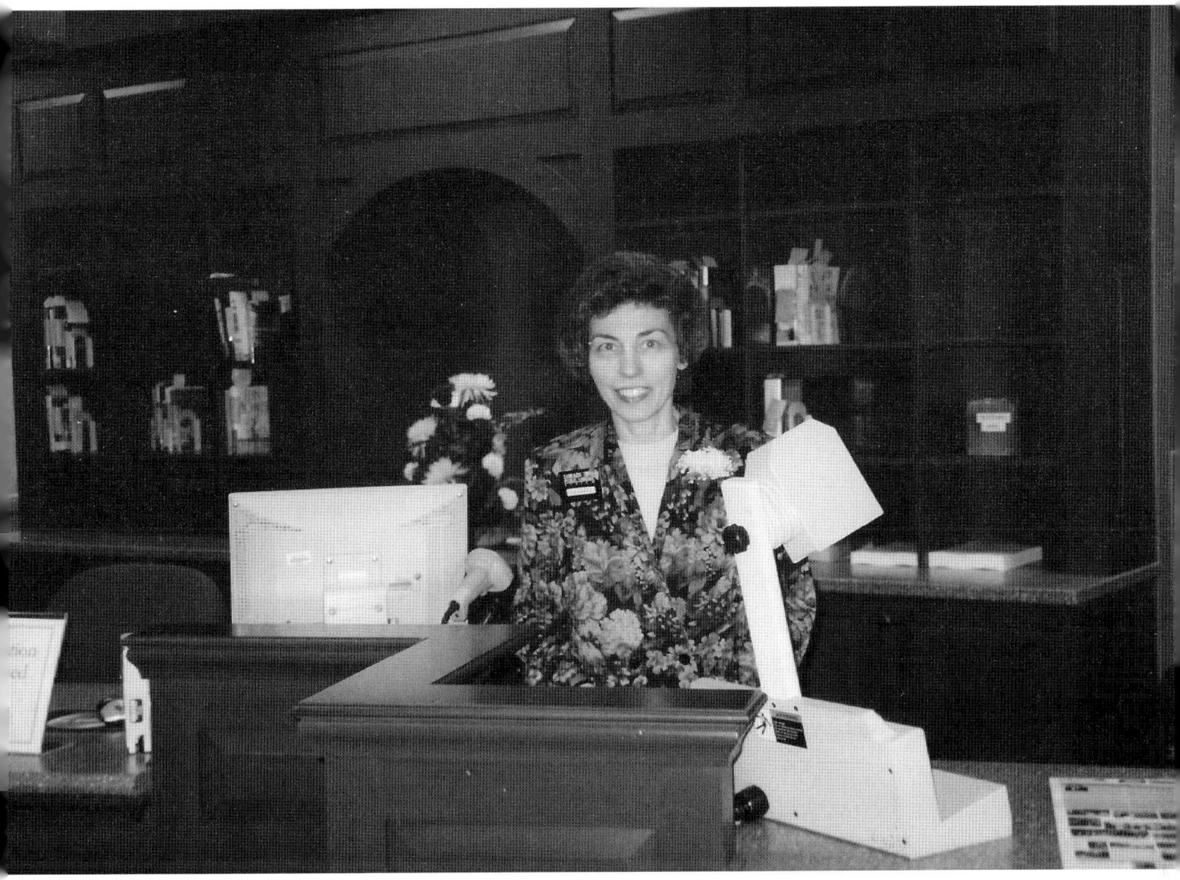

Karen Sigsworth
Everyone knows Karen Sigsworth, supervisor of the North Ridgeville Branch Library. A native of Mansfield, Ohio, Sigsworth graduated from the Ohio State University and went to library school at Kent State. She was hired for a position at the main library of the Lorain Public Library System in 1977, working there for four and a half years. It was there that she met her future husband, Jeffrey. They were married in 1981.

At that time, North Ridgeville was a small rural town. The library was located on the first floor of the Old Town Hall. Sigsworth said she applied and was hired as the branch library supervisor. However, the population was beginning to grow, and it was not long before the library became crowded. In 1989, there was a vacant bank on Jaycox Road. After the building was inspected, it was decided the library would relocate there. Every bit of space in the bank was used, even the vault. Within a short time, space was again becoming a problem, as more and more people were availing themselves of the library. More reading materials and CDs, audio books, and videos were being requested. And, there were no additional rooms for meetings. Decisions had to be made about how to resolve the issue.

As the branch library supervisor, Sigsworth attended many meetings and held many discussions on the situation. Then, Mayor Deanna Hill and other city officials offered the library system a piece of city-owned land on Bainbridge Road, across from South Central Park. On April 13, 2002, city and library officials and residents gathered for the ground breaking. On May 4, 2003, the new North Ridgeville Branch Library opened its doors. Sigsworth said the building was what the city needed. The library staff has been able to offer free programs, children's programs, computer classes, and much more. "We did not envision the technology we have now," Sigsworth said. "It is exciting to keep the library new and fresh." (Courtesy of Karen Sigsworth.)

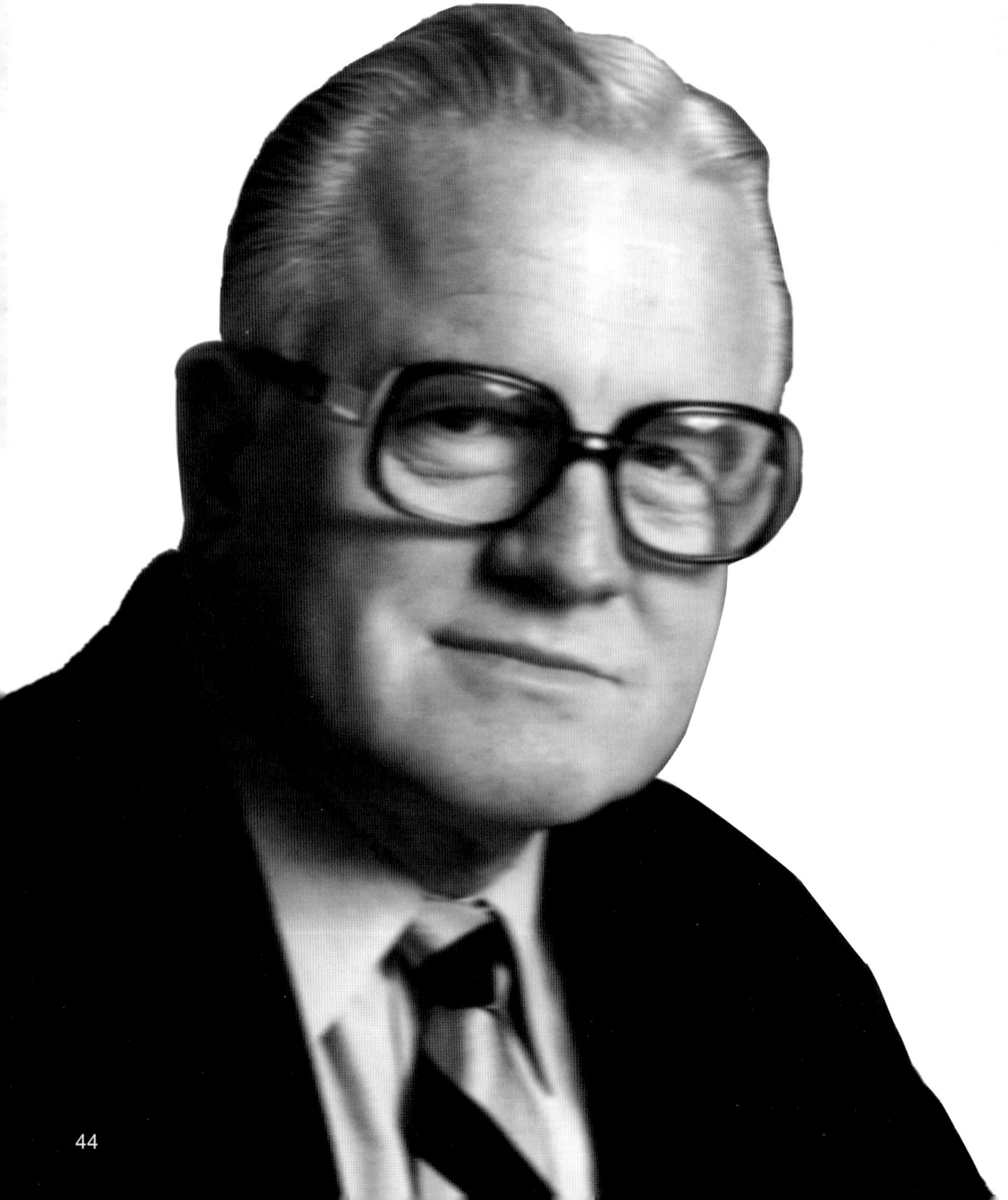

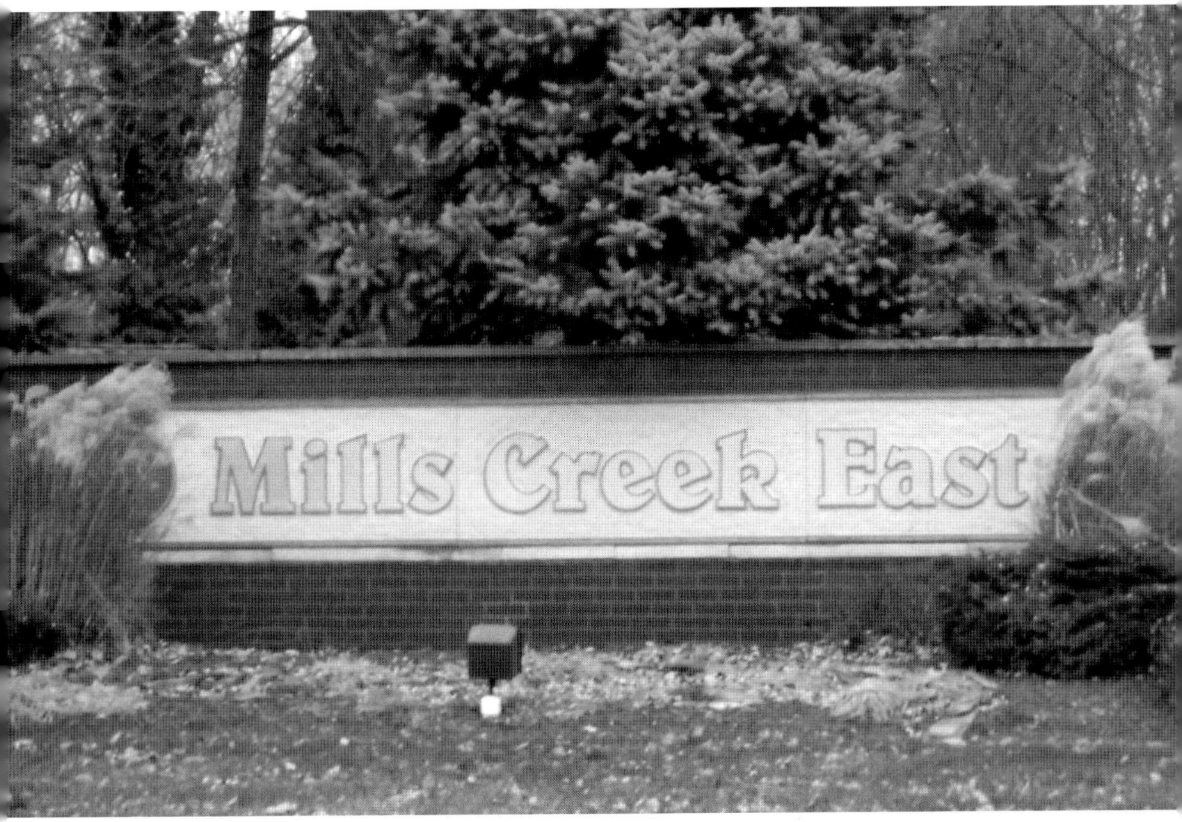

Robert Schmitt

A predecessor company of Bob Schmitt Homes was founded in 1946 by Robert Schmitt in Mansfield, Ohio. Schmitt, a third-generation builder, constructed and sold houses to pay his way through college. He eventually reorganized the approach to building homes.

In 1950, Schmitt began building homes in Berea. Between 1950 and 1972, he constructed 936 single-family homes, 92 condominiums, and 10 townhomes. In 1963, his next location was the City of Strongsville, with easy access to major highways and Cleveland Hopkins Airport. He continued developing and building neighborhoods in Strongsville until 1996.

While Schmitt was building in Strongsville in 1986, Bob Schmitt Homes had a separate crew working in North Ridgeville. Mills Creek was his first neighborhood, consisting of Mills Creek North, South, East, and West, with a total of 737 single-family homes, 165 cluster homes, and 82 townhomes on 453 acres of land. In 1993, Bob Schmitt Homes returned to North Ridgeville and purchased multiple parcels of land that became the Ridgefield neighborhood, complete with single-family lots and detached cluster lots. The neighborhood included a heated outdoor swimming pool, a kiddie pool, a fitness center, and a recreation center for social functions.

Over the years Schmitt won a number of awards, including many from the National Association of Home Builders. In 1976, he was honored by *Professional Builder* magazine as "Professional Builder of the Year." In that same year, he was appointed to the board of directors of the National Institute of Building Sciences by Pres. Gerald Ford. Since 1956, Schmitt and Bob Schmitt Homes have received more than 50 awards.

A lesser-known side of the developer/builder was his generosity in helping Community Care design and construct a new building for the organization, at his cost, after Mark Giacco donated land behind Arby's Restaurant on Center Ridge Road. Community Care helps the less fortunate in North Ridgeville. (Both, courtesy of Kevin Corcoran.)

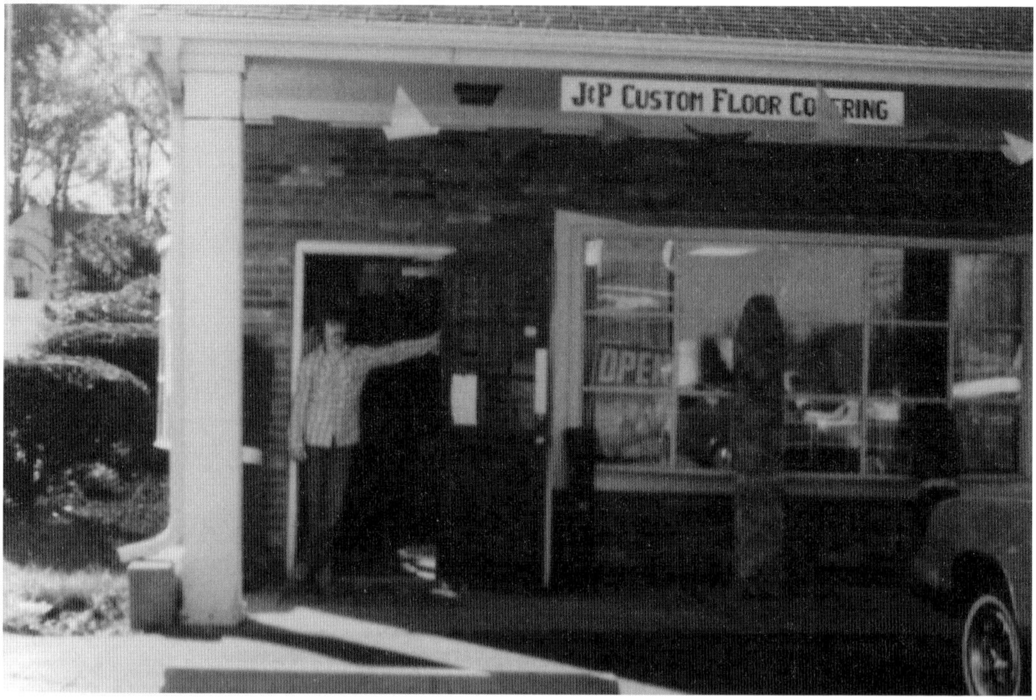

James and Patrick Ginley

The brothers opened their floor-covering store in October 1980, naming it J&P Custom Floor Covering. Their mother, Audrey Ginley, said her sons had initially worked for someone else, but one day asked if they could start their own business. Their first shop was next to Ron's Barbershop on Jaycox Road, but in 1985, they moved into the former location of a Lawson's store on Center Ridge Road. It was larger, allowing the Ginleys to offer more choices to customers. Each brother has his own talent, according to their mother. Patrick is the laborer; James is the businessman. Their parents are proud of their sons, who are hard workers and are always very polite to customers. The brothers offer advice and always come up with a solution, Audrey Ginley said. (Both, courtesy of James and Patrick Ginley.)

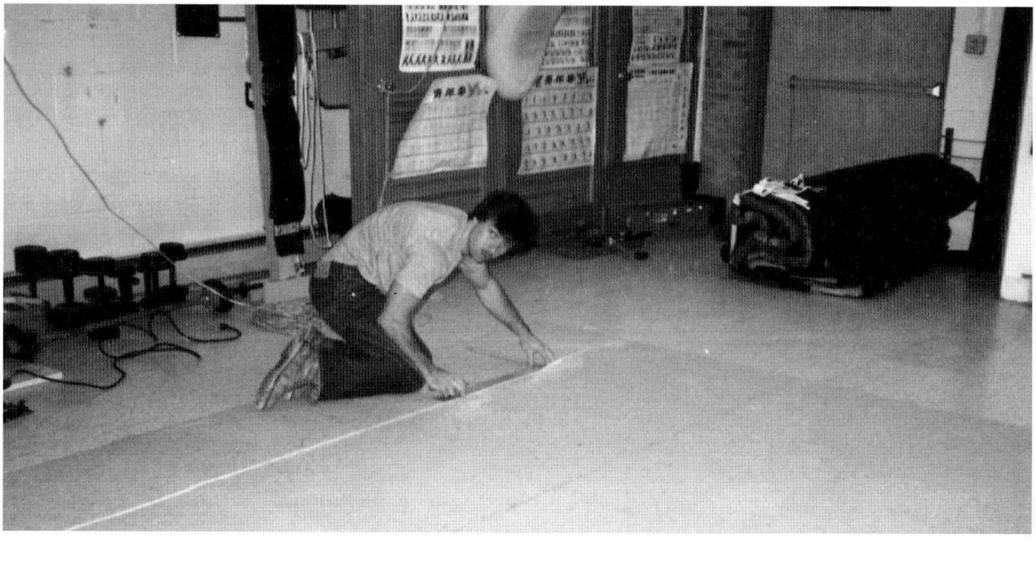

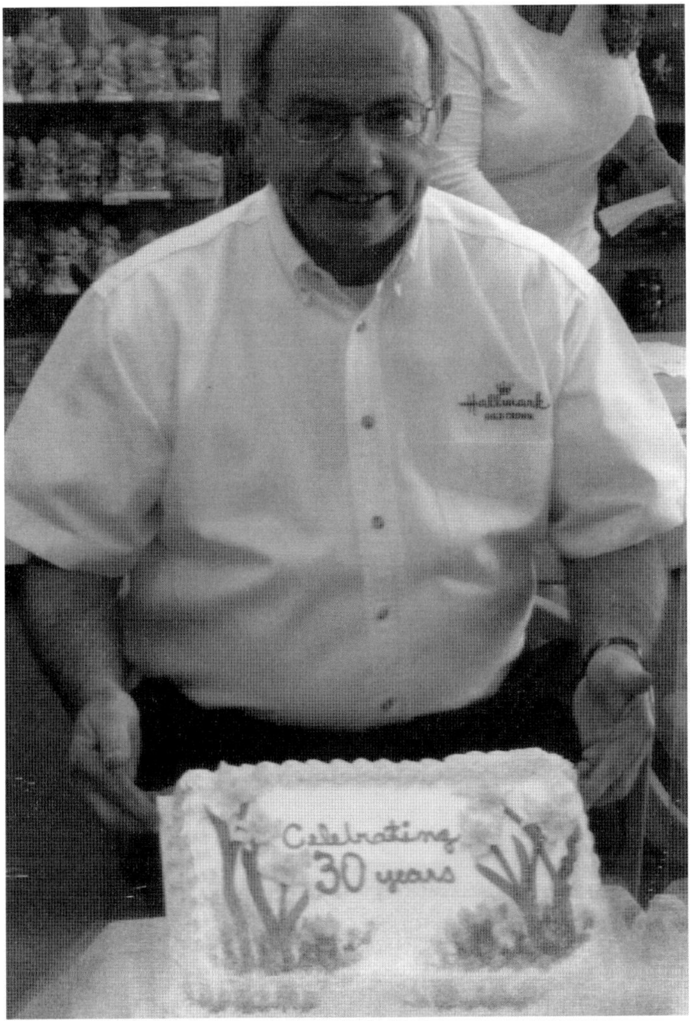

Robert LeHoty

Before opening LeHoty's Hallmark store in May 1981, Robert LeHoty worked for the federal government. He said that he decided on a career change because he could never be sure what the government was going to do.

LeHoty and his wife, Sandra, work together. While in college, she had worked at a Hallmark store. The idea of opening their own Hallmark store was intriguing, and the more they pursued it, the more they liked it. The LeHotys found a 3,000-square-foot building in a good location on Center Ridge Road in the Rini's Shopping Plaza. LeHoty made up his mind. In the weeks leading up to the May 1981 opening, people began peering through the windows. This gave LeHoty a feel for the community.

Hallmark company policy calls for its stores to stock 50 percent Hallmark items and 50 percent from other manufacturers, LeHoty said. "I've never had a problem with that, I like what they do; I'm proud of it." To gauge what people will purchase, LeHoty said he listens to what they ask for and observes what they like. He said that he wants to avoid being a "cookie cutter" type of store. To select what he offers customers in his store, LeHoty attends gift shows and a merchandise show in Chicago in a building 21 stories high that requires five days to cover.

Around 1996, LeHoty made what he calls "a leap of faith" and expanded the store to almost 5,000 square feet. It is going very well. (Courtesy of Robert LeHoty.)

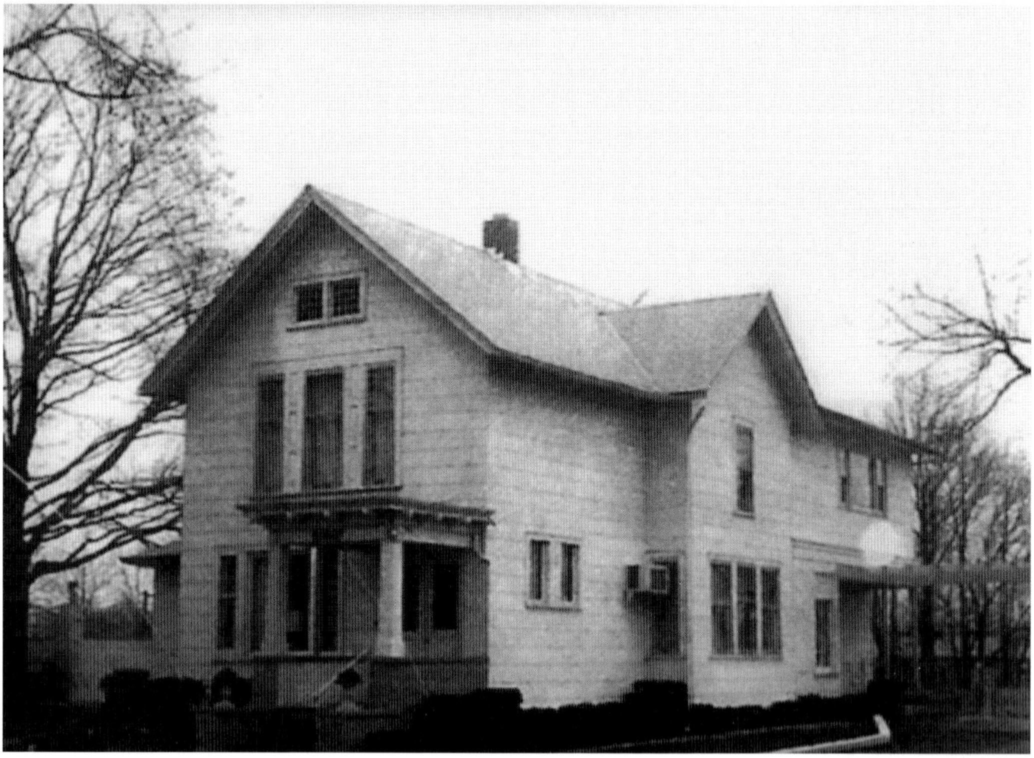

Harold and Kathleen Bogner

The Bogners opened North Ridgeville's first funeral home in 1963, in the historic Snyder house. The home, built in 1878, was located on Center Ridge Road across from the Ridgeville Cemetery. They were on call seven days a week, 24 hours a day. As there was no ambulance service in the community, they initiated that idea as well. Kathleen Bogner said they had not only a personal telephone, but a telephone for the funeral home and another for ambulance calls. Handling the entire operation was quite a feat initially, but, over time, the North Ridgeville Fire Department took over the ambulance service, allowing the Bogners to focus on providing funerals for bereaved families.

The couple lived above the funeral home, with an eye to putting an addition on the rear of the structure for their growing family. This was accomplished after the owner of the house west of the parking lot decided to sell his home to them.

Neither Harold nor Kathleen Bogner were from North Ridgeville, but they began to feel at home as they became involved in the community. Harold Bogner helped found the chamber of commerce and the Knights of Columbus. He also was a past president of the Lions Club and a charter member of the Rotary Club of North Ridgeville. In 2008, Mayor G. David Gillock presented him with a proclamation for the work he had done, including chairing the Voice of Democracy and Patriots Pen essay contests. Harold also served on the executive board of Community Care.

Kathleen Bogner started the Arts Council after having served for some time on the board of the Olde Towne Hall Theatre. The theater was in need of renovation, and she and other board members worked to raise money for the project. "We sold seats for $15 or $20," she said, adding, "The community needed an umbrella for the theater and the fine arts." The Arts Council promotes the arts through an Arts and Crafts Fair held during the Corn Festival. It also offers a scholarship to a high school senior each year.

David Bogner is following in his father's footsteps. With his wife, Mary Beth Bogner, he owns and operates the David Bogner Family Funeral Home on Center Ridge Road. (Both, courtesy of Kathleen Bogner.)

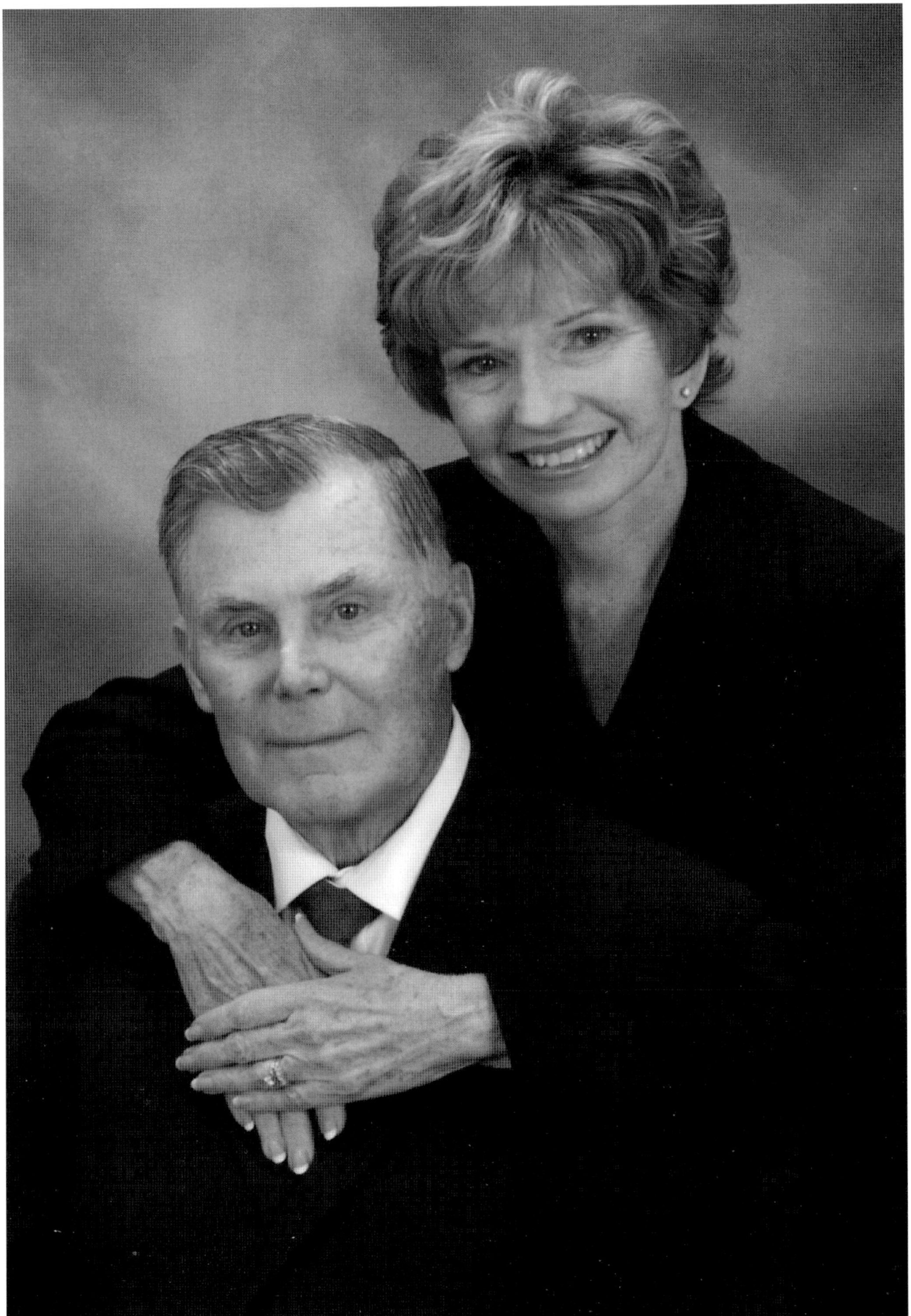

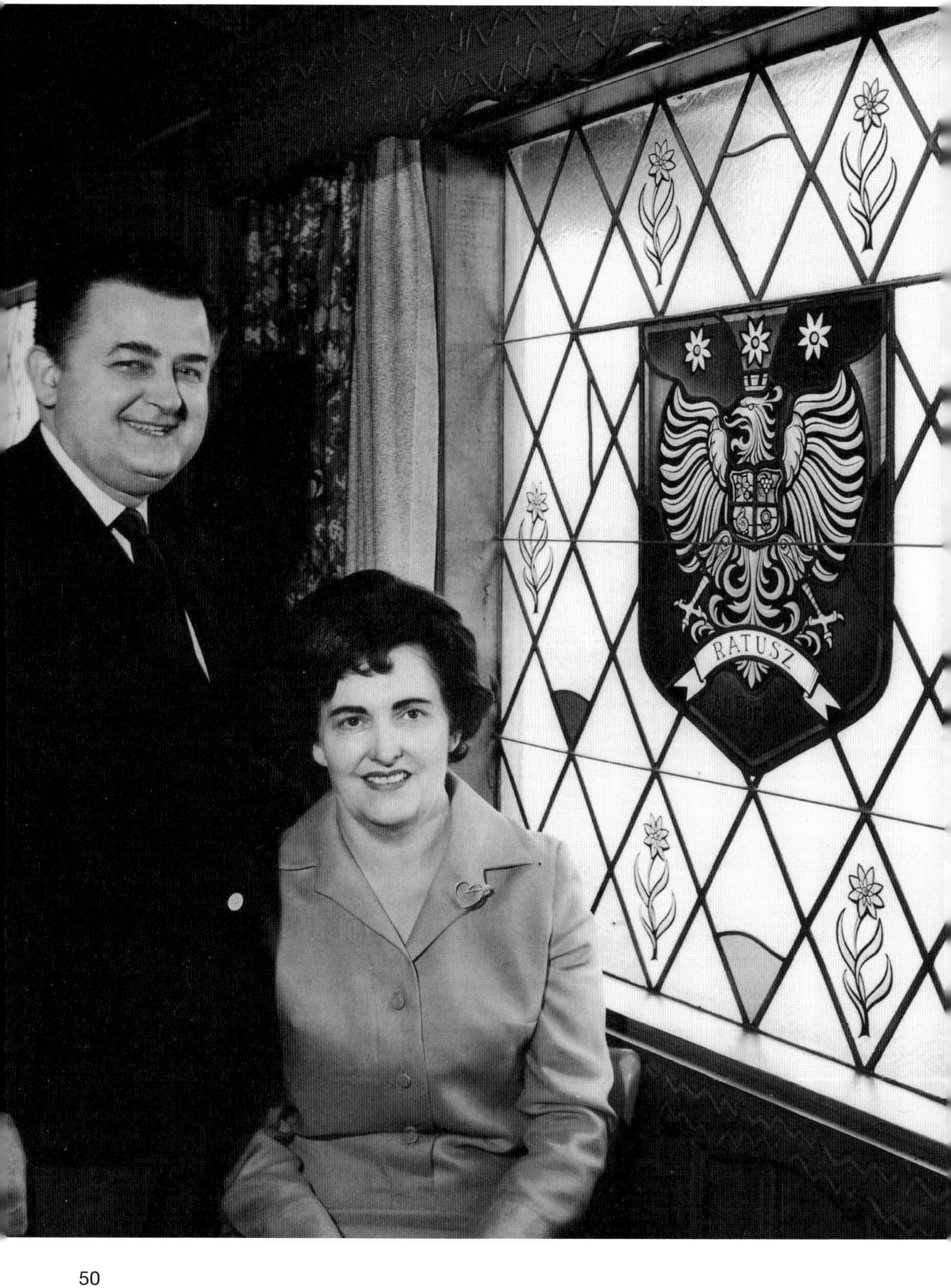
RATUSZ

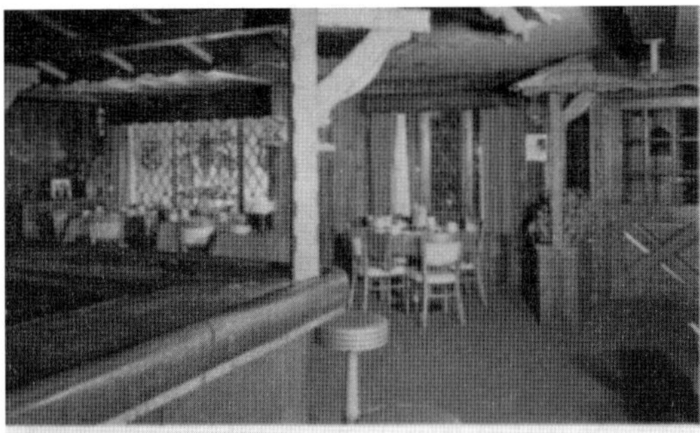

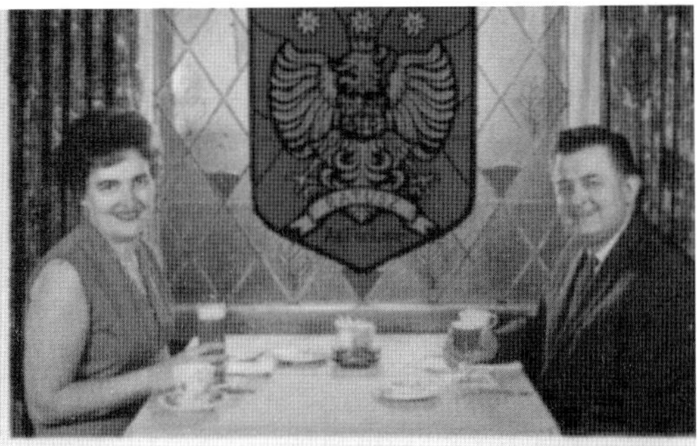

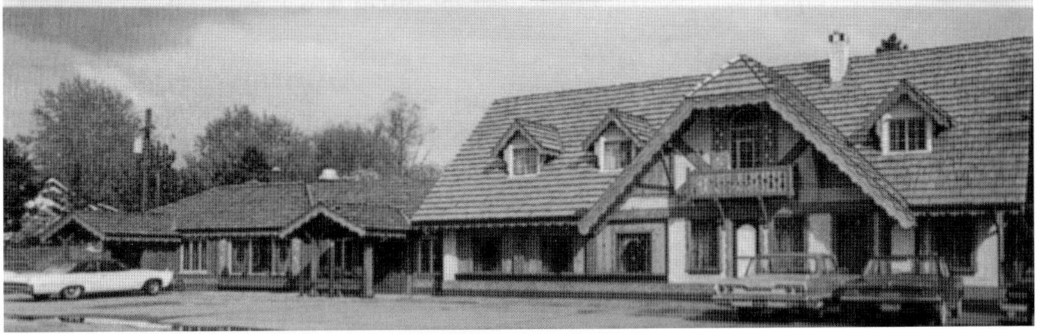

Edward Ratusz
In the 1940s, Frank and Antoinette Ratusz, Edward Ratusz's parents, bought the Green Parrot Restaurant on Center Ridge Road in North Ridgeville. They had previously owned another restaurant, and Edward helped them in the business. The Green Parrot was a popular dining place. It was located on Route 20, a well-traveled thoroughfare in the days before the turnpike was built.

Edward Ratusz was born in Cleveland and lived in Lakewood until the 1940s. When he returned home in 1944 after service in the Army, he and Catherine were married. He was then shipped off to Hawaii, but was soon discharged. Edward and Catherine began their family and had three daughters.

The Ratusz family lived above the restaurant, and Ratusz worked for a food salesman in Delaware. In 1960, he decided to open his own restaurant in Westlake called the Dover Chalet. Customers loved the home-cooked meals. About a year later, Ratusz took over the Green Parrot from his father when the elder Ratusz retired. Edward sold the Dover Chalet in the 1960s and renamed the Ridgeville restaurant Eddy's Chalet West.

Ratusz was a genial host and always took time to visit with diners. The restaurant was such a popular spot that he soon found it necessary to expand, adding the Eidelweiss Room and a bar. As he got older, Ratusz tried several times to sell the restaurant, with no luck. Just before New Year's Eve one year, the chef walked out with all of the food. Ratusz rounded up his family, including his wife and daughters, and, according to one daughter, Kathy Hepp, they cooked all night in order to handle the people who had reservations. In 1994, Ratusz and his wife retired, and the restaurant was sold. It was later destroyed by an electrical fire.

The couple enjoyed their family. Sadly, as they headed home from babysitting grandchildren in Oberlin on December 20, 1996, Edward and Catherine Ratusz were killed in a crash on Interstate 480, east of the Ohio Turnpike. Their family was distraught, and the accident shocked the entire North Ridgeville community. Following a funeral mass at St. Julie Billiart Church, where they were charter members, the husband and wife were buried in St. Peter Cemetery in North Ridgeville. (Both, courtesy of Kathy Hepp.)

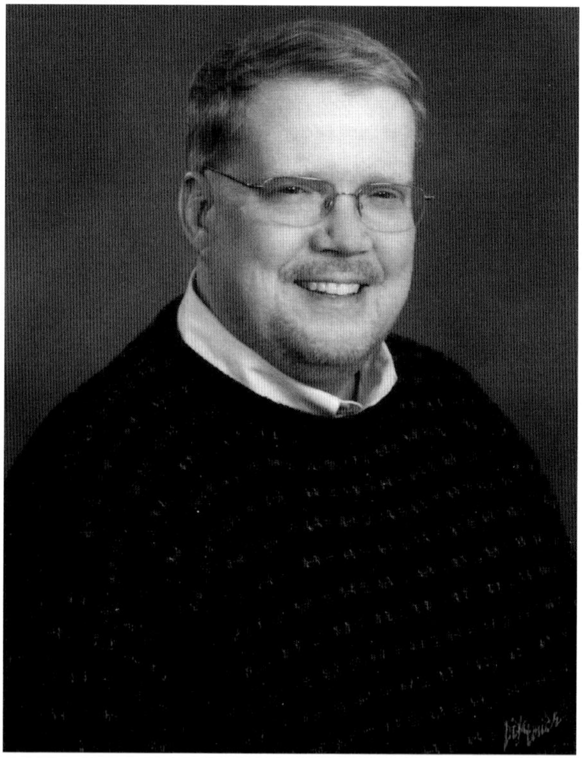

Kerry Mueller
Mueller started his firm, Center Cleaning Services, in April 1980 with just two employees. The company's peak years were from 1999 to 2003, and Mueller had 140 people working for him. With the recession and other economic conditions, the number of employees dropped to 65. The company provides commercial cleaning, residential cleaning, window cleaning, carpet cleaning, wall washing, and other services in five counties.

Mueller's father had been the vice president of a cleaning company, and when Kerry graduated from high school in 1969, he worked for the firm until a position opened up at NASA for a utility man. Kerry changed lights, cleaned, washed windows, and scrubbed floors.

In 1970, he left his dad's company when it lost the former agreement and went to work for the new NASA cleaning contractor, headquartered in New Jersey. Mueller was promoted to day supervisor and then contract manager within one year. At just 18 years of age, Mueller was handling a $600,000 agreement with 135 employees. He worked there for six years until a local cleaning company made him an offer he could not refuse. He stayed until 1980, then went out on his own.

Once, in the 1980s, Mueller had a crew at a restaurant in Beechwood washing the ceiling, vents, and performing a complete kitchen cleaning. The work had to be done on the weekend, and it fell on the same day as the AFC championship game, in which Cleveland's "Kardiac Kids," the Browns, were vying for a trip to the Super Bowl. Cleveland lost the game. The next day, as Mueller's men worked, the telephone kept ringing and ringing. Mueller answered, and a voice said, "This is Art Modell calling, and I would like to make reservations for this evening for 12 people." Mueller told Modell, the owner of the Browns, that the restaurant was closed and that he was just the cleaner and could not take his reservation. Modell replied, "Just the cleaner? You are not just the cleaner; your job is just as important as anyone else's. Don't ever forget that." And Mueller never did. Although his job is demanding, Mueller does like to relax at times. He has a passion for cooking and he collects miniature liquor bottles. He has about 3,000 in his collection. He also loves camping in his motor home and being with members of his Rotary Club. (Courtesy of Kerry Mueller.)

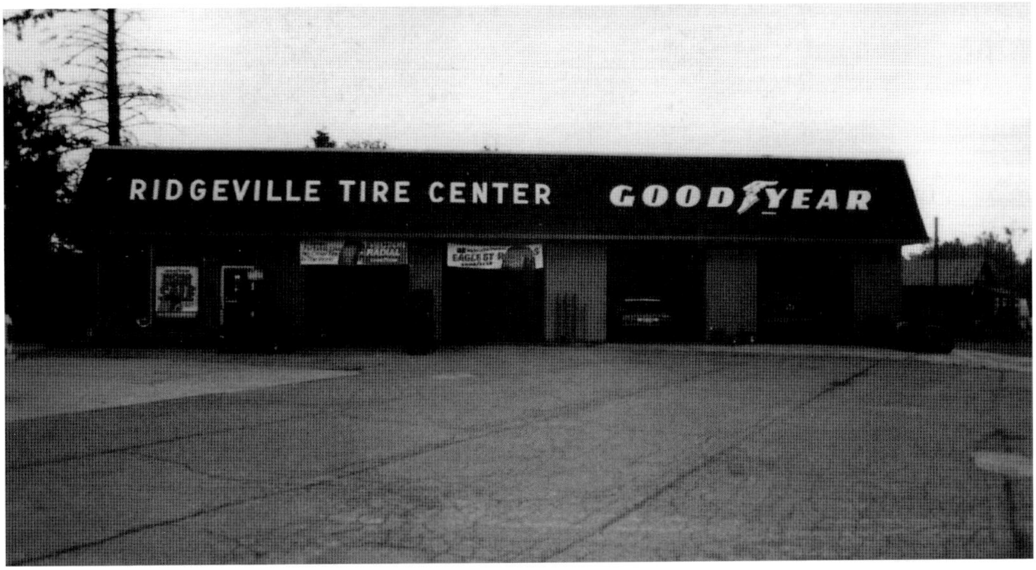

James Johnson

James Johnson opened the North Ridgeville Tire Center in 1972, later adding another section. In the beginning, Johnson tried to stock four of every kind of tire. With the advent of radial tires, however, this was impossible, because the radials lasted longer. Johnson initially only handled tires and sent the vehicles out for alignments. Eventually, the store began stocking fewer tires and started hiring mechanics to repair cars. The federal guidelines for mechanics increased, requiring Authorized Service Center certification. Johnson's son Greg is ASC certified and runs the store as a full-service operation. In 1988, when the Johnsons lived next to the store, Joyce Johnson woke to see the building on fire. "It was a $160,000 setback," James said. The next year, a tornado tore the roof off. "We started over in 1990," Johnson said. (Both, courtesy of James Johnson.)

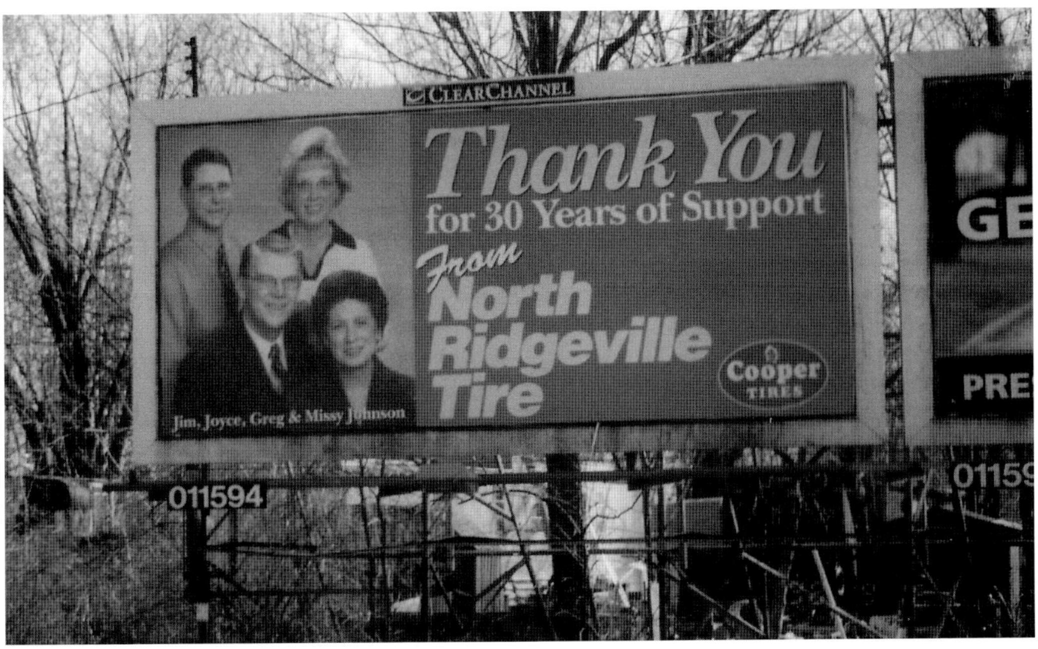

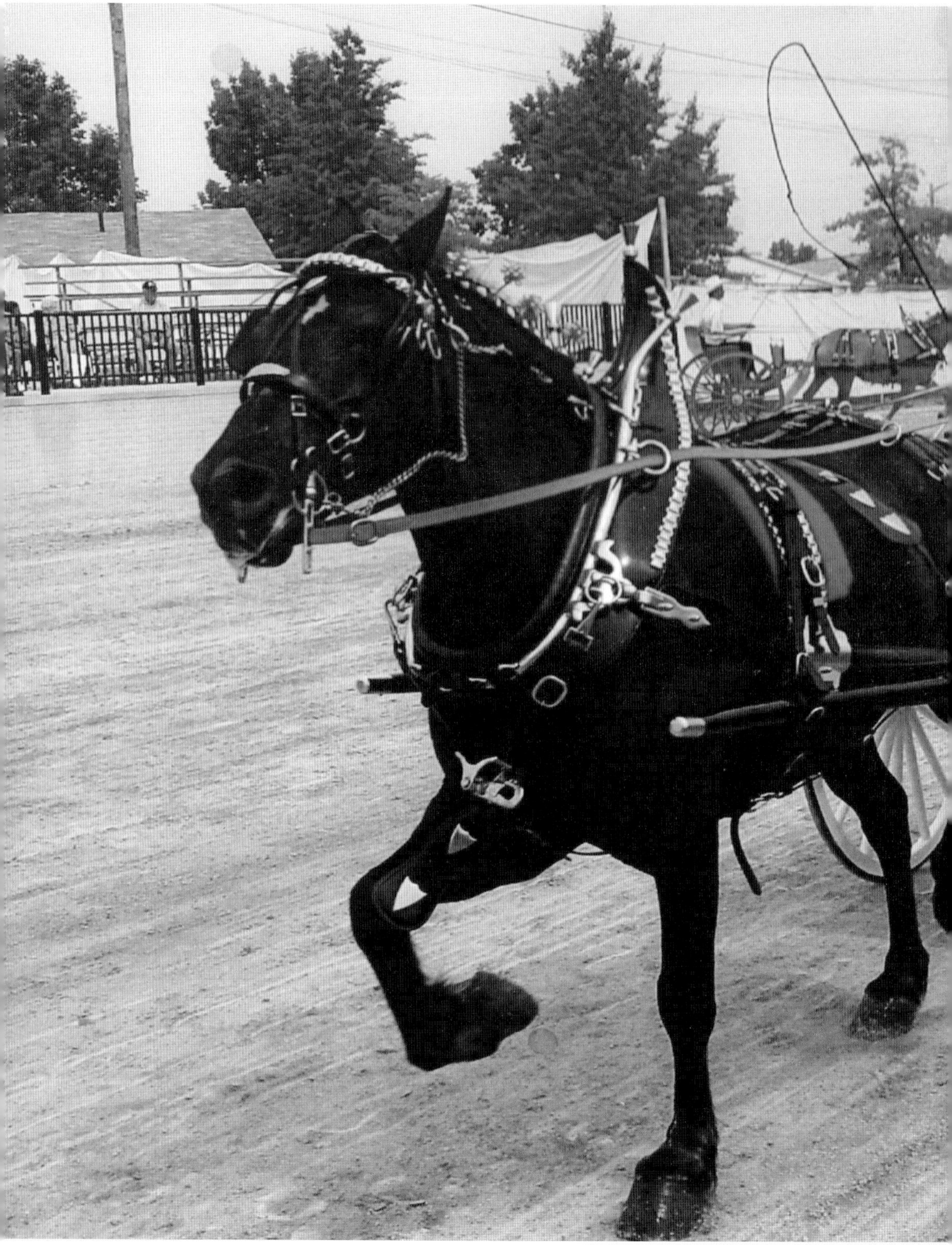

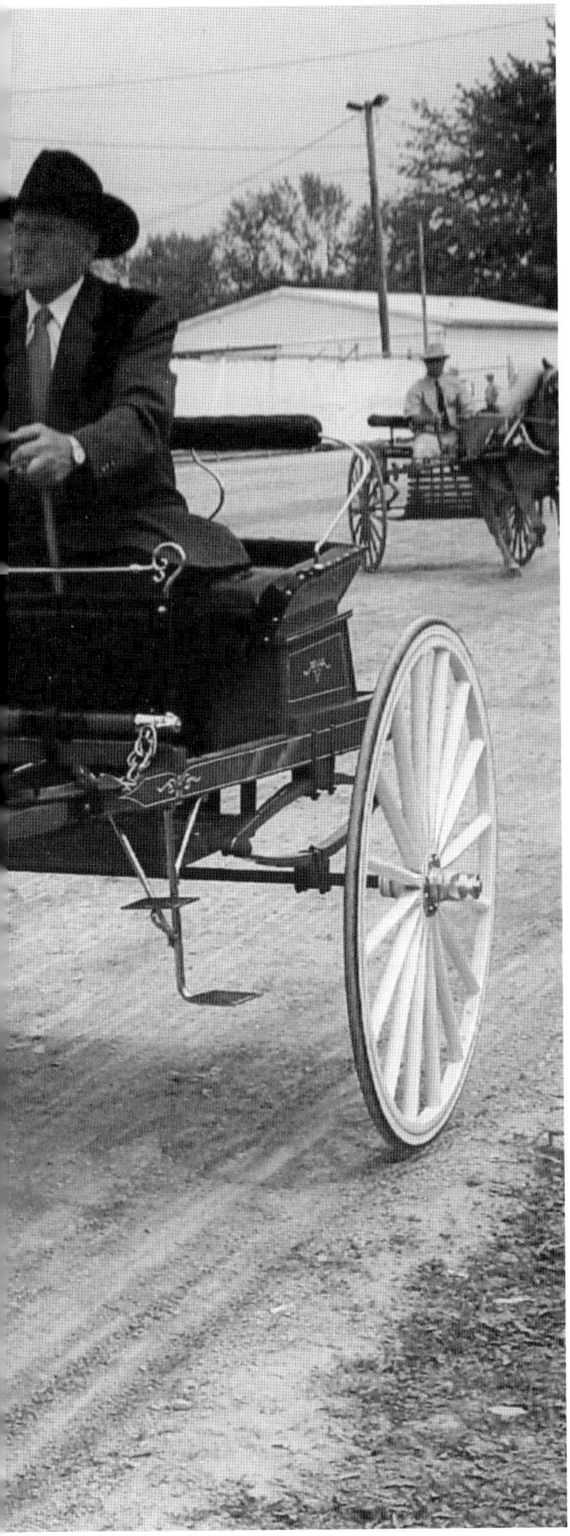

Laurence Kuchenrither
Born in Elyria, Kuchenrither moved to North Ridgeville in 1965. He transported mail from 1965 to 1975. When his employer went defunct, he bought his first mail truck. By 2013, in his 39th year in business, he had 20 trucks and nearly 30 employees on the road 24 hours a day from Cleveland to Lorain County, Akron, Canton, and Mansfield. He and his wife, Peggy, also own Percheron horses and raise ponies for the Lorain County Fair. They have a wagon they use with the Percherons, as well as a 20-year-old carriage for weddings. (Courtesy of Laurence Kuchenrither.)

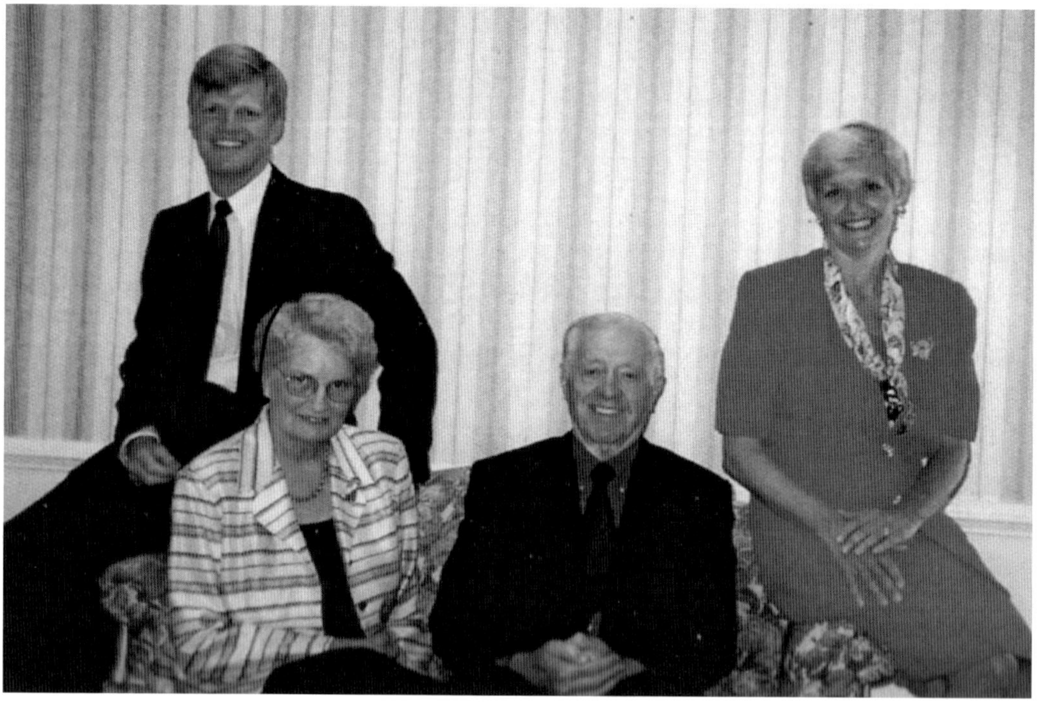

John T. O'Neill

The O'Neill family has owned and managed local skilled nursing, rehabilitation, and assisted-living facilities since 1962, providing excellent, comprehensive care. Shown here are, from left to right, John T., Alva, John O'Neill, and Doreen O'Neill Ziska.

John and Alva O'Neill both became licensed nursing home administrators and utilized a family approach to their clientele. Their son, John T. O'Neill, manages facilities in several cities, including the Center Ridge Health Campus in North Ridgeville. Through the West Shore facilities, seniors are provided with the diverse, personal, and quality care they need, from independent living to Alzheimer's care to outpatient services.

The O'Neill family built the 100-bed Center Ridge Nursing Home, now known as Center Ridge Health Campus, in 1986. Over the years there have been several expansions, including a 50-bed memory support unit in 1990, a 40-unit assisted-living unit in 2010, and a 16-station dialysis center in 2011. The younger O'Neill has introduced one of the area's newest assisted-living residences, featuring private suites, recreation programs, a library, a theater room, and an activity room. The Center Ridge Road facility is also pet-friendly. In addition to offering professional care, John T. O'Neill is involved in the day-to-day operation of the facility and carries on the legacy that his parents started 50 years ago.

Center Ridge Health Campus hosts several community events for North Ridgeville residents, including a Fourth of July Picnic, a community dog show, a trick-or-treat celebration, and breakfast with the Easter Bunny. The health campus has been approved by the Ohio Department of Health as a training site for certified nursing assistants as well as certified medication aides.

Members of the team at Center Ridge Health Campus are part of the North Ridgeville Board of Education Business Advisory Committee and the Lorain County Chamber of Commerce. The facility has been a member of the chamber for more than 25 years, and John T. O'Neill at one time served on the board of directors. Employees have participated in every Corn Festival.

The O'Neill family gives thousands of dollars in scholarships to high school seniors who are planning to go into the healthcare field, including those attending North Ridgeville High School. The company also sponsors a number of churches in the area, including St. Peter and St. Julie Billiart Catholic Churches. (Courtesy of John T. O'Neill)

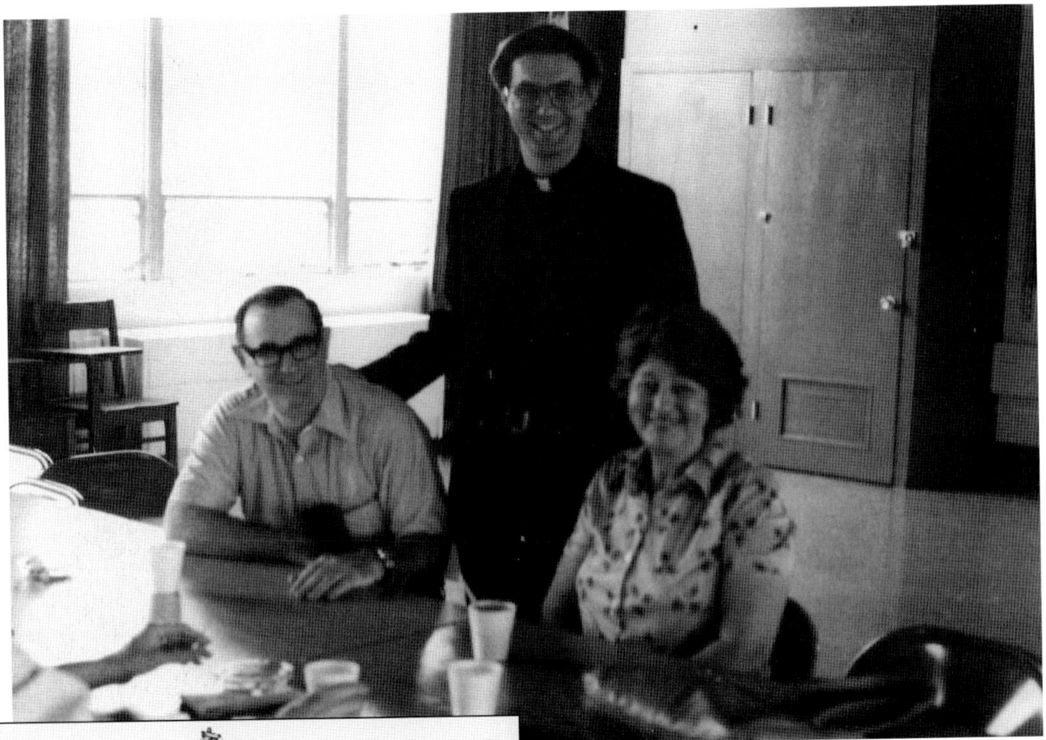

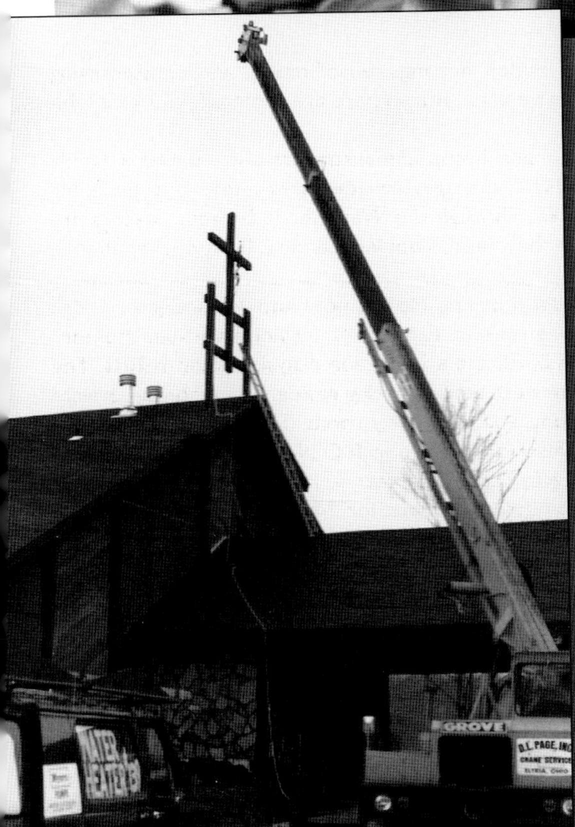

Rev. Dr. Richard A. Gonser
Gonser, shown above with his parents, was ordained a Catholic priest in 1962. In 1978, he was appointed founding pastor of St. Julie Billiart Church with the directive, "find a place to live, find a place to have church, and find people." There were 14 acres of trees and swampland on the proposed church site on Lear Nagle Road, and Gonser learned firsthand about the vandalism in the area when damage to the church property occurred from time to time, such as at Christmas when lights were stolen. He wanted the church to be "practical, functional, welcoming, and cheerful." The ground breaking took place in July 1981. The dedication and first Mass were held five months later, on Christmas. St. Julie Billiart Parish has been active in social justice, serving Thanksgiving dinners and working with Habitat for Humanity, the youth ministry, and more. Since 2012, Gonser has been a senior priest retired in residence at St. Jude Parish in Elyria. (Both, courtesy of Rev. Dr. Richard Gonser.)

Barb Mamrak

It was around 1946 when Barb Becker Mamrak's father returned home from service. He and his three brothers opened Becker Brothers Restaurant and Donut Shop in Cleveland. Unfortunately, as sometimes happens in family-owned businesses, the brothers couldn't get along. Each went a separate way and opened individual shops. Although they couldn't agree in business, Mamrak said the uncles had respect for one another.

When Barb married Frank Mamrak, her father taught the couple the secret to making those very special Becker's donuts. "Dad taught Frank and I, all of the children, their spouses and the seven grandchildren," she said, adding, "all pitched in at one time or another for awhile."

Money was tight for the Mamrak family, so Frank Mamrak was always looking for side jobs to supplement their income. He had been hired to clean up and mow weeds behind Fisher's Big Wheel, now Marc's. It was July 8, 1982, when the 31-year-old husband climbed onto a tractor to take care of the mowing. According to reports, he was cutting the weeds in a fenced retention basin behind the shopping center. Not long after he started, Mamrak apparently hit a piece of concrete, causing the tractor to overturn on the slope of the retention basin, wedging him between the vehicle and a tree for about 10 minutes. When firefighters arrived, they cut down the tree, freed Mamrak, and transported him to the hospital. He showed no signs of life at the scene and died 23 days later. "It was too long without oxygen," his wife said, adding that she felt he was gone at the scene.

The family business has continued in the shop on a strip on Avon Belden Road, eventually expanding into a coffee shop. However, in 2008, Barb Mamrak learned she was going to have to downsize her space and upgrade her equipment at a cost of $18,000. Looking into other locations, she realized that it would cost twice as much to move. Becker's is still in business, selling donuts made by a fourth-generation Becker. (Courtesy of Barb Mamrak.)

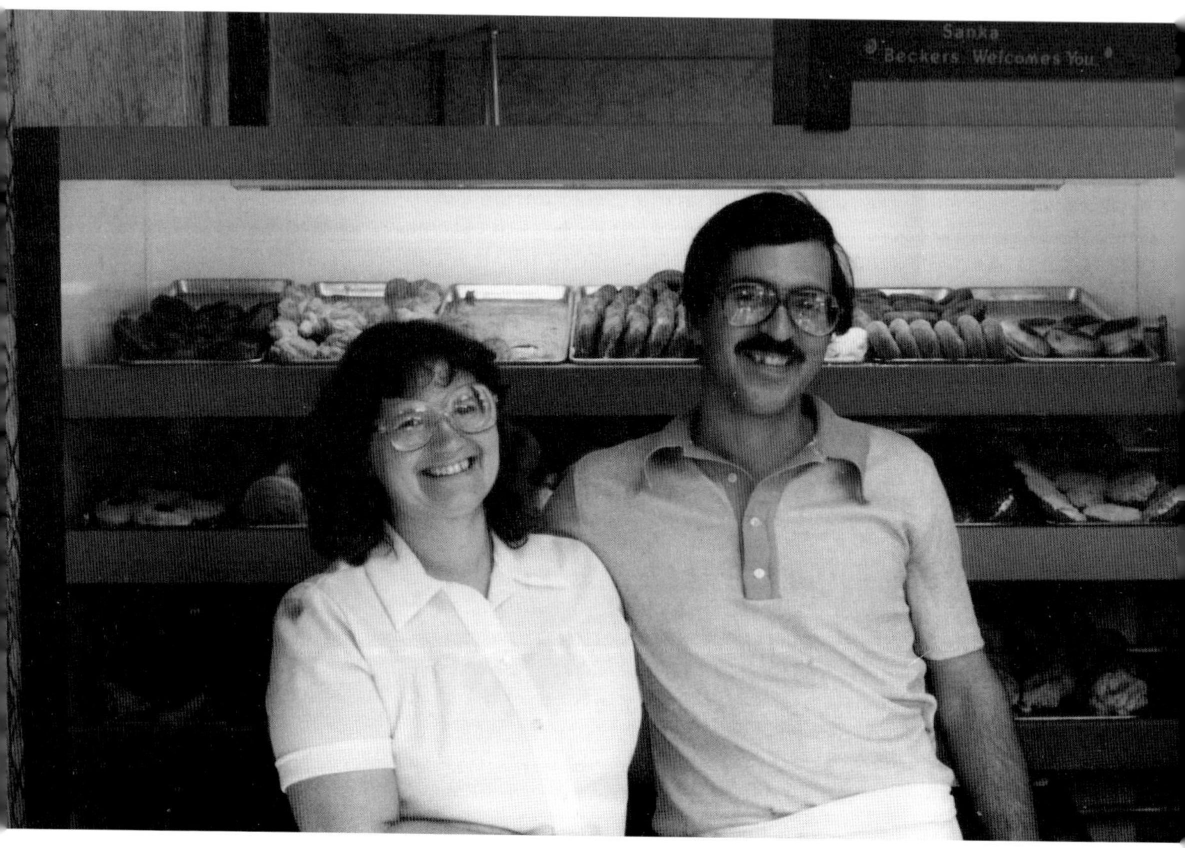

CHAPTER FIVE

Working Together

Regardless how affluent or impoverished a community may be, its heart lies in the people who live there. North Ridgeville is no different. The city is a blend of wealthy and moderate-income residents as well as those who, regardless of the reason for their circumstances, must rely on others, such as Community Care, to help provide for their welfare.

There are many organizations in the city with a philosophy of working together for the sake of others, such as the Rotary Club of North Ridgeville, whose members believe in "service above self" and spend time and money following that creed. But it isn't just about passing the hat and giving the funds to a worthy cause. It is also about helping young scholars work toward going to college, or providing dictionaries to schoolchildren. Other groups, such as the Lions Club and the Kiwanis, also do what they can to help their fellow men and women. Other organizations are designed for specific groups of people, such as the chamber of commerce, which works with the business community with a goal of providing programs and activities that will benefit the entire city, making it more vibrant and energetic.

A group in town brings sheer joy to residents by performing plays and musicals in the Olde Towne Hall Theatre; another group of hard workers hosts the annual Corn Festival, which draws people from across the state. The city's historical society invites residents and nonresidents alike to enjoy a bit of the community's history through regular monthly meetings and open houses at the museum, located in the Old Town Hall and the schoolhouse on Jaycox Road. In 2010, members presented a variety of activities to promote the bicentennial and stir pride in the place that residents call home.

For each of these groups, and others as well, the key to success is working together. This is the core of a happy, productive community.

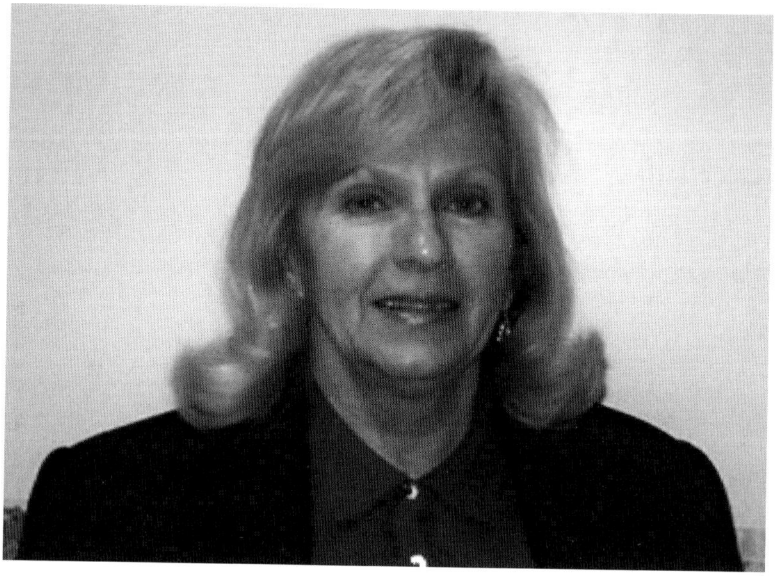

Dayle Noll

Noll was hired as a part-time secretary to the chamber of commerce in 1985. The job included signage for the Ohio Turnpike and obtaining toll-free calling to Cuyahoga County. Noll stressed her communication skills and membership in organizations such as the Junior Woman's Club. "I was connected with the community," she said. Her first project was a haunted house, then updating the city map and membership directory. In 1988, a visitors' bureau was developed. Noll is now the chamber CEO, and she enjoys it, saying, "There is a lot of personal satisfaction." Pictured below are the members of the 1996–1997 board of directors. They are, from left to right, (first row) Dayle Noll, Jack Smith, Jo-Ell Jacobson, Marian Gardner Stafford, and Thomas Klear; (second row) Don Hoffman, Gary Sweet, Paul Klein, Fred Dorow, Scott Hosler, Dixie Mazer, and Thomas Rockwell. (Both, courtesy of the North Ridgeville Chamber of Commerce.)

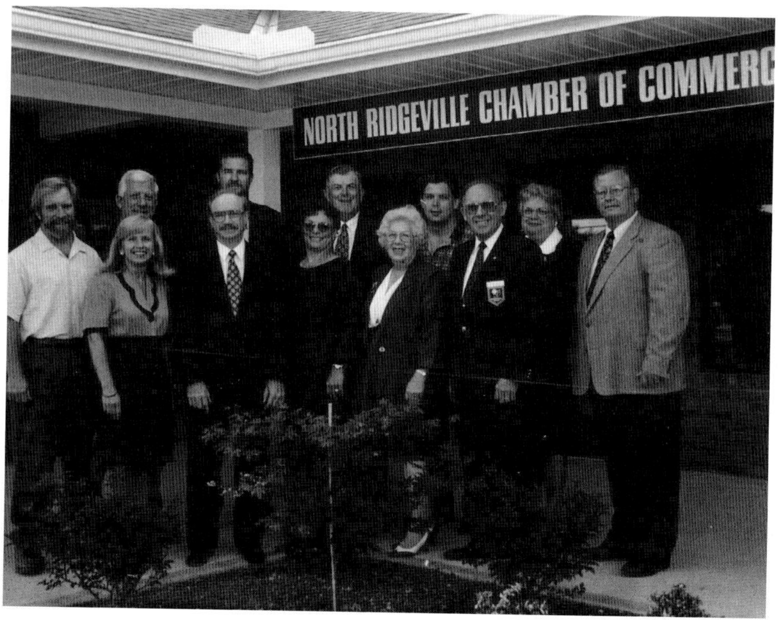

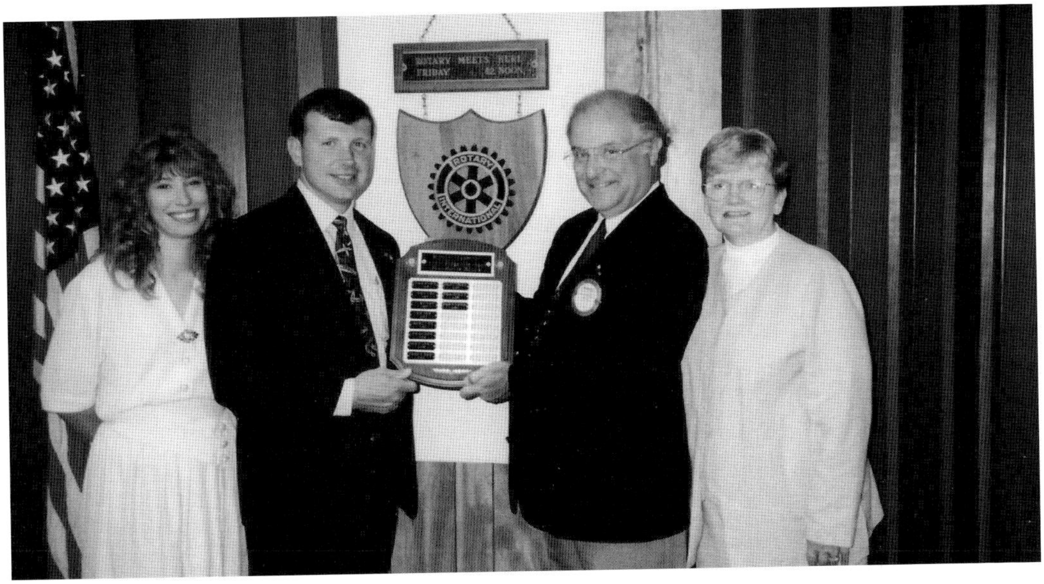

Warren and Patricia Blakely

The Rotary Club of North Ridgeville is a big part of the Blakelys' lives. Warren Blakely joined and then encouraged his wife to become a Rotarian. She supported what her husband was doing, and decided to join. The couple was so active that each earned a Paul Harris Fellow Award, at the time the highest honor a Rotarian could receive. Above, the Blakelys (right) present the award to Douglas Charboneau, as his wife, Bambi, stands with him. Below, the Blakelys are attending an Indians game. The North Ridgeville club was chartered on April 10, 1981, and members initiated projects to demonstrate the motto, "Service Above Self." The community Easter egg hunt ranked high with children, distributing dictionaries was a favorite with teachers, and Safetyville helped youngsters to be cautious. Reaching beyond the city, Rotarians also filled shoe boxes with necessities for children in Nicaragua. (Both, courtesy of the Rotary Club of North Ridgeville.)

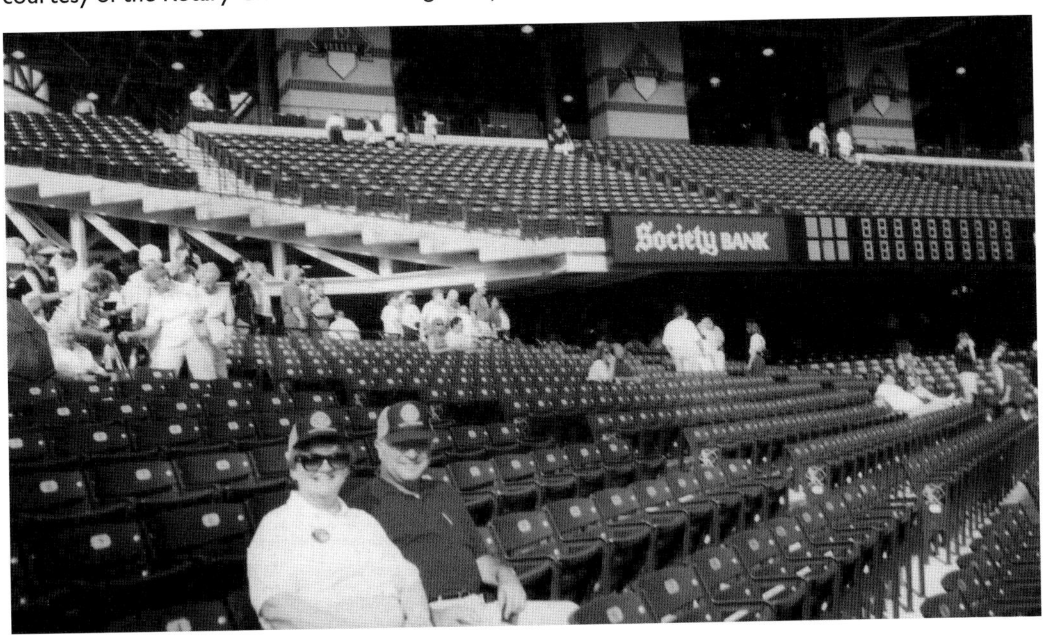

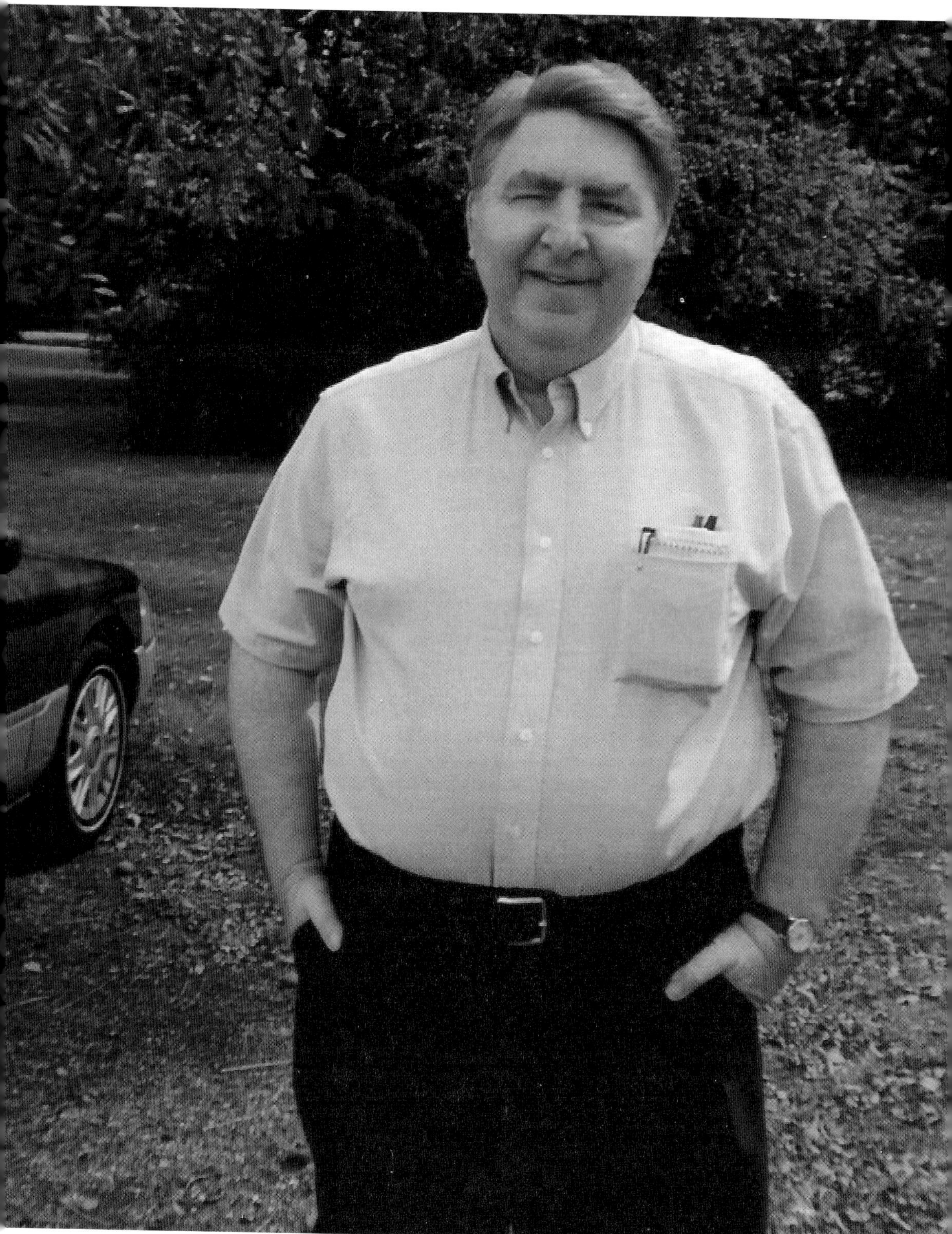

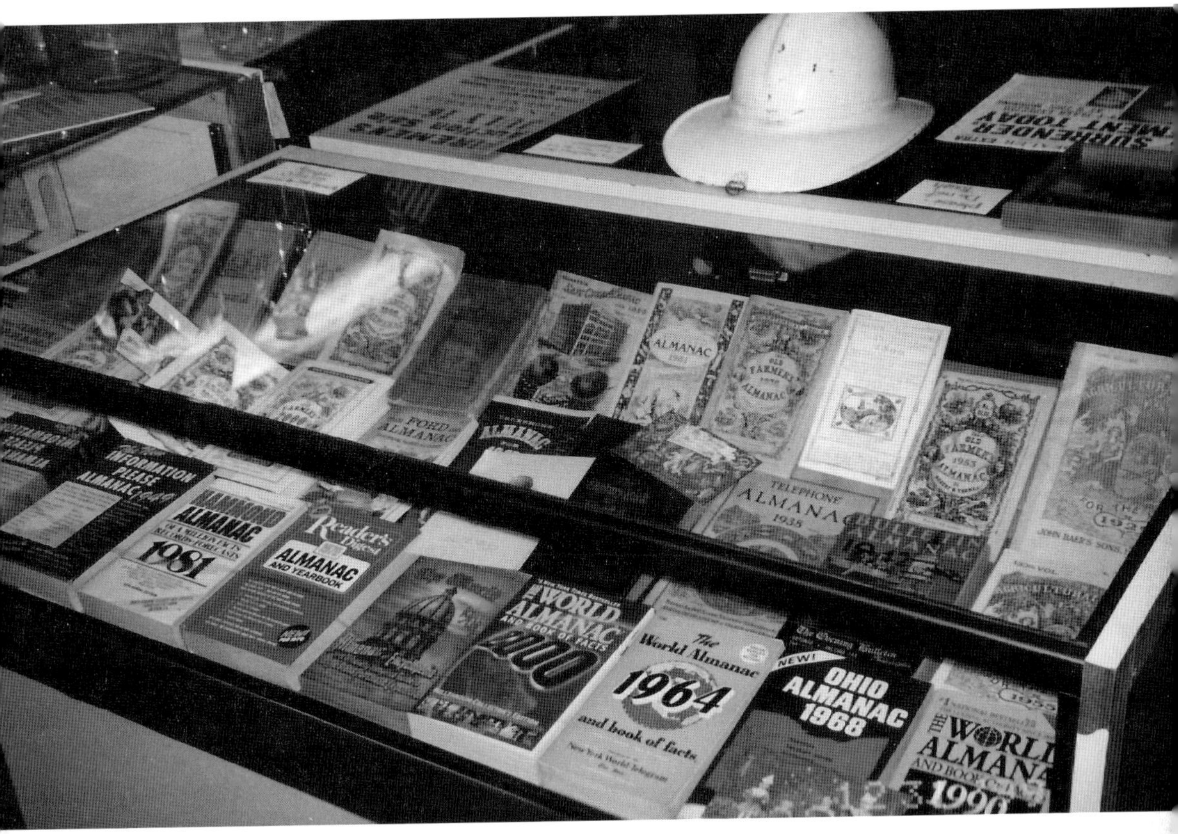

Jeffrey Sigsworth

When he was about nine years old, Jeffrey Sigsworth began making lists. He started with the names of all his cousins and their birthdays. He said he probably came by the list making naturally, as one of his grandmothers did the same. He soon also began collecting things. His small collections numbered about 100, and they included stamps, coins, feathers, and pencils. As he grew older, the groups of collectibles also expanded. "Anything that was more than one of a kind" became part of his collections, he said.

Sigsworth became interested in history and soon gathered boxes of historic headlines from newspapers. He also has what he terms "presidential boxes," which contain all sorts of items related to US presidents. He started a new assemblage of commemorative plates, and the list goes on to include long-playing and 78 rpm records, especially 1920s dance music. Sigsworth even began accumulating almanacs, which he displayed at the First Night New Year's Eve celebration in 1999.

In addition to his treasures, which he sometimes displays in the showcase at the North Ridgeville Branch Library, Sigsworth has researched ancestors. When he was 11 or 12, he and his grandmother Sigsworth went to the cemetery to look at the names on the grave markers. She would pack a picnic lunch, and they would have a good time. At that young age, though, Sigsworth did not know much about the study of genealogy. But he later began joining genealogical groups, many based in Elyria. He also heads the North Ridgeville Historical Society and has a wealth of knowledge about the city's early pioneers.

At one point, he had to line up a speaker for an organization he had joined. He knew that the director of the Lorain Public Library System was starting a Sons of the American Revolution group. Through the program, Sigsworth learned that he was eligible to join, and he got to know the speaker. However, he then lost his job and lost touch with the speaker. Fortunately, he was able to get a position with the Lorain Public Library System as a library assistant in the technical services department and has been there for 37 years. He continues to join various genealogy groups and participates in five or six historical societies. (Both, courtesy of Jeffrey Sigsworth.)

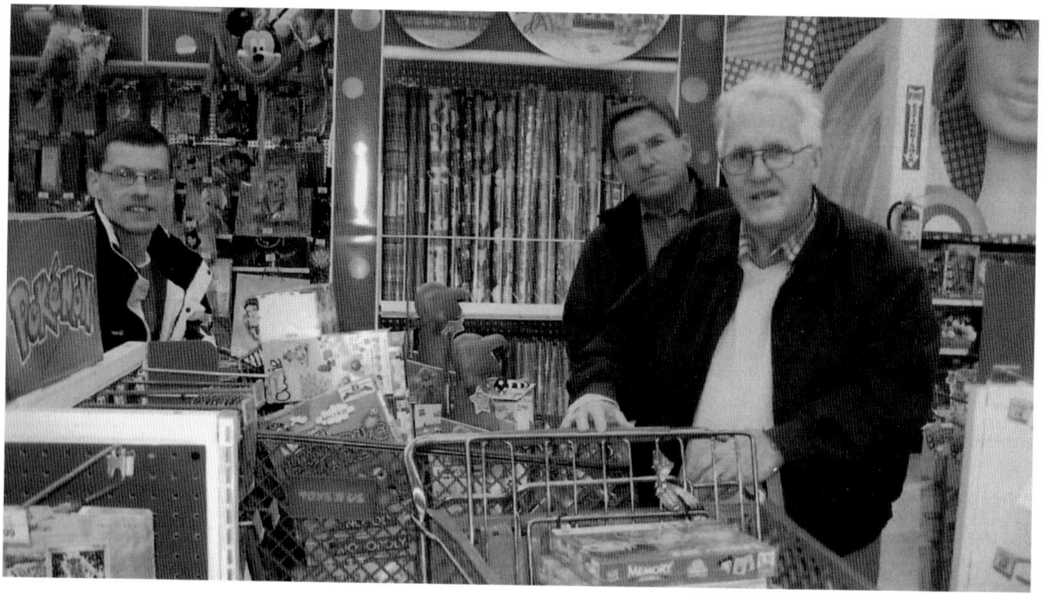

Lions Club

The North Ridgeville Lions Club was chartered in 1961, with Robert Schmittgen as its first president. Members prescreen children's eyesight. They also offer scholarships to handicapped youngsters for Echoing Hills Camp and work with the community by sponsoring ball teams and cleaning on Pride Day. Shown here are Lions Danny White (left), Daniel White (center), and Robert Franks. They are shopping for toys for Community Care. (Courtesy of the Lions Club.)

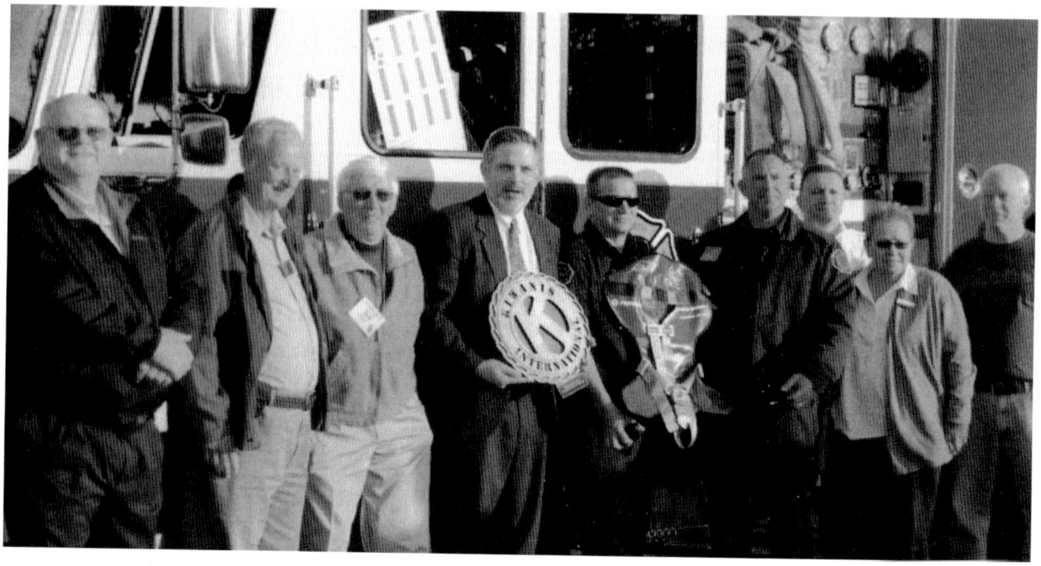

Kiwanis Club

Kiwanis has long been active in the community, including in 1947, when members built a Boy Scout cabin at Camp Kiwanis on Westwood Drive. In 2013, the club donated a Pedi-Mate Unit to the Fire Department for transporting young children. Shown here are, from left to right, Mayor G. David Gillock; Kiwanians Bob Williams, Bob Fortune, and Scott Hosler; firefighters Robert Knowlton and Andy Castle; Chief John Reese; Jan Schneider; and Hugh McQuillan. (Courtesy of Scott Hosler.)

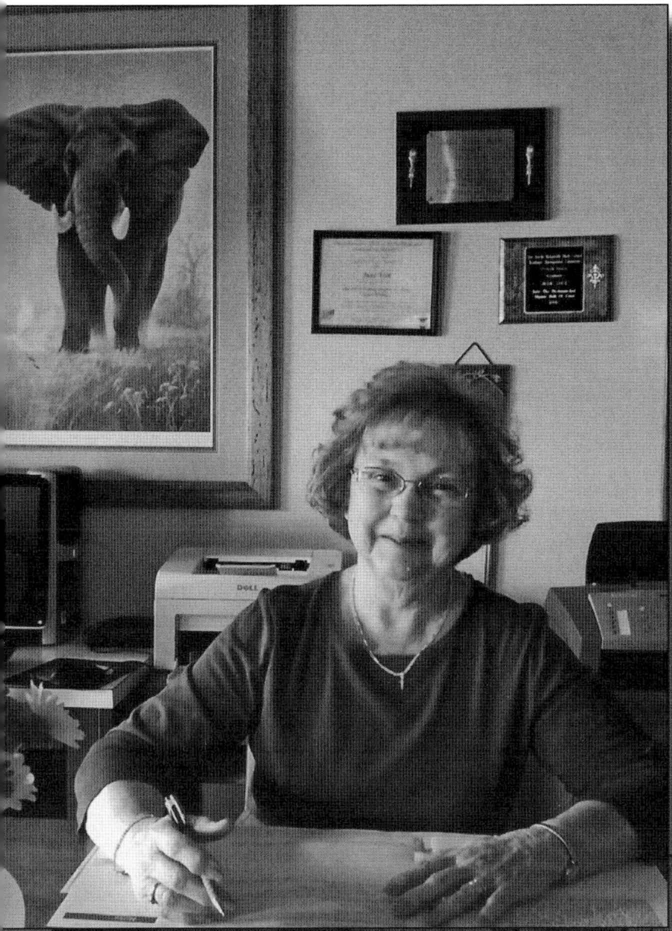

June Yost
For more than 25 years June Yost has headed Community Care, an organization that helps North Ridgeville's less fortunate with clothing, food, and other necessities. For much of that time, Yost and her volunteers used buildings belonging to others, working in churches, in a space on Jaycox Road, in a beauty shop on Center Ridge Road, and in a warehouse on Lear Nagle Road. But in 2000, Mark Giacco, the owner of Arby's on Center Ridge Road, donated a parcel of land behind the restaurant and the group began making plans for a facility of its own. As Community Care's board of directors began discussing the structure, developer Bob Schmitt stepped in to offer assistance. Yost explained what was needed, and Schmitt constructed the building at his cost. (Both, courtesy of the *North Ridgeville Press*.)

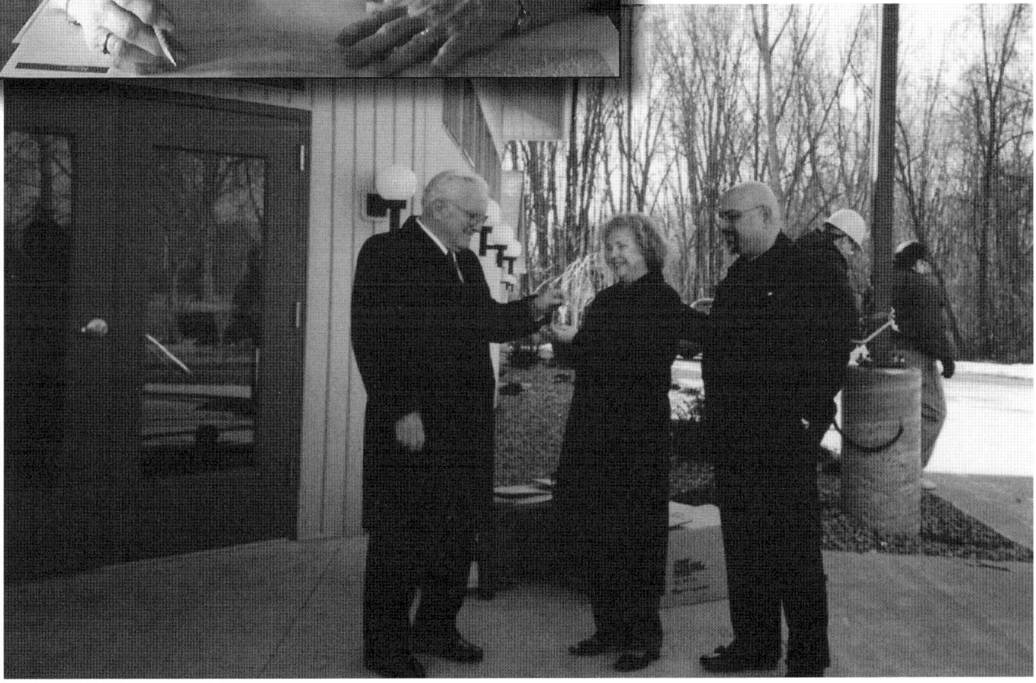

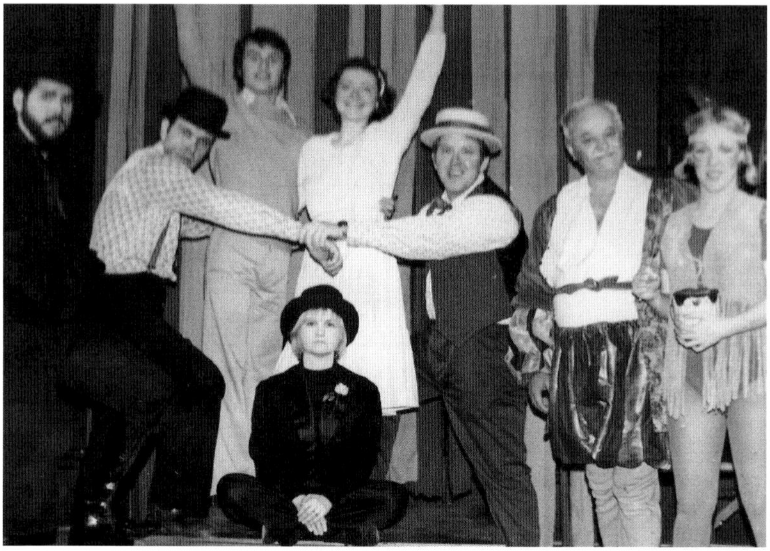

Olde Towne Hall Theatre

In the 1970s a group of women, including Kathleen Bogner, Kathleen Forthofer, Marilyn Grimm, Joyce Solomon, Branka Malinar, Nancy Scott, and Nancy Ziegman, wanted to save the Old Town Hall from demolition and establish a theater. Mayor Charles H. Stuart permitted them to work on restoring the 90-year-old structure. They held fundraisers, including "restore a chair." The first production was held at the Olde Towne Hall Theatre in 1977, and the group joined the Ohio Community Theatre Association. However, there were issues with electrical codes, and it took time for the situation to be resolved. For a time, plays were staged at schools and at the Lorain Palace Theater. In March 1979, *The Fantastiks* was performed at the Olde Towne Hall Theatre. For decades since, theatergoers have enjoyed productions at the vintage venue. (Both, courtesy of the Olde Towne Hall Theatre.)

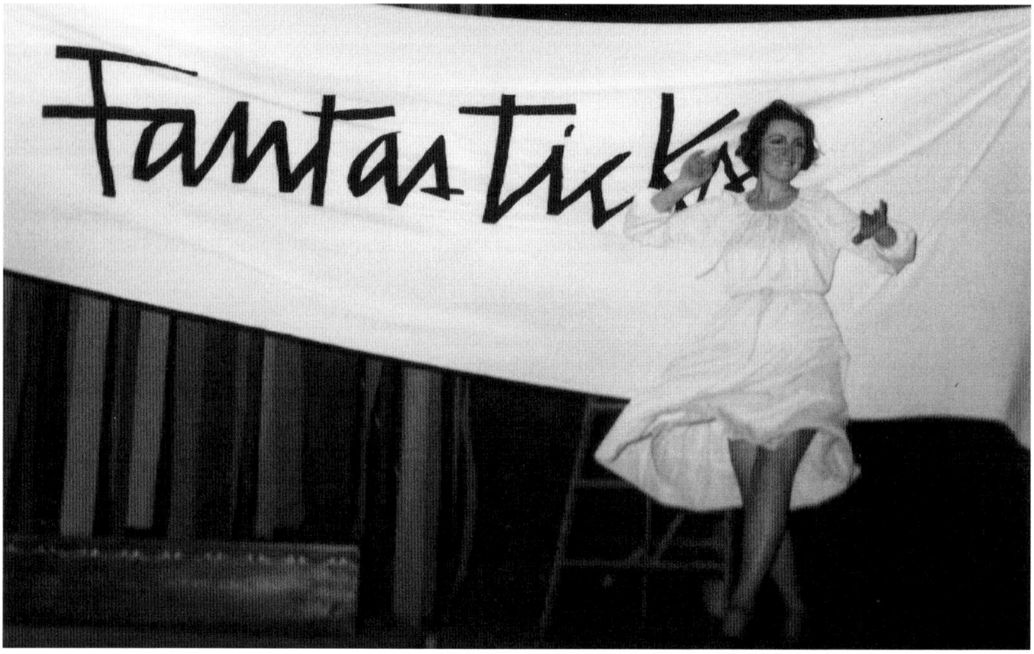

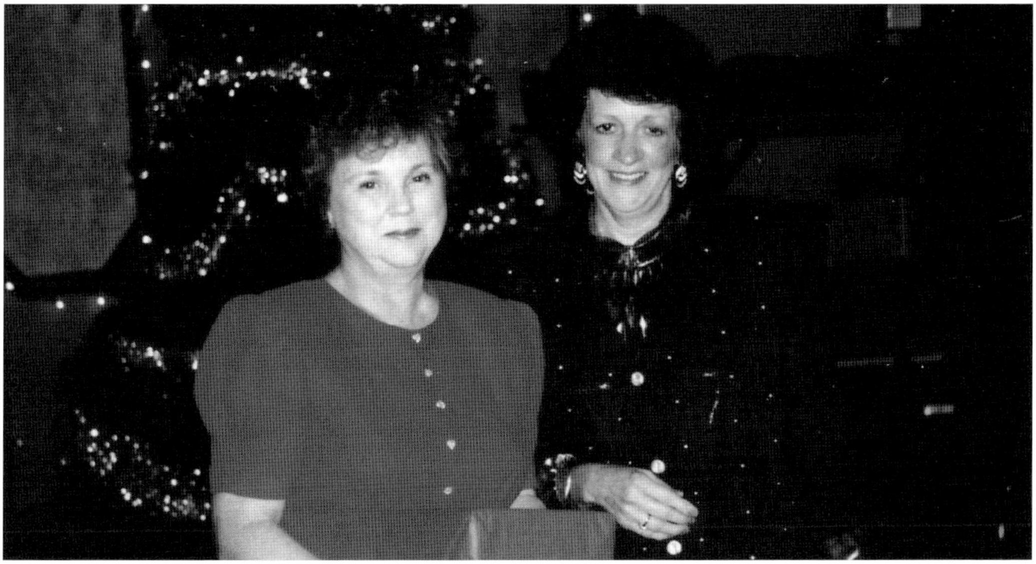

Regina Comerford
In a 1985 newspaper article, Comerford was tagged a "super volunteer." Things have not changed. If she is asked to help with just about any project, she will probably say "yes." When her three daughters were in school, she was a room mother and was asked to join St. Peter's Parent Teacher Union; from there, she became an officer. After school, Comerford and her husband, William, coached CYO basketball. Men were not permitted to coach girls, so Regina appeared to coach while her husband told her what to do. She also got involved in City Baseball and Boosters, having her own trading card. Comerford then became Arts Council president and helped June Yost with Community Care. Above, Comerford (right) and Yost pose together. In 1999, Comerford won the Golden Kernel Award. Below are, from left to right, Jo-Ell Jacobson, Mayor Deanna Hill, Comerford, and Jeffry Armbruster. (Courtesy of Regina Comerford.)

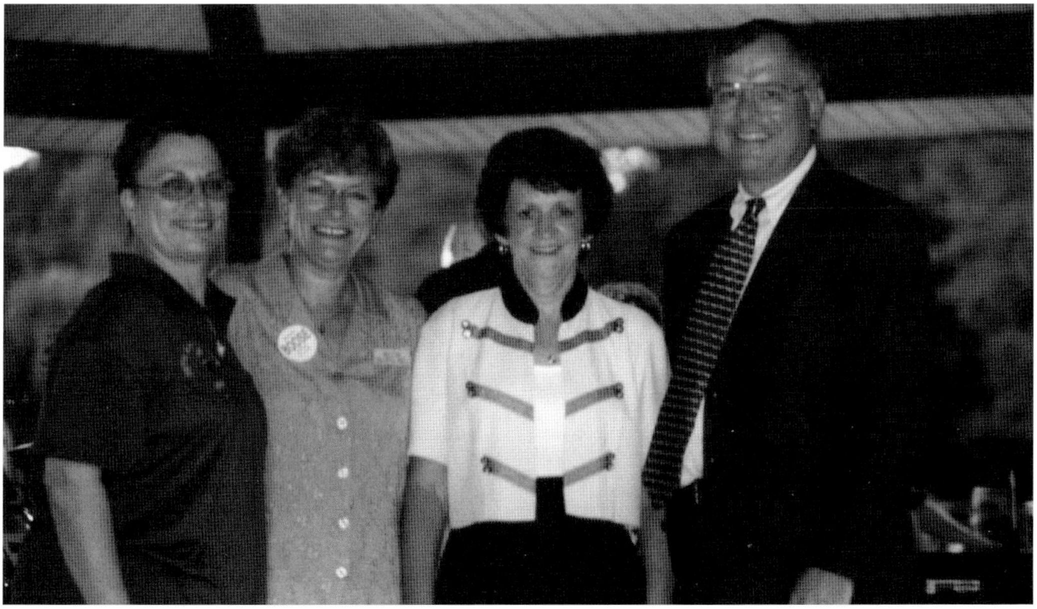

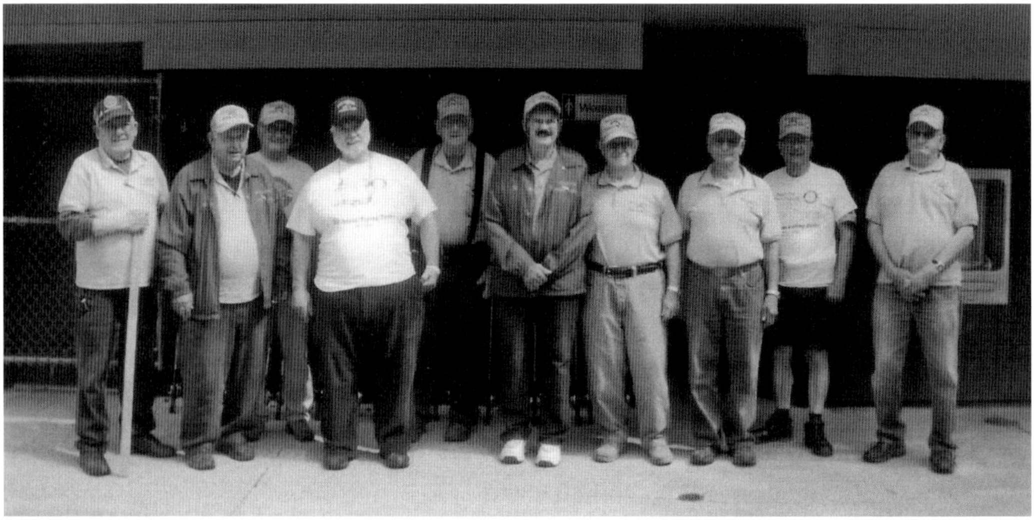

Robert Kirkpatrick

Fishing has always been a part of Kirkpatrick's life. His late wife, Audrey, enjoyed it as much as he did. "She was a fisherwoman," he said. The Kirkpatricks started a fishing club in North Ridgeville. "She was really involved," Robert says. Above, Kirkpatrick (second from left) poses with the club. Members would help nursing-home residents at the fishing lake at South Central Park. In 2013, the parks and recreation department offered sessions on fishing, and Kirkpatrick was right there to help youngsters bait the hook or take fish off the line (below). "We were almost like grandfathers," he said. Kirkpatrick is a charter member of the Rotary Club, which co-sponsors fishing derbies with the fire department. The children love learning the sport, and Kirkpatrick enjoys teaching them as much as they like catching the fish. (Both, courtesy of Thomas Klear.)

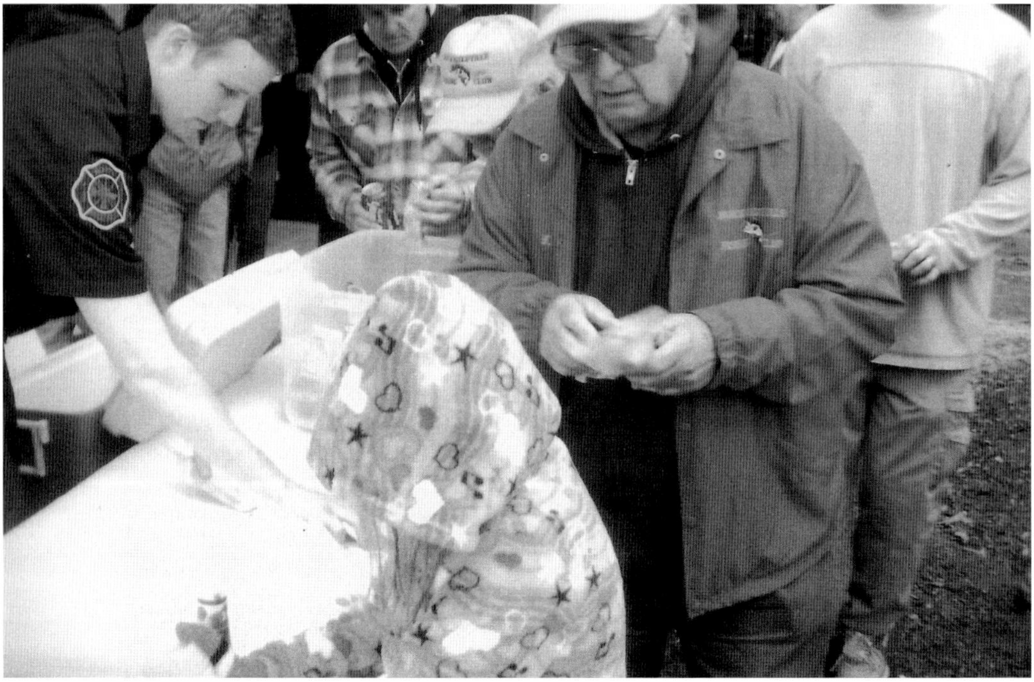

John Butkowski

In 1975, former mayor Charles Stuart wanted North Ridgeville to be recognized as a bicentennial community when the country celebrated its 200th birthday in 1976. Butkowski chaired the committee that was created. A requirement was that a lasting memorial for the bicentennial be established. Butkowski suggested that an annual Corn Festival be formed, since much corn and popcorn was grown in the town. The festival was given a trial run in August 1975 so that the town would be ready for the real thing in 1976. The first official Corn Festival was held on the track area behind the middle school on August 23, 1976. It honored Harold Sweet, a longtime resident and corn farmer. The festival grew from a one-day to a three-day event, and it will celebrate its 40th anniversary in 2014. (Courtesy of John Butkowski.)

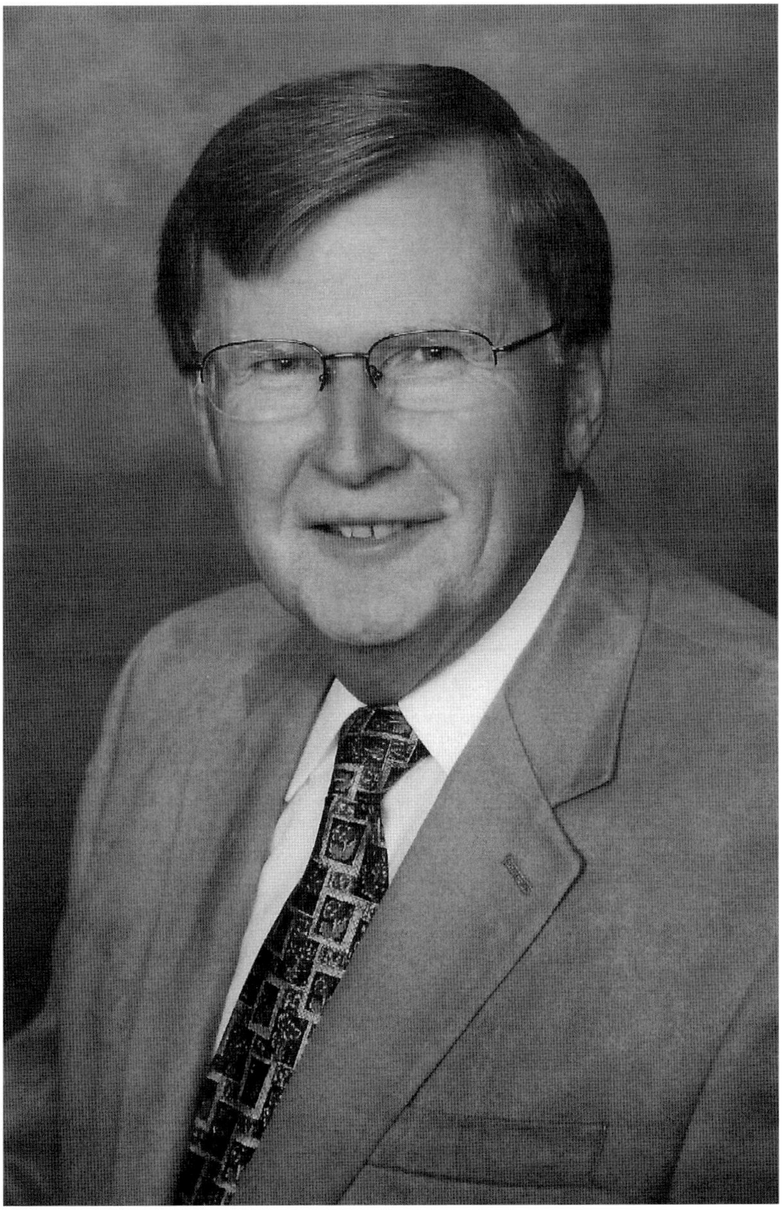

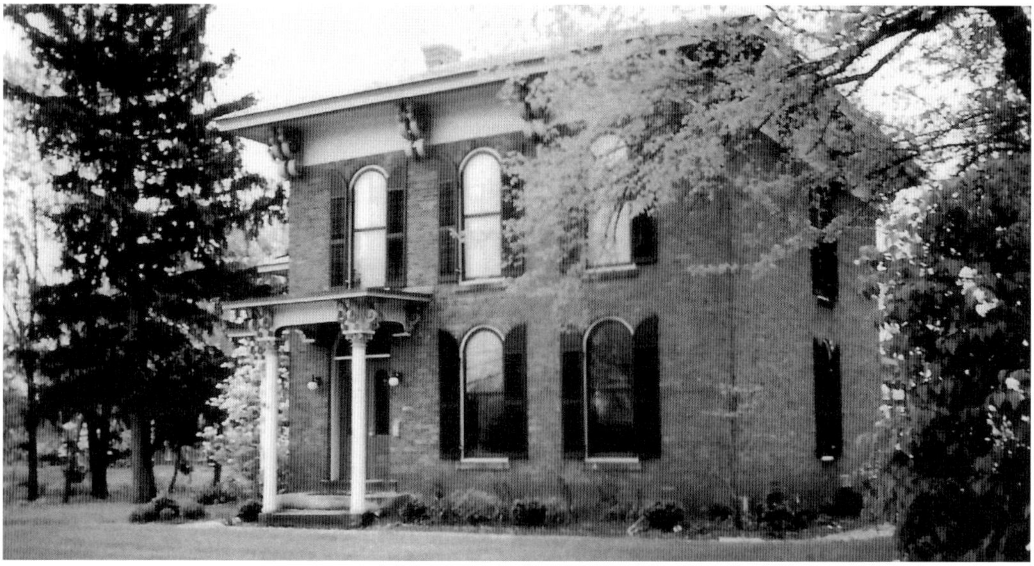

North Ridgeville Historical Society

The organization was founded in 1977 by Marcellen Lengel, Harry and Dorothy Painter, Frances Smith, Jerry and Branka Malinar, and others. The first president was Harry Painter. In 1978, the R.W. Beckett Corporation allowed the use of three rooms for meetings and museum space in the Samuel Cahoon House (above). The museum was there from 1978 to 1987, then moved temporarily to the Lunas Professional Building. In 1989, city officials offered the first floor of the Old Town Hall for a museum. Donations resulted in a collection of farming and military items, furniture, a 1976 bicentennial quilt, and more. The first open house at the museum took place on May 30, 1992. Shown below are, from left to right, Jeffrey Sigsworth, Pauline Kellogg, John Vessalo, John Mahl, Dorothy Painter, Barbara Reining, Dale Kellogg, and Frank Nesbitt. (Both, courtesy of the North Ridgeville Historical Society.)

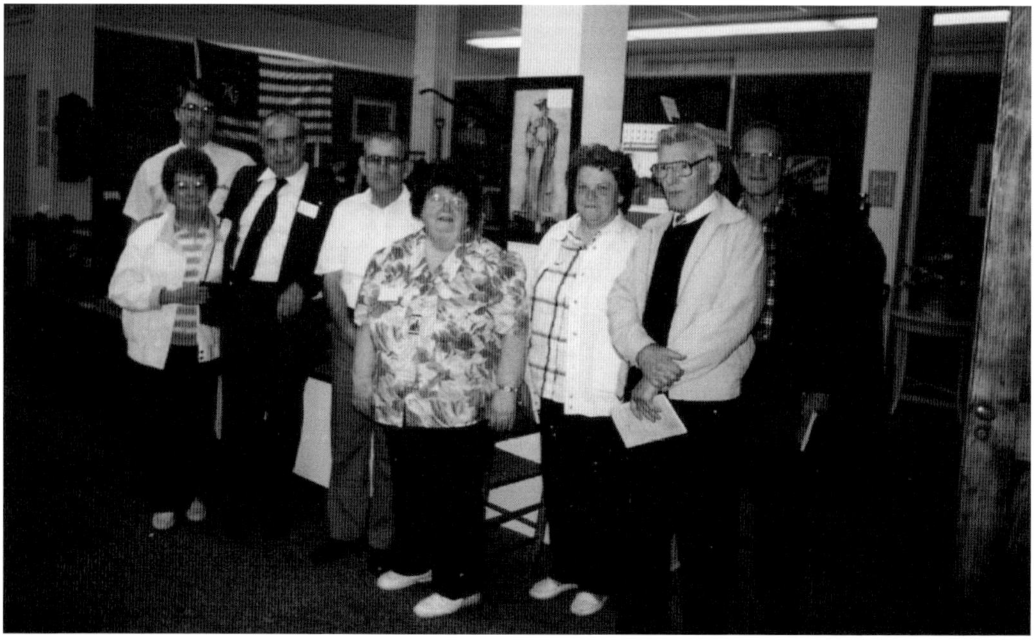

CHAPTER SIX

Serving Others

The City of North Ridgeville is no more unique than any other; or maybe it is. The community is a pillar of strength in trying to serve others, regardless of age, race, or creed. If there is a need, there is someone, or a group of "someones," ready to offer service.

Safety forces are on alert 24 hours a day, seven days a week. The warning sirens can be heard wailing no matter the hour, as emergency vehicles race to an accident, a fire, or a violation of individual rights. While the people in the situation are confused or panicky, the uniformed personnel provide service under a veil of calm. Men and women who are now retired can relate tales of unimaginable situations, and, as they retell the events, listeners wonder how they handled the pressure. But they were on the scene to serve, and they did.

An organization that focuses on the military is the Veterans of Foreign Wars. Most members of the North Ridgeville Post 9871 have seen warfare up close and personal and are aware of the true meaning of the phrase "war is hell," spoken to a graduating class in 1879 by Civil War general William Tecumseh Sherman.

There are those in the community who may not don protective suits or carry weapons, but instead offer service of a spiritual nature to weary souls. People can be served in many different ways. Church services sometimes require musicians to accompany the spoken words, and organists add their talents. Wanda Jurco plays the organ at St. Peter Church on weekdays. Without saying a word, she is serving others. There are choirs of many denominations who prepare hymns of praise for special occasions. They, too, are serving.

There are individuals who work tirelessly for the good of an entire city, like William Comerford, who recognized that residents should have access to 911 for emergency aid and did all he could to see that it was implemented.

"Service" is a short word that can have a profound effect on the lives of others.

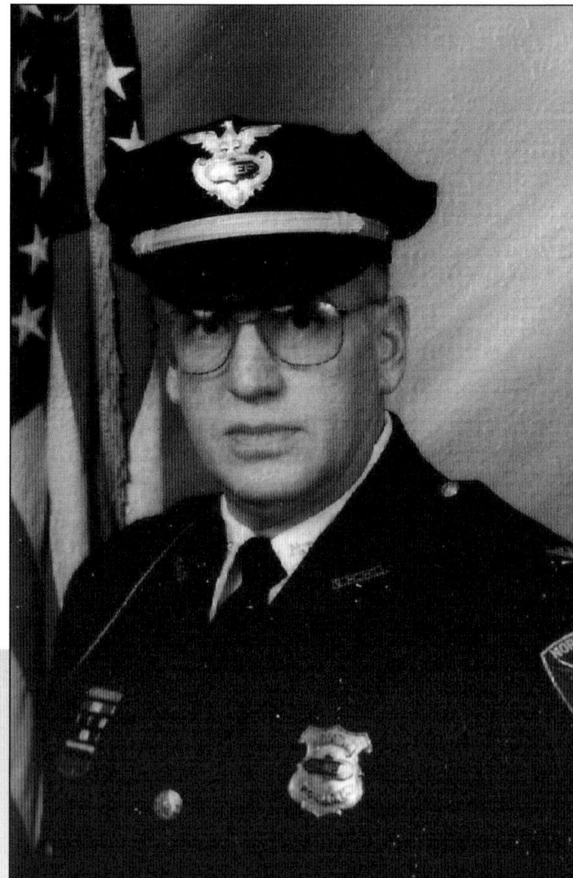

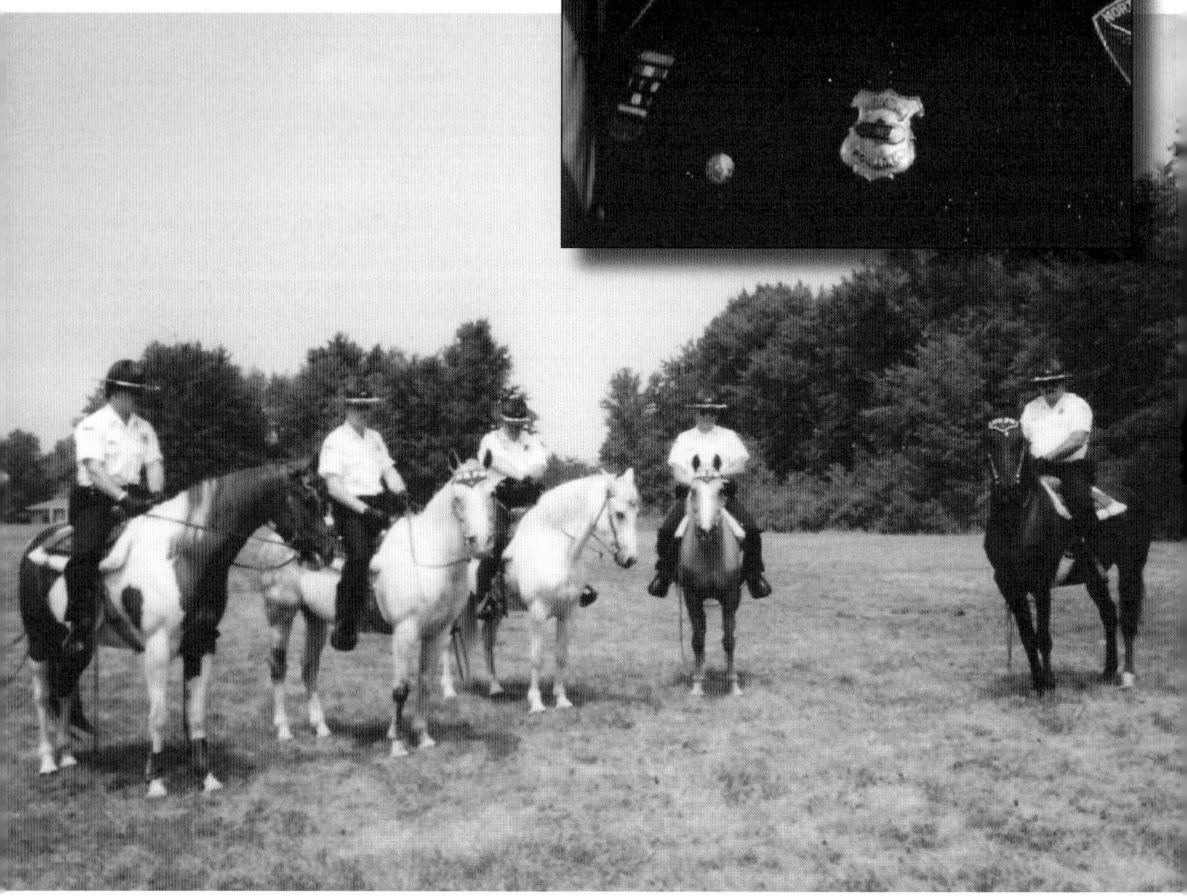

Ronald Bauer

Bauer, a native of North Ridgeville, graduated from North Ridgeville High School in 1964. His first job after graduation was at EST Bank, which lasted a little over a year before he was drafted into the Army. When he was discharged from the service, Bauer took the test for the police department, but then went to work for Sears in November 1967. In the spring of 1968, he was sworn into the North Ridgeville Police Department. In 1989, he became police chief and remained for 12 years.

An incident that stands out for Bauer happened in 1977. "Everybody remembers the blizzard of 1978," he said, "but during the blizzard of 1977, I was run down by a car while investigating an accident." Bauer had knee surgery and was off duty for a month.

The former police chief accomplished a number of things to improve the department and the city during his tenure, including starting a youth bureau and a diversion program for juveniles. If the parents and the youngsters agreed, they could do community service or write an essay as a punishment for what they had done. If they did their assignment correctly, their record could be expunged.

Before he was chief, Bauer was the head of the detective bureau, and morale was low. There were budget problems and also the issue of whether or not officers should take their support cars home. From 1989 to 1991, there were police officers on horseback (opposite). Bauer said it was sort of a public relations idea and that residents liked it. About 20 years ago, Bauer said there was a work program at the middle school to help students build junior dragsters. Bauer and former police officers Skip Hoffstetter and Thomas Schultz worked with the youngsters. "I built the racers and Tom Schultz did the welding." In the bottom photograph on the opposite page, Bauer (left) and Schultz work on a car.

Bauer liked his time with the department, especially as chief. "I really enjoyed it," he said, adding that from time to time, men would go to him for advice. He also received a number of awards while a member of the department, including being named to the North Ridgeville High School Hall of Fame. (All, courtesy of Ronald Bauer.)

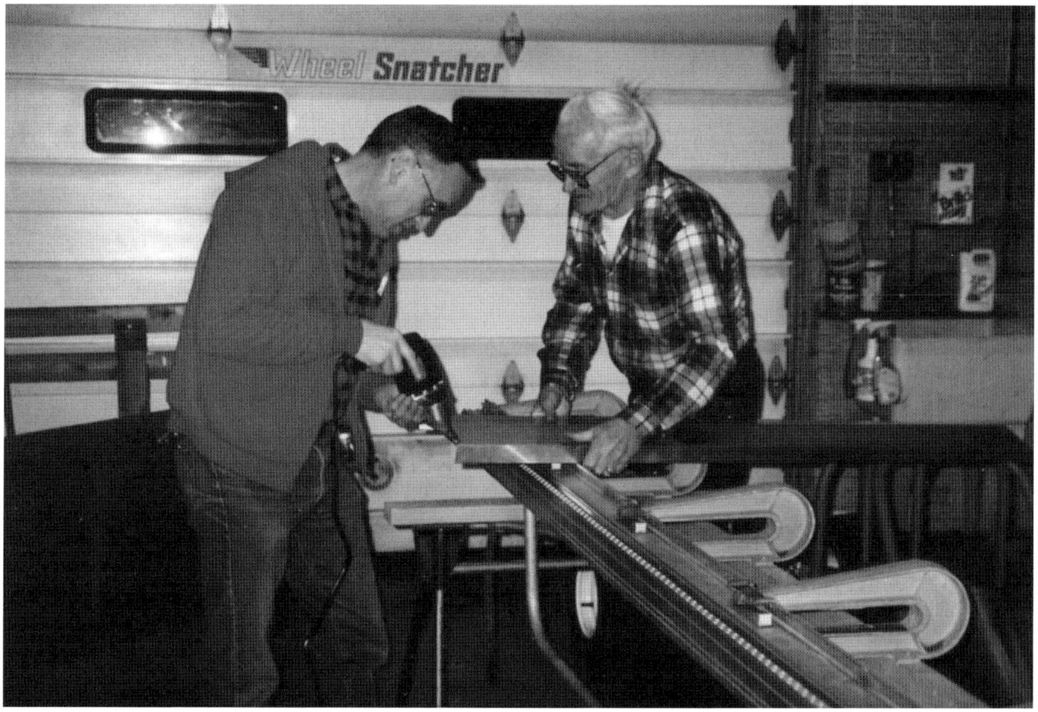

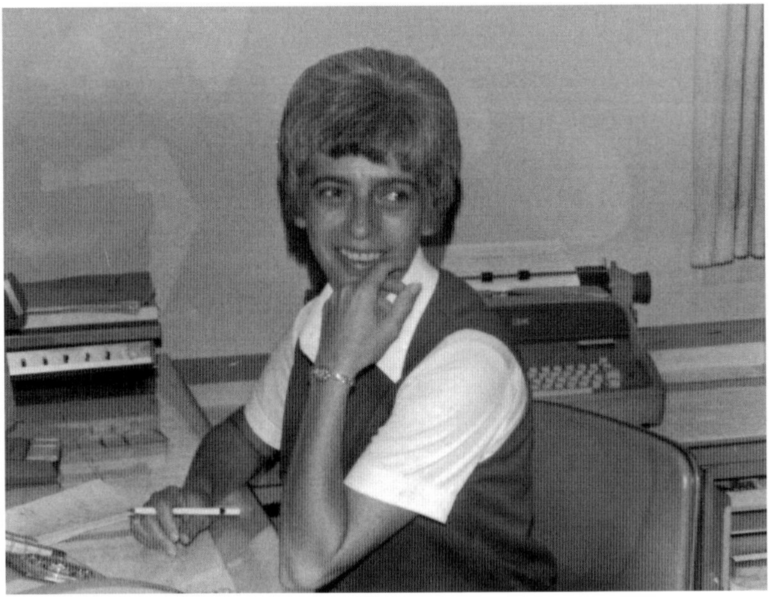

Audrey Ginley

It was 1971, and Audrey Ginley's husband, Patrick, had a serious accident. With four children to raise, it was up to her to get a job. For the next 24 years, she spent her days answering the telephone as a dispatcher for the police department. The police department supported Community Care. Shown below are, from left to right, Ginley, June Yost, Officer Larry Swenk, and Ilona Manista. Ginley retired, then three years later, Chief Ronald Bauer called and asked, "Could you give us a hand part-time?" As Ginley tells it, "I was there for 10 years." By that time, Ginley was 74 years old and ready to leave, especially because computers were arriving. Ginley worked under a number of chiefs, including Thomas Sigsworth, Richard Kreps, Bauer, and Richard Thomas. "I thank the Lord. It was a wonderful experience," she said. (Both, courtesy of Ronald Bauer.)

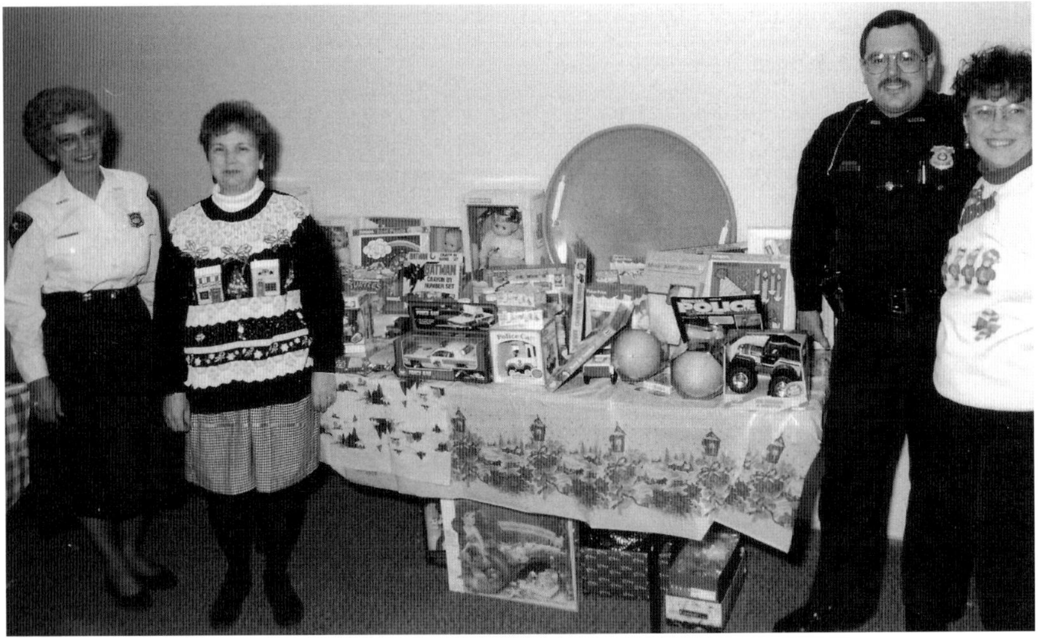

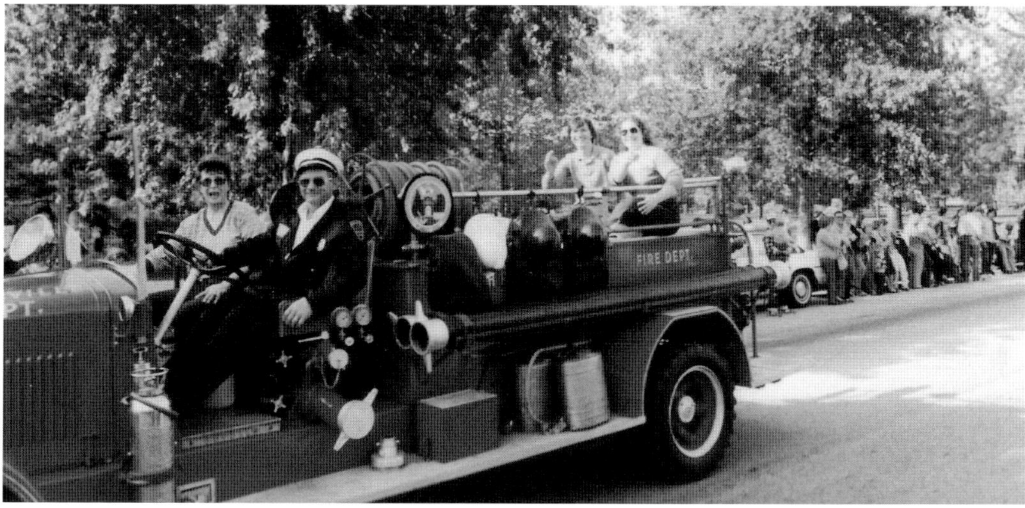

Eugene Diederich

Diederich became fire chief in 1982, retiring in 1989. Of his 42 years with the department, over 19 were in part-time service. The men "worked together," then they became unionized, he said. The worst fire he recalled was at Independent Oil, located on the Elyria line. "All the tanks blew," Diederich said. There were fun times as well. Shown here riding in the Corn Festival parade are, from left to right, Zoe Ann Diederich, Eugene Diederich, Pete ?, and Beth Ann Diederich. (Courtesy of Eugene Diederich.)

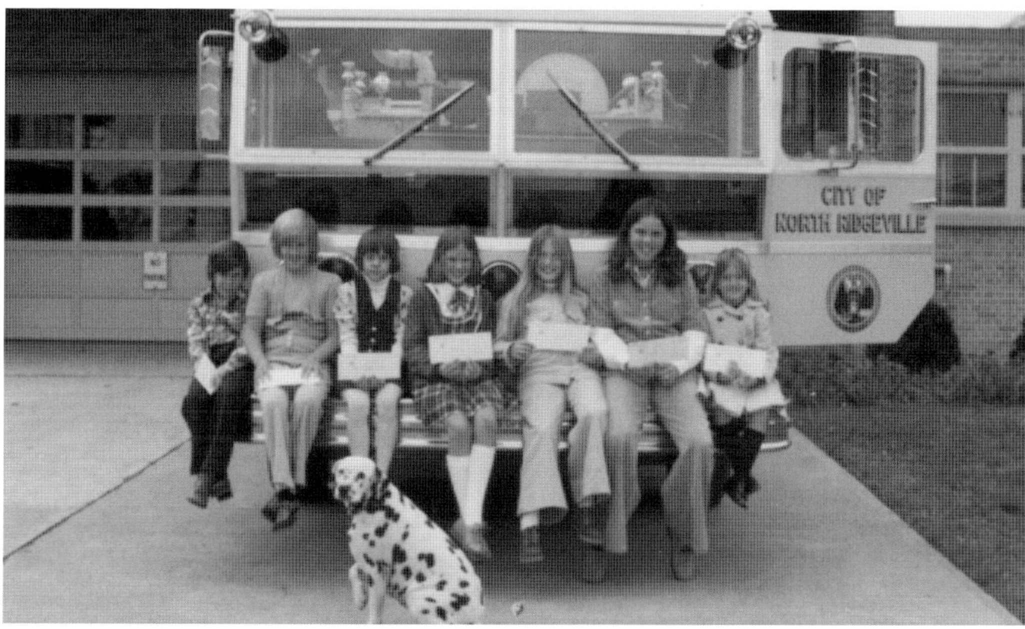

Freckles

In earlier eras, stagecoach drivers used dalmatians to protect against horse thieves. It is not known how long Freckles was the North Ridgeville fire station mascot, but there are fond memories of the black-speckled friend. Martin Thibo took chocolate-covered cherries to the station, putting them on Freckles' nose. The dog would not touch them. In this undated photograph, Freckles is pictured with schoolchildren. (Courtesy of the North Ridgeville Fire Department.)

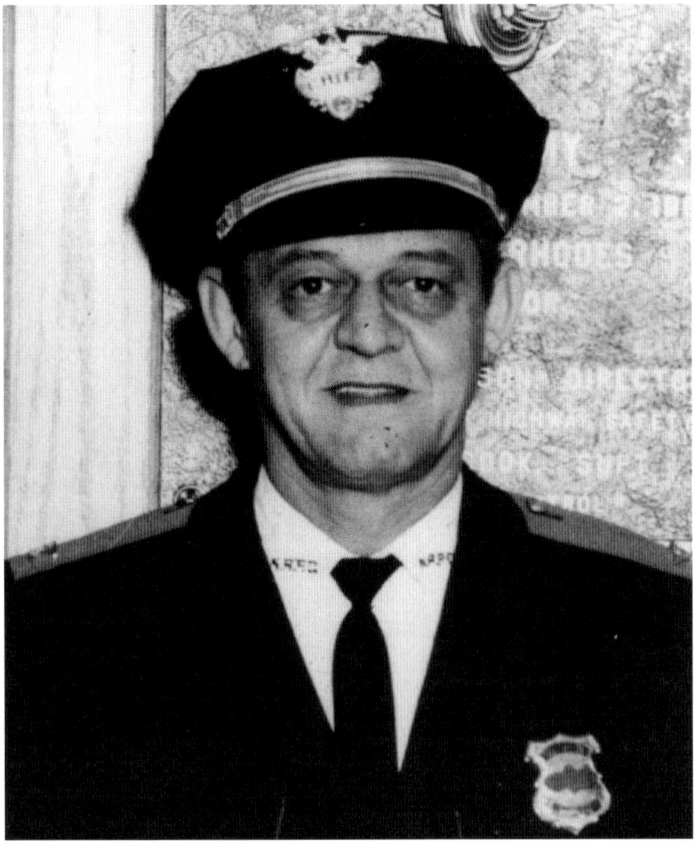

Thomas P. Richards

Hired as the first patrolman on the North Ridgeville Police Department in 1959, Richards was promoted to sergeant in 1960 and captain in 1965. On January 1, 1966, he was made police chief, a post he resigned from after four years, effective on June 3, 1970. Capt. Thomas Sigsworth became the acting chief and remained in that position until a civil service exam was given. Richards was 47 at the time and sent letters of resignation to Mayor Marcellus Diederich, safety service director Gerald B. Hansen, and the city civil service commission, telling them he had been mulling the idea for some time. He said he enjoyed working in the department, but felt he could do better elsewhere.

According to a newspaper report, the departing chief cited personal reasons for leaving. He also stated that the department was understaffed in 1965, when it went full time, and continued to be undermanned. He stated, "The department and myself continually requested more manpower to meet growing demands. Our requests have fallen on deaf ears or have been shoved into one committee or another until they have been forgotten." Richards also said the 10-man department should have been double the size to cover the city's 25 square miles and population of 13,500.

He also criticized some of the orders given to police officers, including "chasing stray dogs, making deliveries and enforcing zoning infractions," stressing that those duties were degrading to officers and took them away from important duties. Richards insisted that police work was technical but that some public officials thought the police operated for their benefit and expected them to carry out orders that had nothing to do with their responsibilities. The former chief asked residents to support the police department and speak out, stressing that the residents were the ones who would benefit. Hansen said he knew Richards's decision was difficult, one he himself had made the previous year. "Richards served the community well for the past 10 years," Hansen said, "giving much of himself to it—more than most people realize and appreciate." (Courtesy of Ronald Bauer.)

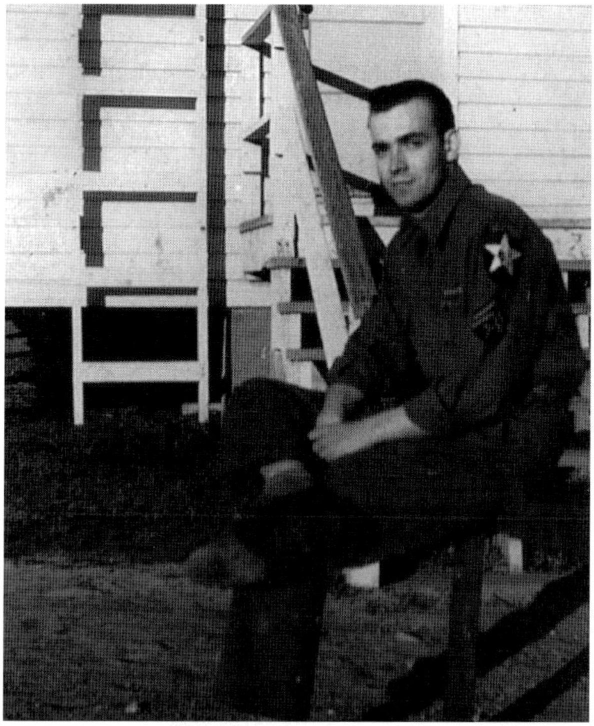

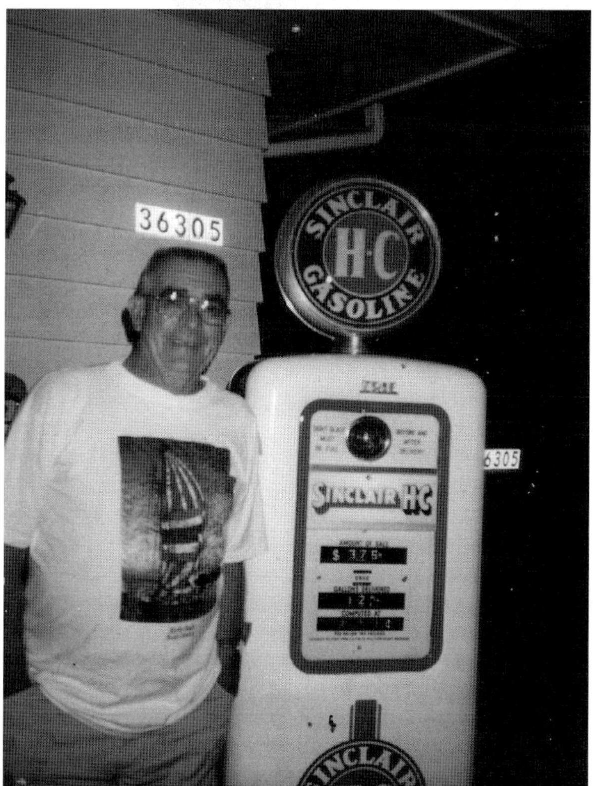

Robert Gilder
Gilder, born in 1926, graduated from North Ridgeville High School and was proud of being from North Ridgeville. On August 12, 1944, Gilder joined the Army and served in the Battle of the Bulge.

He owned and operated Gilder's Gas Station and was a member of the fire department from 1947 to 1986, attaining the rank of captain. He was a member of several organizations, including VFW Post 1079 in Elyria, the American Legion, and the historical society. "He was like a small businessman," his daughter, Nancy, said. "He helped so many people." She said he loved the historical society, but that even more, "he was history." Gilder enjoyed refinishing furniture. Following her husband's death, Jean Gilder said she discovered 10 suitcases, each containing a Black & Decker saw. (Both, courtesy of Jean Gilder.)

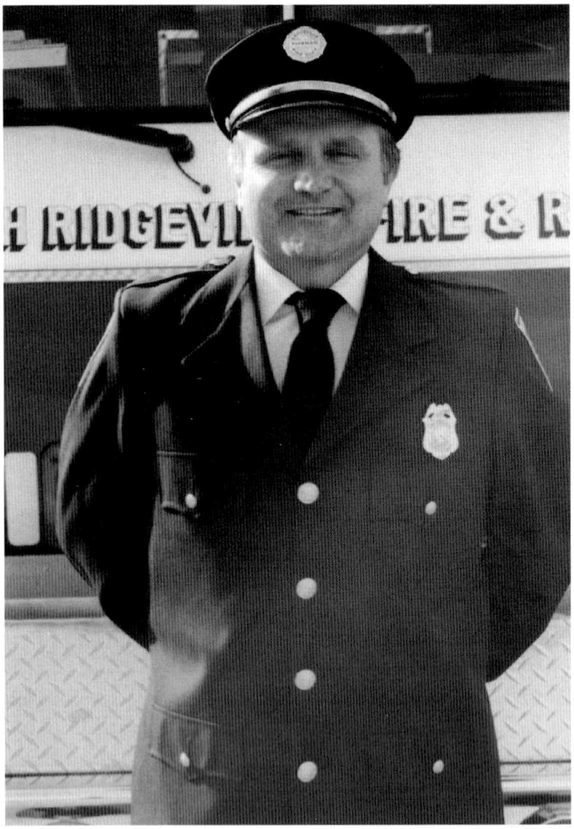

Eugene Kleinholz

While a city employee, Kleinholz worked under eight different mayors. He got a summer job before 1970, but in 1972, he was drafted. When he returned from the service, he worked for the parks and recreation department, followed by a job in the streets department doing sewer work. Ridgeville began growing so fast, Kleinholz said, that in 1979 he joined the fire department and stayed there until he retired. He agreed with former fire chief Eugene Diederich when he said the explosion at Independent Oil was one of the worst disasters he was called to. But the worst motor vehicle accident was in 1981, involving a Honda Civic with four people in it. Ironically, the 1980 Corn Festival Committee had just purchased the Jaws of Life, but the car was so mangled that the equipment did not help. (Both, courtesy of Eugene Kleinholz.)

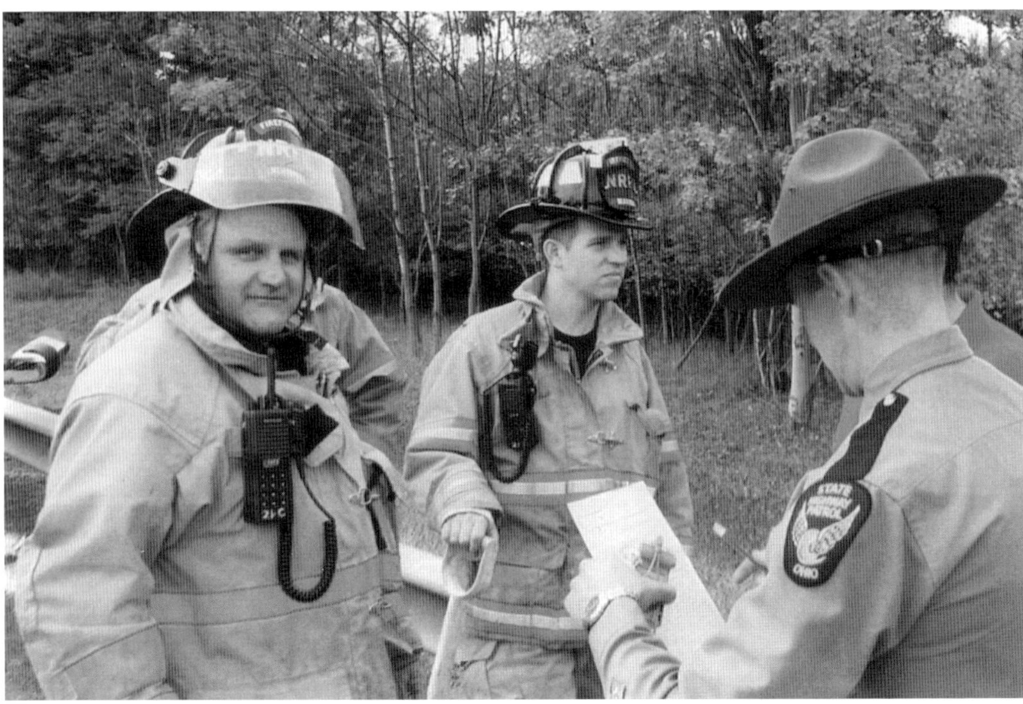

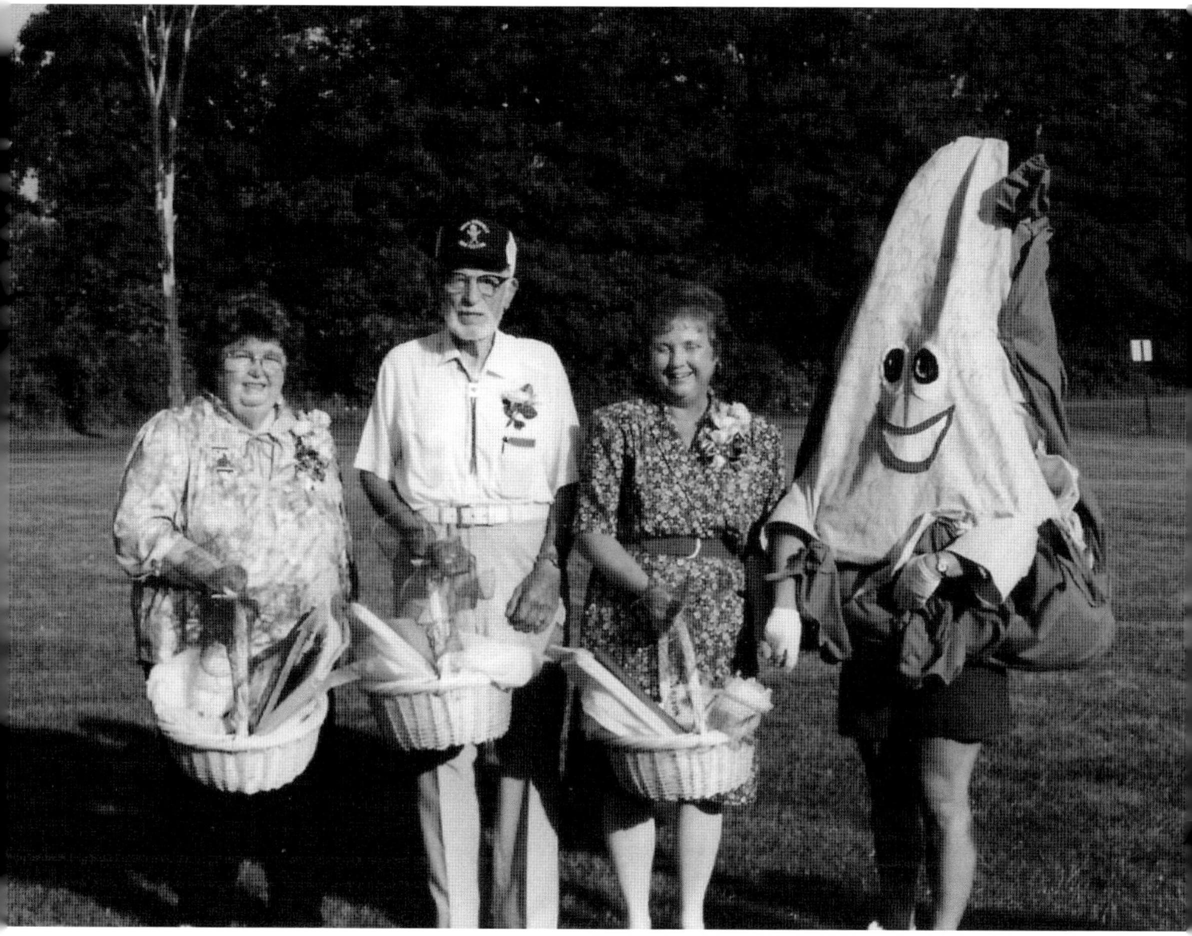

Harry and Dorothy Painter
Harry and Dorothy Painter were born in Michigan and moved to North Ridgeville in the 1940s. Harry worked for 34 years for the Air Force in Cleveland. Although she had taught school in Michigan, Dorothy was content to be a homemaker in her adopted hometown. The couple was active in the Beekeepers Association and county historical and genealogical groups, and were charter members of the North Ridgeville Historical Society. Harry Painter was the organization's first president. Dorothy Painter worked with the Girl Scouts for 50 years and compiled a three-volume set of information about the organization, including photographs and newspaper clippings. The Painters were given the Golden Kernel Award in 1993. Shown here are, from left to right, Dorothy Painter, Harry Painter, June Yost, and the Corn Festival mascot. (Courtesy of the North Ridgeville Historical Society.)

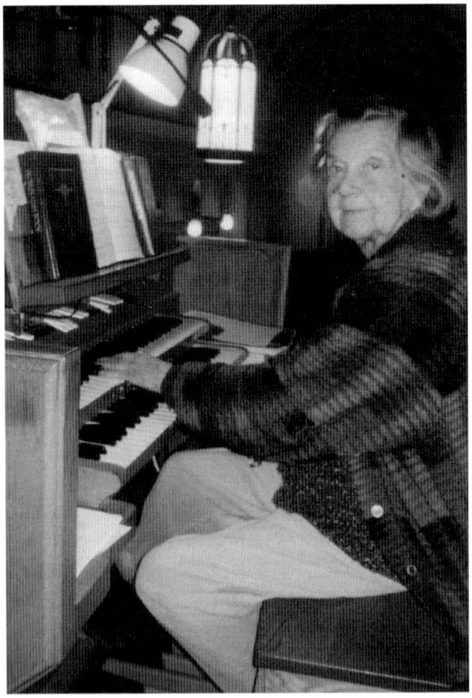

Wanda Jurco

The late Albert Jurco owned Al's Market, on Route 10 at Route 83, for years. Wanda Jurco, his widow, lives next door and keeps the market going. In addition, each morning, Monday through Friday, she climbs the winding stairs to the choir loft in St. Peter Church, where she plays the organ for weekday Mass, remarkable for a woman in her 90s. (Courtesy of Carol Klear.)

Folk Mass Musicians

Norman Rak leads musicians who play for the folk Mass every other Saturday at St. Peter Church. The idea started around 1975, and Rak joined two years later. He selects music based on the readings. If he hears something at another church, they give it a try. Members of the group are, from left to right, Rak, Hilary Sundheimer, Jetta Niemojewski, Ruby Niemojewski, Beth Price, and Don Sundheimer. (Courtesy of Norman Rak.)

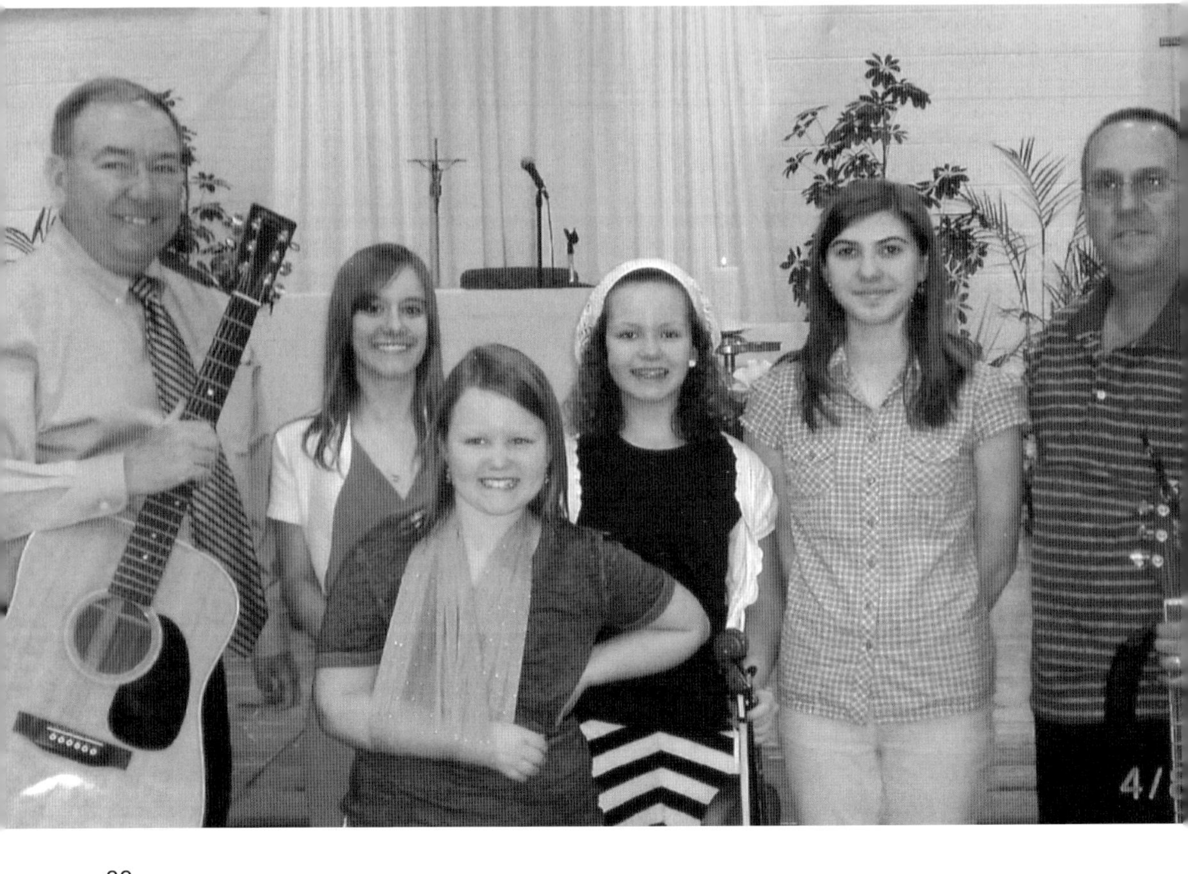

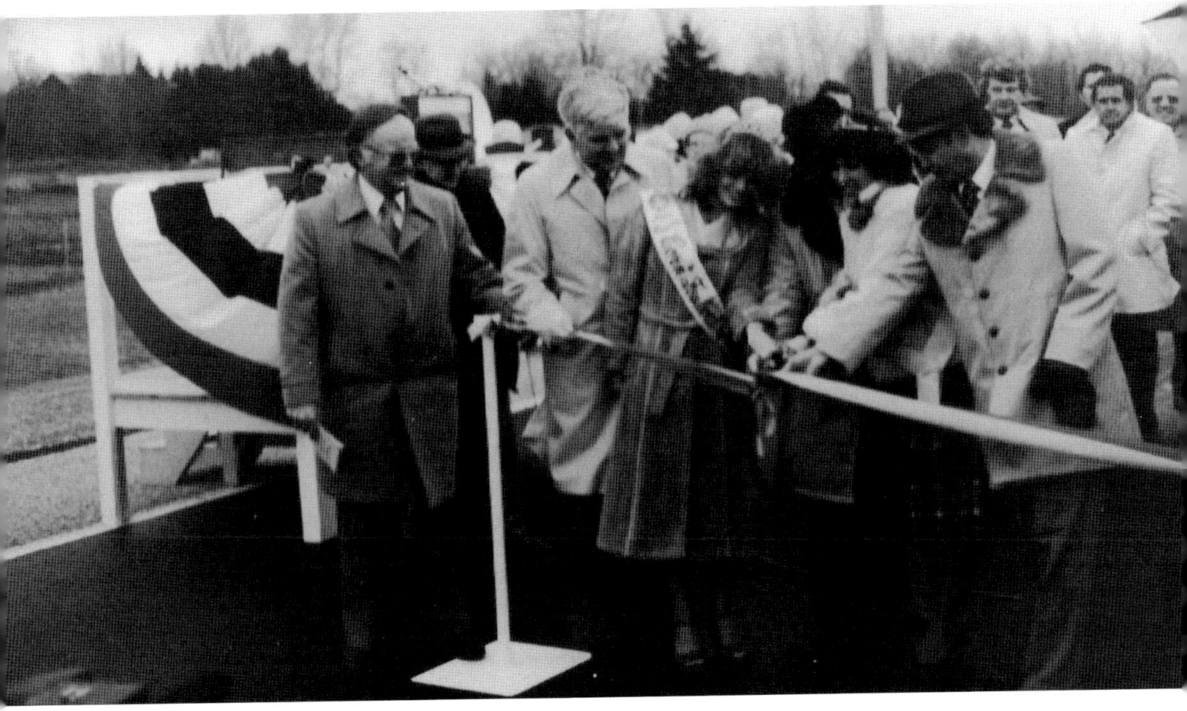

William Comerford

Comerford graduated from North Ridgeville High School in 1959, and in 1997, he was inducted into the high school's hall of fame honoring former graduates. The owner of Hovey-Kaiser Insurance served with the Army paratroopers and then became active in the community, especially in the chamber of commerce, which he helped found in 1976. As chamber president, Comerford worked tirelessly to implement the 911 emergency phone system in the city. In 1983, the city council's finance committee approved the funding. Comerford was also a charter member and first grand knight of local Knights of Columbus Council 7970. He was named the Melvin Jones Fellow, the highest award for humanitarian service to the Lions Club in 2013, as well as countless other honors, including being named "Mr. Baseball." Above, Comerford is at far left, attending the I-480 ribbon cutting. Below, Comerford (left) accepts a plaque from Lions past president William Shaffer. (Above, courtesy of Regina Comerford; below, courtesy of Lions Club.)

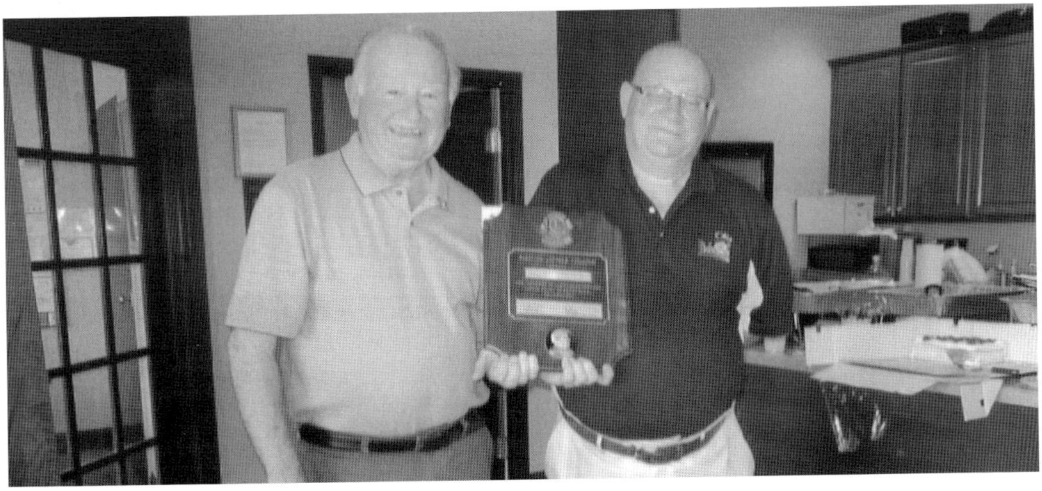

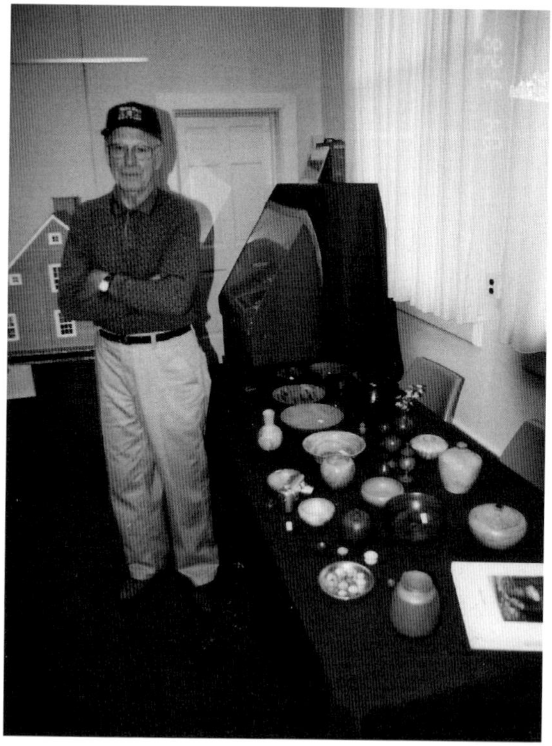

Joseph Lesnick

Lesnick graduated from Scott High School in Pennsylvania in 1937, where he learned woodworking. Jobs were scarce, but he worked as a server at a restaurant, where customers knew him well. A Westinghouse division opened in 1940, but World War II broke out, and Lesnick joined the Marines, serving until 1945. He returned and worked at Bendix Westinghouse for 41 years and continued his woodworking. (Courtesy of Marge Lesnick.)

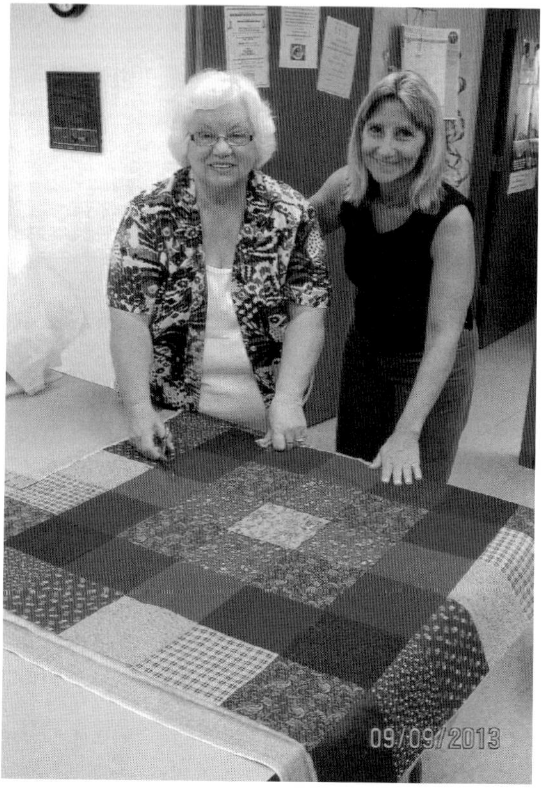

Rita Price

Price, the director for the Office of Older Adults, welcomes seniors to use the services and join the fun, fellowship, and meals. Since the Senior Center opened in 1976, there have been increases in staff, services, activities, and visitors. In addition to serving those in need, the center has line dancing, card playing, volunteers, and crafters, like Nancy Tangar (left), shown here with Price. (Courtesy of Rita Price.)

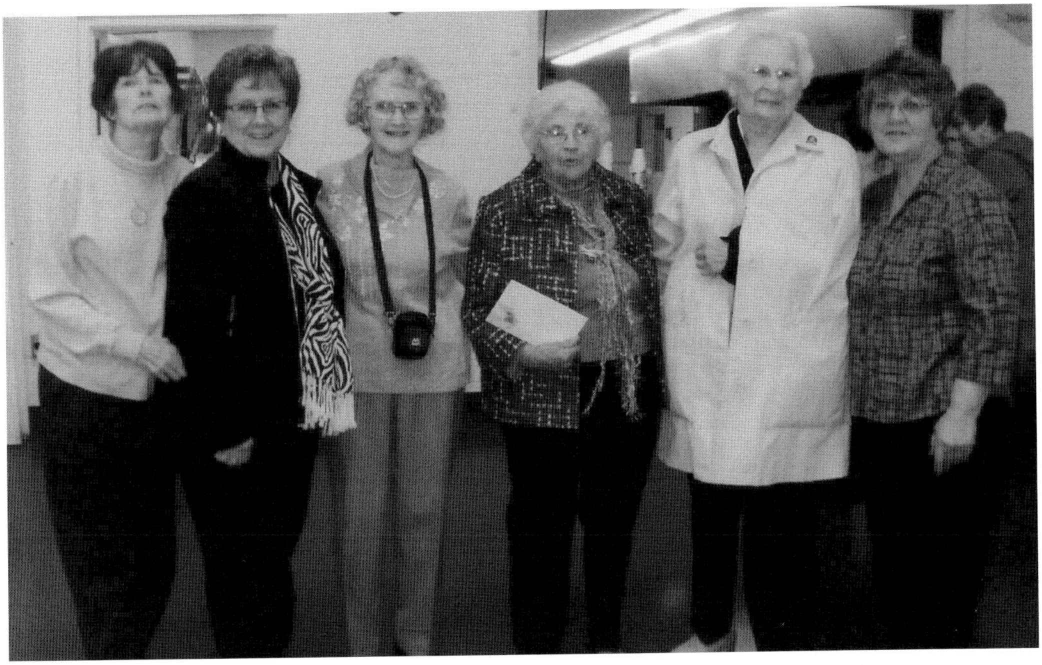

Frances Edwards
When Edwards (fourth from left) turned 90 in 2013, she celebrated with relatives and friends, including some from Birthright of Lorain County, where she volunteered for 40 years, 12 of them as the director. A registered nurse, Edwards learned that Birthright counseled women who had unplanned pregnancies and were contemplating abortions. The agency provides clothing and other baby items to help women in need. (Courtesy of Carol Klear.)

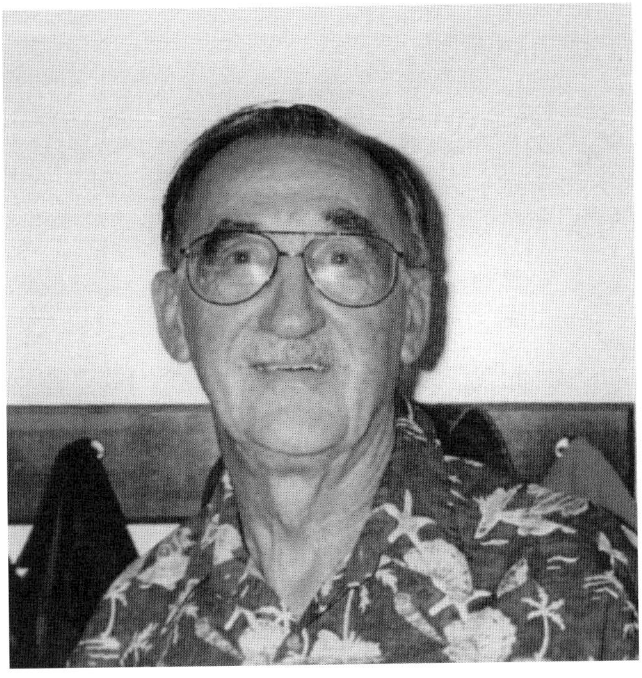

James White
White loves to visit people, especially those in hospitals or nursing homes or wherever he can serve.

"I especially like to do hospice." He also transports people to places they couldn't otherwise reach. White said he visits nearly every day, though he never knows what he will encounter when he meets people who are ill. Ironically, White has never taken a pill in his life. (Courtesy of James White.)

John Sigsworth

John Reid Sigsworth, eldest of four sons of John H. and Mabel Ann (Worcester) Sigsworth, was born on September 7, 1922, and died on February 8, 1985. He married Margaret Ellen Ritsko in 1945 at Fields United Methodist Church in North Ridgeville. Sigsworth served from 1943 to 1945 as a second lieutenant in the US Army Air Force as a B-17 copilot based in England, flying over Germany and France. In early August 1944, while flying with the 600th Squadron of the 398th Heavy Bomber Group, Sigsworth was shot down and was transported to Stalag Luft III, a Nazi prison camp near Sagan, Poland. He was held there for nine months and released when the European war ended in May 1945.

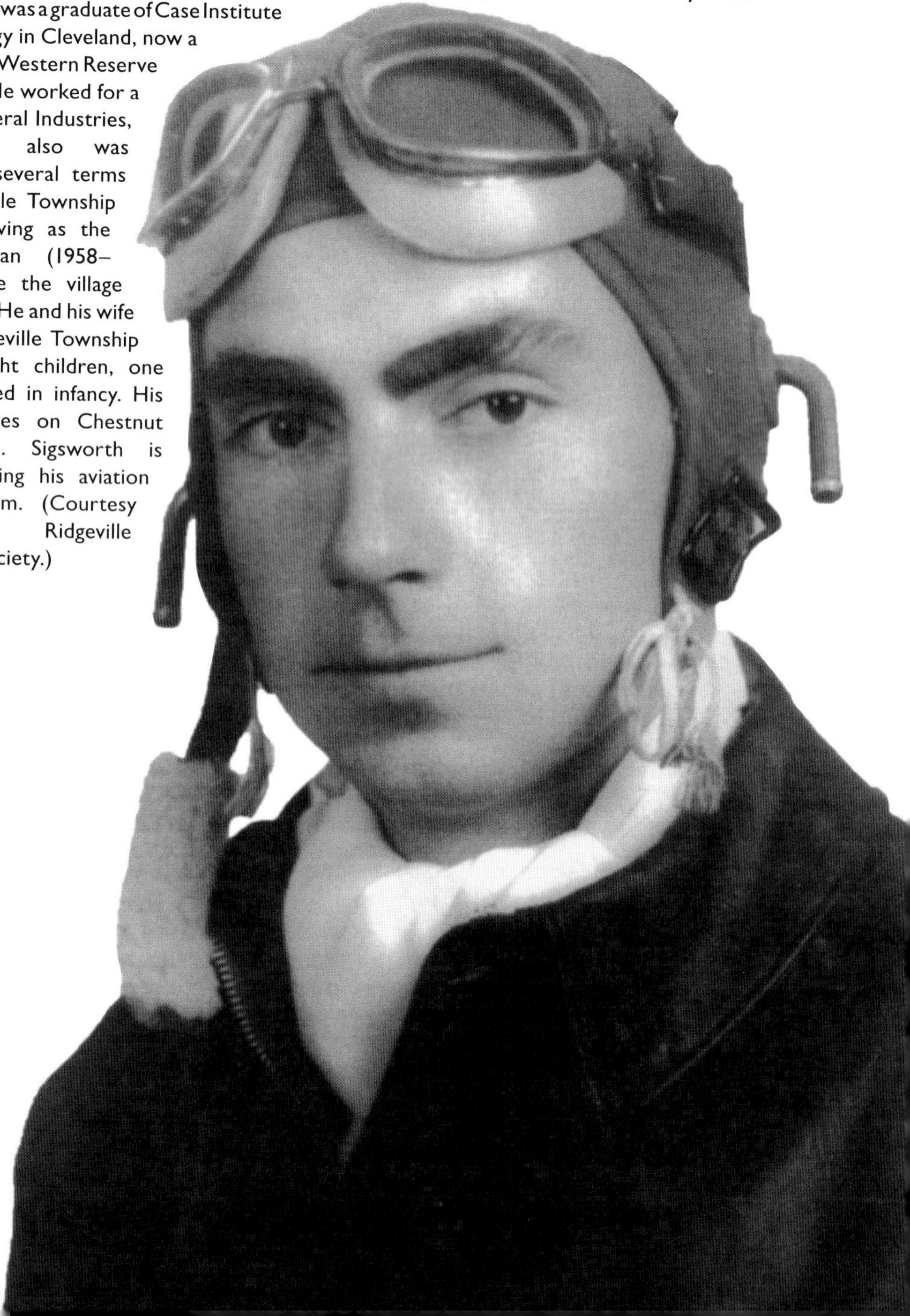

Sigsworth was a graduate of Case Institute of Technology in Cleveland, now a part of Case Western Reserve University. He worked for a time at General Industries, Elyria. He also was elected to several terms as a Ridgeville Township trustee, serving as the last chairman (1958–1959) before the village was formed. He and his wife lived in Ridgeville Township and had eight children, one of whom died in infancy. His wife still lives on Chestnut Ridge Road. Sigsworth is shown wearing his aviation cadet uniform. (Courtesy of North Ridgeville Historical Society.)

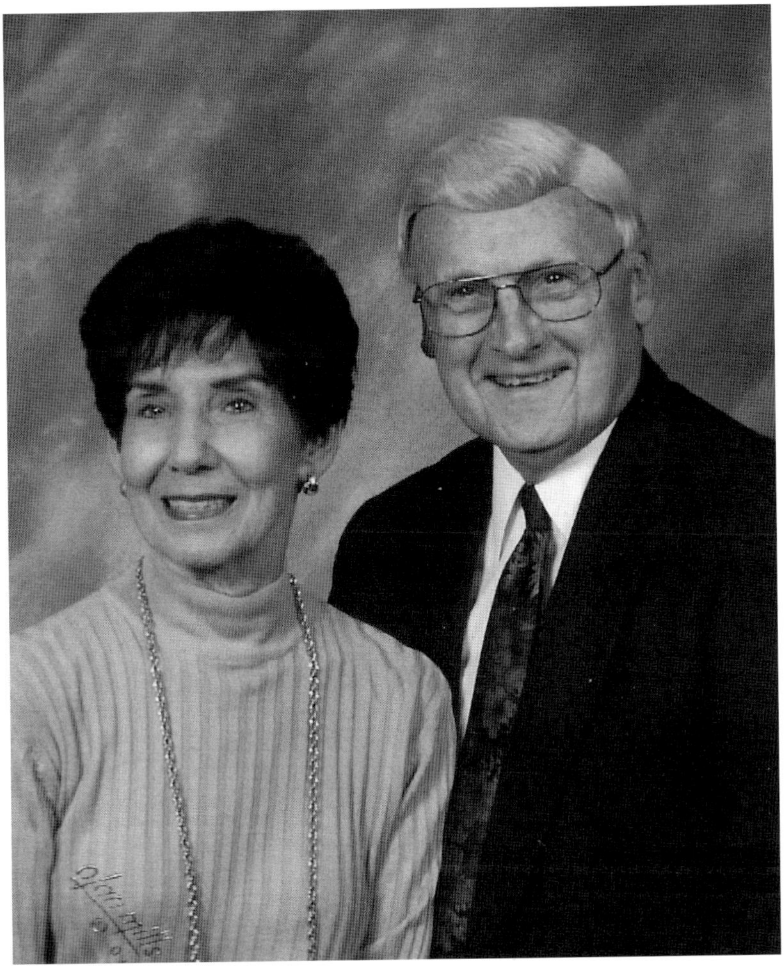

Robert and Evelyn Schmittgen
Robert Schmittgen and his late wife, Evelyn, grew up in North Ridgeville; she was in the third grade when he was in the fifth. The Schmittgen home is next door to the house he was born in on Case Road, but at the time, it was near the corner of Case and Center Ridge Roads, eventually being moved to its current location. He recalled a gas station at the top of nearby Dyke Road and some cabins the Dyke family owned.

Robert Schmittgen said that his father, William, was on the school board around 1923. Former school board president Maria Sycz said in 2013 that she found some records indicating that William served from 1929 to 1935 and was president of the board until 1934. They also noted that Robert Schmittgen was on the school board from 1958 to 1969, serving as president in 1961 and 1965.

Schmittgen was a manager of employee relations for 25 years at Luxaire York. In 1945, he worked in a clothing store in Elyria. His wife was a homemaker and raised their three children. Evelyn Schmittgen was one of the first members of the North Ridgeville League of Women Voters. She was also a soloist at church and sang at weddings. Her husband said his wife was also a model at Higbee's Store in Elyria. Robert was a member of the Civic League and worked to get water for the city in the early 1950s. He was a trustee at the Congregational Church and won the Golden Kernel Award in 2012.

Robert Schmittgen said his father built the house he has lived in for 62 years. It had the first poured basement in the area. One morning around two o'clock, Robert was putting shingles on the roof. Dr. Fred Markham, who lived nearby, yelled up at him, "Get yourself a light bulb." (Courtesy of Robert Schmittgen.)

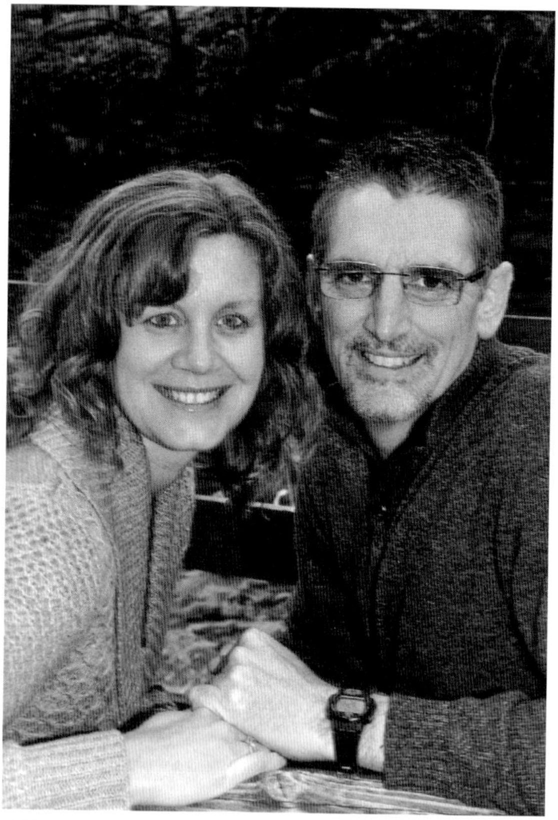

Pastor Kevin and Robin Crow
Kevin Crow and his wife, Robin, arrived in February 1992, which Kevin Crow referred to as a "parachute drop." He said, "We had no land, no money and three months support," but by April, they had 12 people in their congregation. Harvest Ridge Church Assembly of God was begun on May 2, 1992, in Liberty School. Robin Crow, also ordained, held Bible studies in their one-bedroom apartment. In 1995, they purchased over five acres of land on Lorain Road. The first service was held in their church on November 16, 1997. There have been three additions to the building since then. There are services and activities for everyone, including HarvestPalooza on Labor Day weekend. Kevin Crow coaches baseball, basketball, and football. He is seen below with his son, Matthew. A core value is to connect people with Jesus, Crow said. (Both, courtesy of Kevin Crow.)

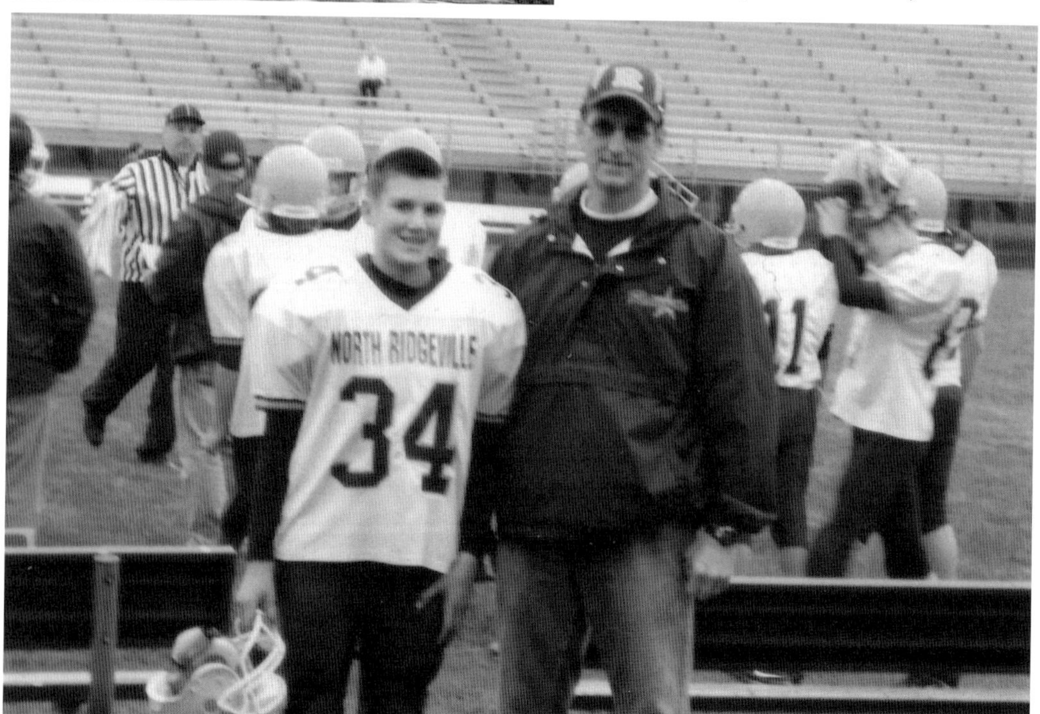

Charles Bowman

Born in Euclid in 1932, Chuck Bowman worked at Euclid Beach while in high school and met his wife, Nancy. They had four children. He served in the Navy during the Korean War and raised the American flag at his home every day. In 1973, they moved to North Ridgeville. He was the chief usher at Fields Methodist Church for 25 years, a Red Coat at Playhouse Square for 17 years, and a member of the Rotary Club of North Ridgeville, where he received the Paul Harris Fellow award. Bowman was also the Easter Bunny at the egg hunt. He won the Golden Kernel Award in 2010. Every morning, Bowman walked his neighborhood, putting newspapers in front of neighbors' houses. He completed the ritual on the morning he died, September 22, 2012. Below, Bowman (right) poses with Douglas Charboneau. (Courtesy of Nancy Bowman.)

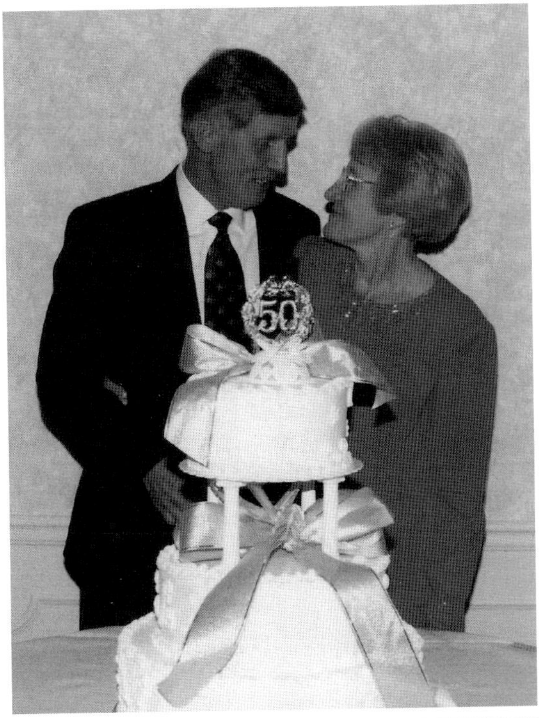

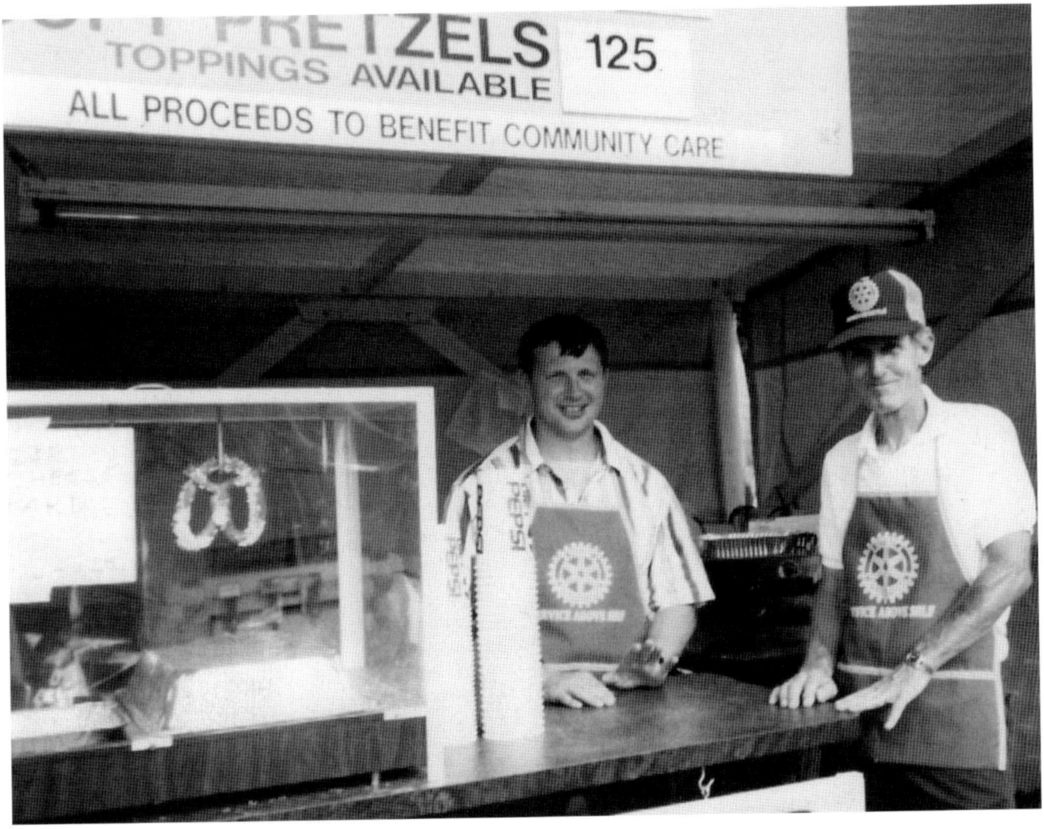

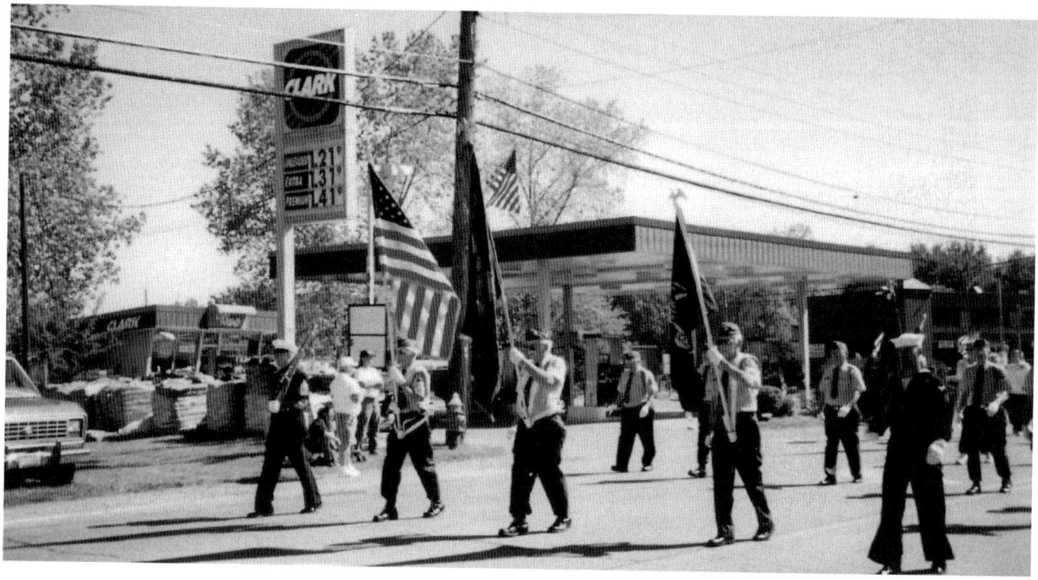

Veterans of Foreign Wars
The VFW serves veterans in many ways. North Ridgeville member Jack Huber said that in 1925, the VFW founded the National Home for Children, where families whose husband or father is serving overseas can remain together. Challenges to veterans often include post-traumatic stress and rehabilitation from battlefield injuries. The organization attempts to meet those needs. If called upon, members provide an honor guard during funerals of veterans. (Courtesy of the North Ridgeville Historical Society.)

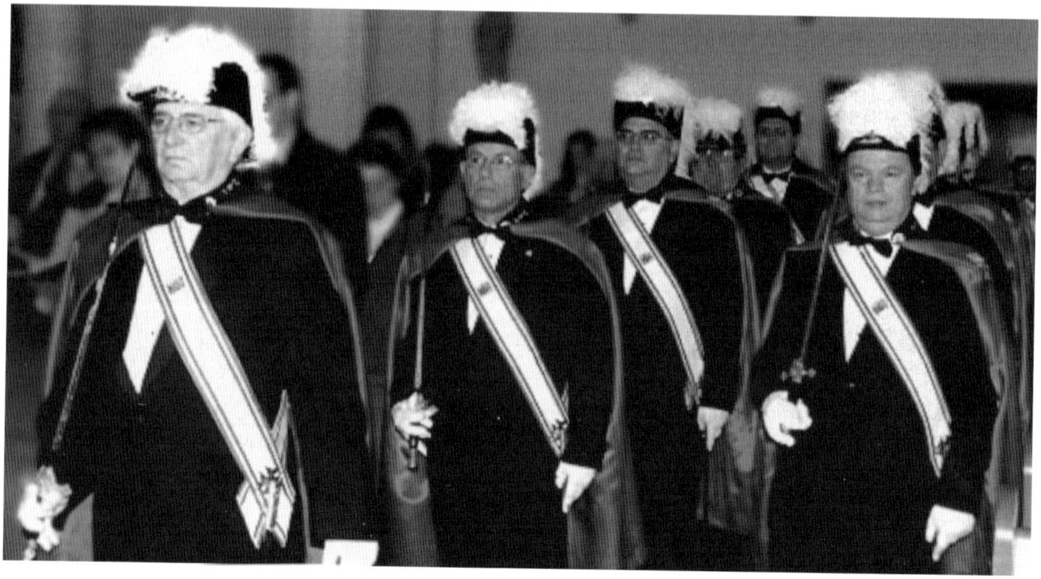

Knights of Columbus
Knights of Columbus Council 7970 was founded in 1982. William Comerford and Gary Krone were the first Grand Knights. Rev. Dr. Richard Gonser is the chaplain. Members help St. Peter School physical education teacher Pamela Nolan with the program Hooked on Fishing, Not on Drugs. They also help with St. Julie Billiart's annual Thanksgiving dinner and support Birthright and Right to Life. (Courtesy of St. Peter Parish.)

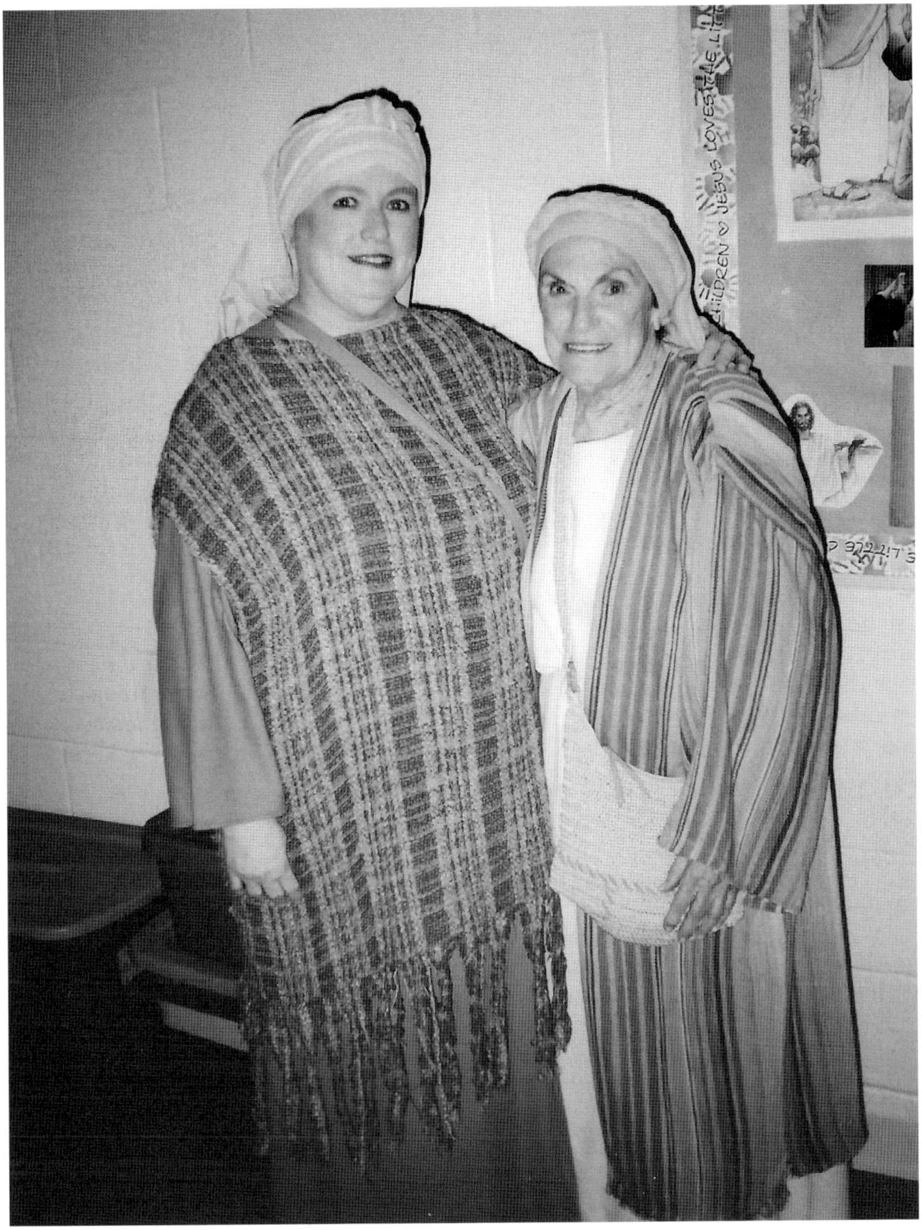

Patricia Fallon
Fallon, one of 13 children, learned early on to help people. She moved to North Ridgeville in 1977. Fallon was a Girl Scout leader, helped with Breakfast with Santa, and provided layettes for newborns at EMH Regional Medical Center. A member of St. Peter Church, she sings in the choir, coordinates volunteers for community meals, and helps with Vacation Bible School.

For 19 years, she has participated in Telestai, a nondenominational Passion Play produced by the Cleveland Performing Arts Ministry. Fallon (left) is seen here with Amy Gransfor. "You do not audition for a part, and costumes are provided, but you should be in it for the right reason," she said.

Fallon, a breast cancer survivor for five years as of November 2013, wants to give back to society. (Courtesy of Patricia Fallon.)

Brother Ray Carpenter

After 44 years as pastor of Faith Baptist Church on Lorain Road, Brother Ray Carpenter retired. The church had a history all its own before Carpenter began serving his congregation there. He said the building had been in Avon before being moved to North Ridgeville. It was Fields United Methodist Church then, before a new church was built farther east for that assembly. "We did not have money, but the Lord blessed us," he said.

When Carpenter, the founding pastor, and his wife, Brooks, started at Faith Baptist, they began meeting on Wednesday nights in people's homes. But children got into residents' things, so Ray and Brooks were anxious to begin holding services in the church. They did not have enough seats for all the worshippers, but Harold Bogner came to the rescue and lent them chairs. Carpenter said he rented a grange hall for nine months, but some people had been drinking wine and beer in there. "It was not fun," he said.

During Sunday School, they used a nursery at the house they stayed in. The floor sloped, but the Carpenters made do, and they lived there for over a year. "I have been in some rough places," he said. He said he was saved in the early 1970s, and it is obvious that he couldn't be happier.

The early days were quite interesting, he said, but during their 44 years at Faith Baptist, the Carpenters have met some very nice people, and it was not easy to leave. The Carpenters will always remember Faith Baptist and all the friends they made there. (Courtesy of Brother Ray Carpenter.)

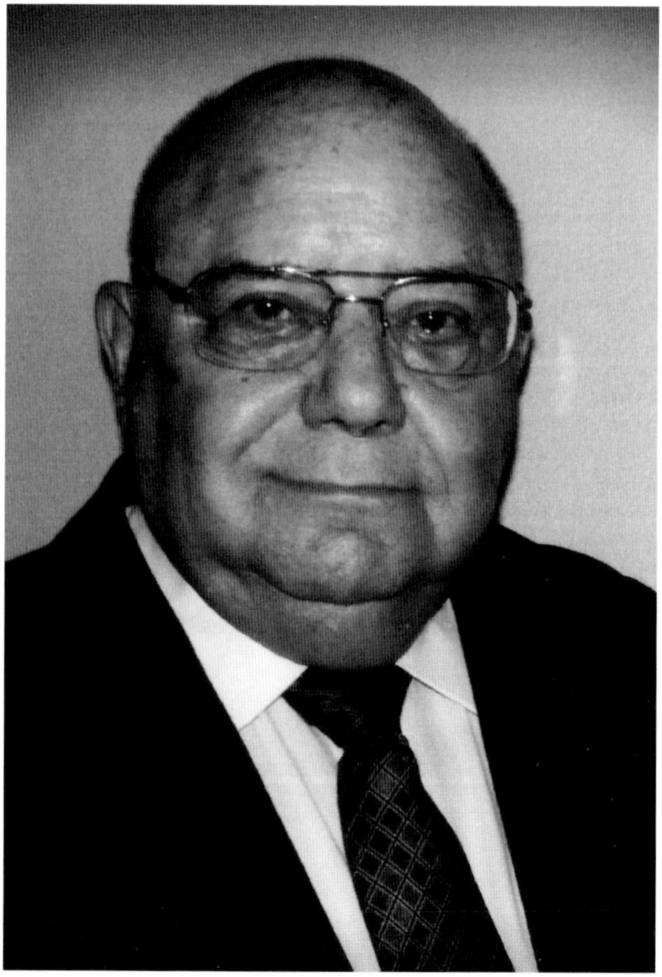

CHAPTER SEVEN

Talented People

An old saying advises, "Don't hide your light under a bushel." There are many people in the community that adhere to that time-worn thought, sharing their gifts and abilities with friends, neighbors, and even people they have never formally met, spreading pleasure as they go.

Talents are exhibited in a variety of ways. Dennis Boose has an aptitude for figures and has carved out a career in the banking profession, but he learned many years ago that he has a flair for acting. When he is not working in his world of finance, he entertains audiences with his Mark Twain characterization.

Groups of people often shy away from performing solo, but put several of these talented people together, and their voices and personalities blend into delightful entertainment. Once in a while, someone uncovers a talent they did not know they possessed, like making music with kitchen tools, as with North Ridgeville's Kitchen Band. They were a joy to watch. If someone wanted to join the group, that person was welcomed with open arms, as long as they had a couple of spoons or ladles to clink together. Another group that has stood the test of time is a quartet of men who harmonize their voices into barbershop singing; one of them is a bona fide barber, as well. They continue to give the gift of music to others at a variety of venues.

Not everyone's ability involves singing a song or playing a musical instrument. One woman has become very popular throughout the city and beyond through telling stories. They can be happy recollections, sad tales, true events, or the kind of retellings that are just too preposterous to be real. But no matter the story of the day, Barbara Sutton's gift of narration carries her audience to another world for a short time, something everyone needs once in a while.

Whatever the bent, skill or forte, each person has something to share. The key is to find it and shine the light for all to see.

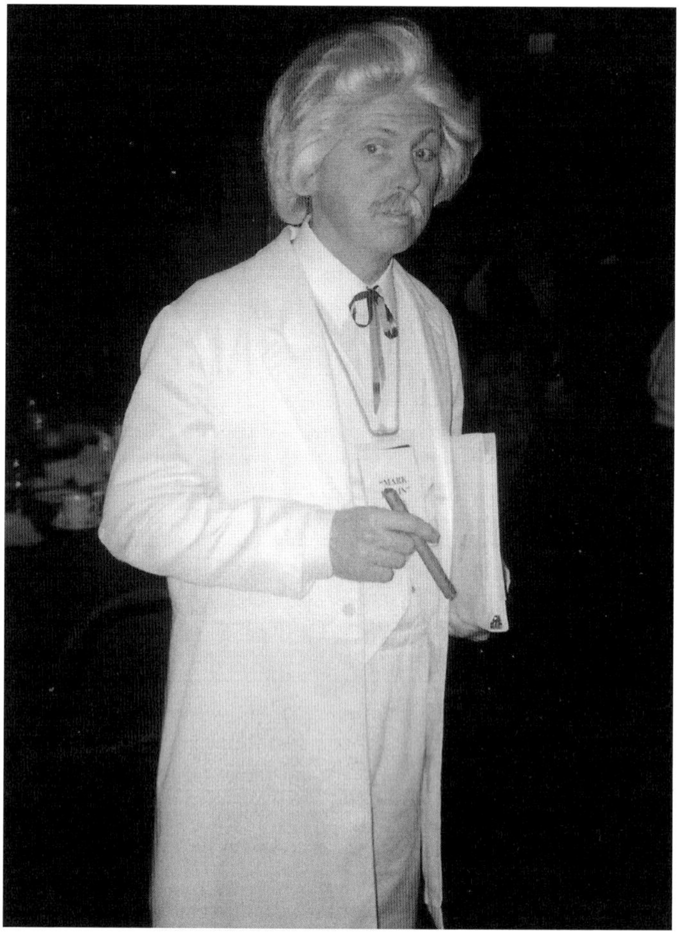

Dennis Boose

Boose has worn many hats in his lifetime. He worked on his dad's farm, toiled in a factory, and sold insurance. But his true love was theater. He graduated from Edison High School in Milan, then went to Bowling Green State University, where he majored in theater and won many awards for his performances. Armed with an Actors' Equity Association card, Boose headed to New York City, but, he said, "I struck out." He tried off-off Broadway for a few months, then began his banking career.

Wanting to settle down, Boose and his wife, Lisa, were looking for a place to live. They were considering four houses in different locations, and he told his wife, "pick one." She picked North Ridgeville, and in 1991, they moved in.

Recalling his work in theater in college, Boose said as a sophomore he played young Mark Twain in *Twain by the Tale*. Several years later, in Milan, he was asked to do Mark Twain again, this time at an Arts in the Park event. He was hooked. Since then, he has been doing Mark Twain impressions for programs every so often, perhaps three or four times a year. The last few times, he said, it has been to a standing-room-only audience.

He also moved up in banking and now is a vice president with Dollar Bank.

When his daughter was growing up and playing baseball, he got to talking to people and, before long, became involved with the baseball board and the parks and recreation commission. He is also a Ward 2 councilman and attributes being on council to Mayor Deanna Hill. He continues to play Mark Twain, always to a captive audience. He has appeared several times at the North Ridgeville Branch Library and may be there again sometime. (Courtesy of the Rotary Club of North Ridgeville.)

Helen Cotterman

In the late 1970s or early 1980s, Cotterman visited her son in California. He took his mom many places, including a senior center, where older adults were playing in a band using kitchen utensils and kazoos. She loved the idea and took it back to North Ridgeville and presented it at a senior meeting. Members liked it and decided to give it a try.

Cotterman gathered 12 women between 60 and 80 years of age to join her. One of the women had a portable keyboard and played the songs, and the others followed along with their kazoos and kitchen items, as well as with their voices. Of course, Cotterman used a wooden spoon to conduct the members, who all wore long dresses and bonnets.

The Young at Heart Kitchen Band played at the Avon Antique Festival and then began playing a regular circuit, including nursing homes, the mall during Senior Days, and other events throughout Lorain County. Before long, they were planning for their appearance at the Corn Festival and even thought it would be fun to be on a float in the Corn Festival Grande Parade. Between numbers, the women tossed candy to the children. When the awards were announced, the band had won a trophy.

In 1987, comedian Martin Mull visited the city to film an HBO special in the town where he spent part of his childhood. He was also the grand marshal of the parade that year. He and the band performed on stage, and the event was filmed. T-shirts were printed with a picture of Mull and Cotterman on the back and the Corn Festival logo on the front. These were sold as souvenirs. After the performance, Mull presented the band with a check for $1,000, which went to the Retired Senior Volunteer Program, an organization the women represented. The band played in just one more Corn Festival, as some of the women had dropped out.

When Cotterman died, she was buried in one of the dresses she often wore when performing. (Courtesy of the North Ridgeville Historical Society.)

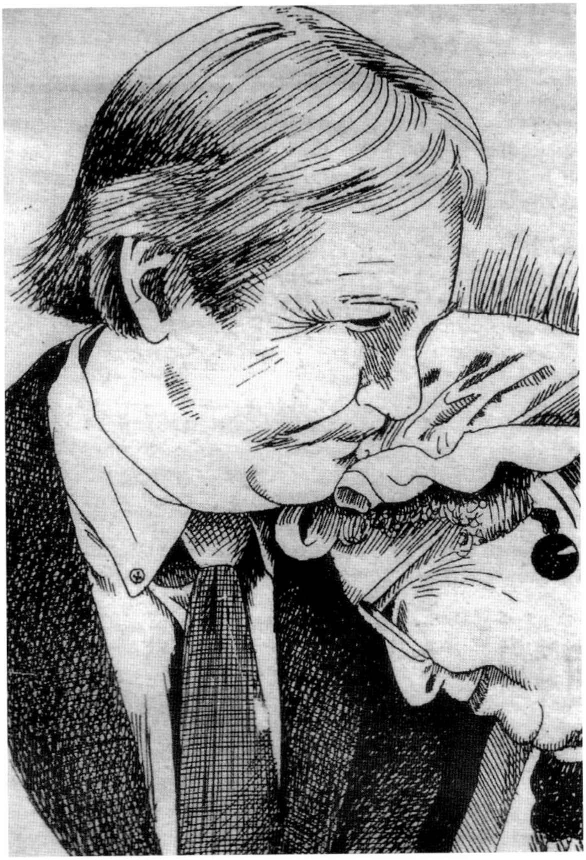

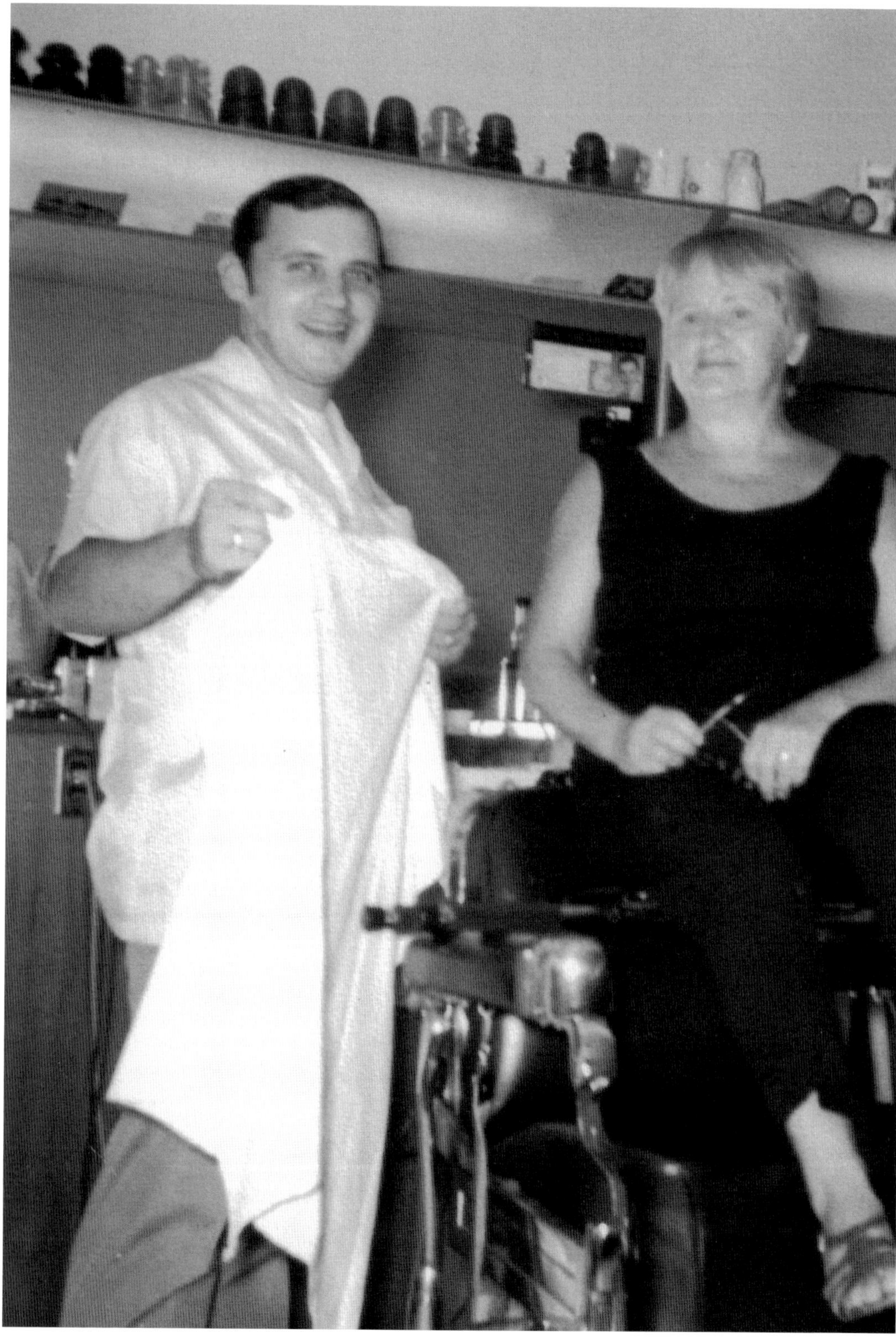

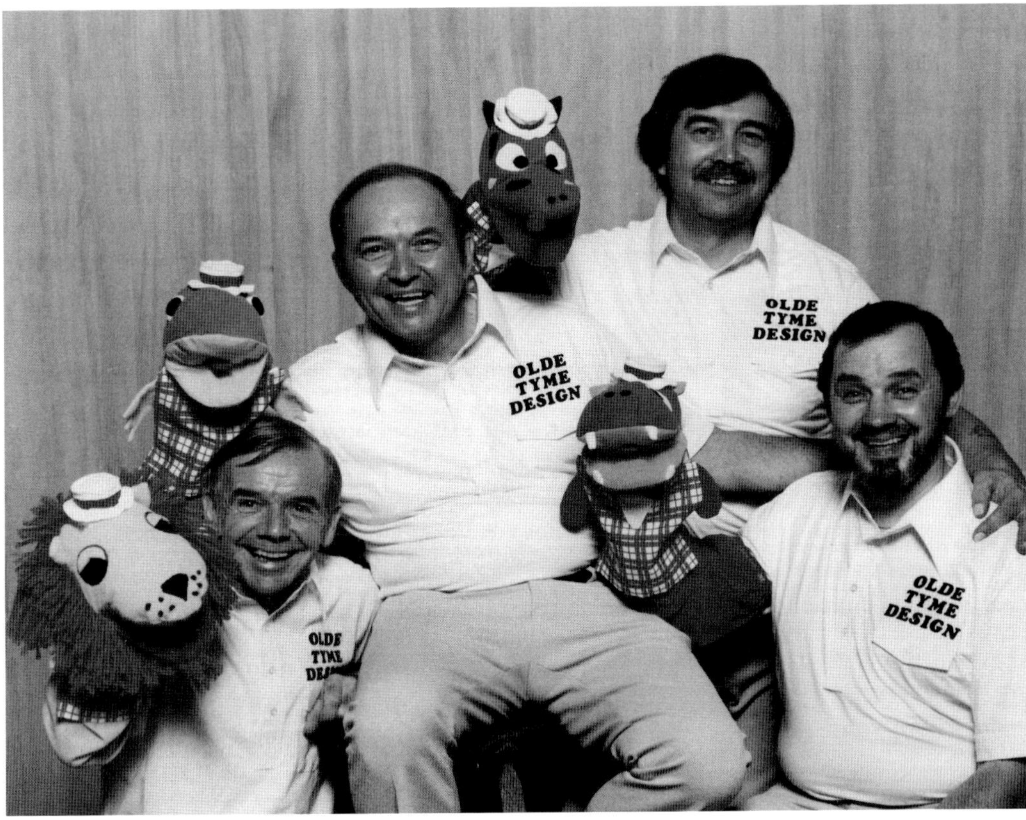

Ronald Granneman

Being a barber doesn't necessarily mean you belong to a barbershop quartet, but Ron Granneman is an exception. He belonged to Olde Tyme Design, an honest-to-goodness barbershop quartet.

Granneman got his barber's license in 1961 and started his first job in the Ridgeview Shopping Center. He served as an apprentice for 18 months and is now a master barber. He is seen on the opposite page with Millie Imler in the barber chair.

Hairstyles have changed over the years. In the 1970s, it was the Beatles' look. But in 1971 and 1972, the profession lost about 800 barbers, Granneman said, because the longer styles became less popular. The cuts got shorter, including crew cuts. What kept area barbers afloat in the early 1970s was the fact that Lorain County is primarily a blue-collar area, with many men working at Ford Motors and Chevrolet, Granneman explained.

The veteran barber said things are changing in the barbershop. The government is attempting to direct the business. "State laws have changed," he said. "There are a lot of diseases and state violations and inspectors stop by." Thinking back to when he began barbering, Granneman said that, around 1961 or 1962, a neighbor was getting his hair cut and asked Granneman, "Have you done any singing?" And that was the start of his involvement in a barbershop quartet, something he has been doing for about 50 years. The group he is with now meets on a weekly basis in the Methodist Church on Abbe Road. There is a director, and a music committee that selects the songs. The men have performed at a number of places, including the North Ridgeville Branch Library and at First Night. Granneman feels he is with a great group of men, and he loves the stuff of which barbershop quartets are made. The above photograph shows members of Olde Tyme Design in the 1970s. They are, from left to right, Tom Clemens, Gene Wise, Casey ?, and Ronald Granneman. (Both, courtesy of Ronald Granneman.)

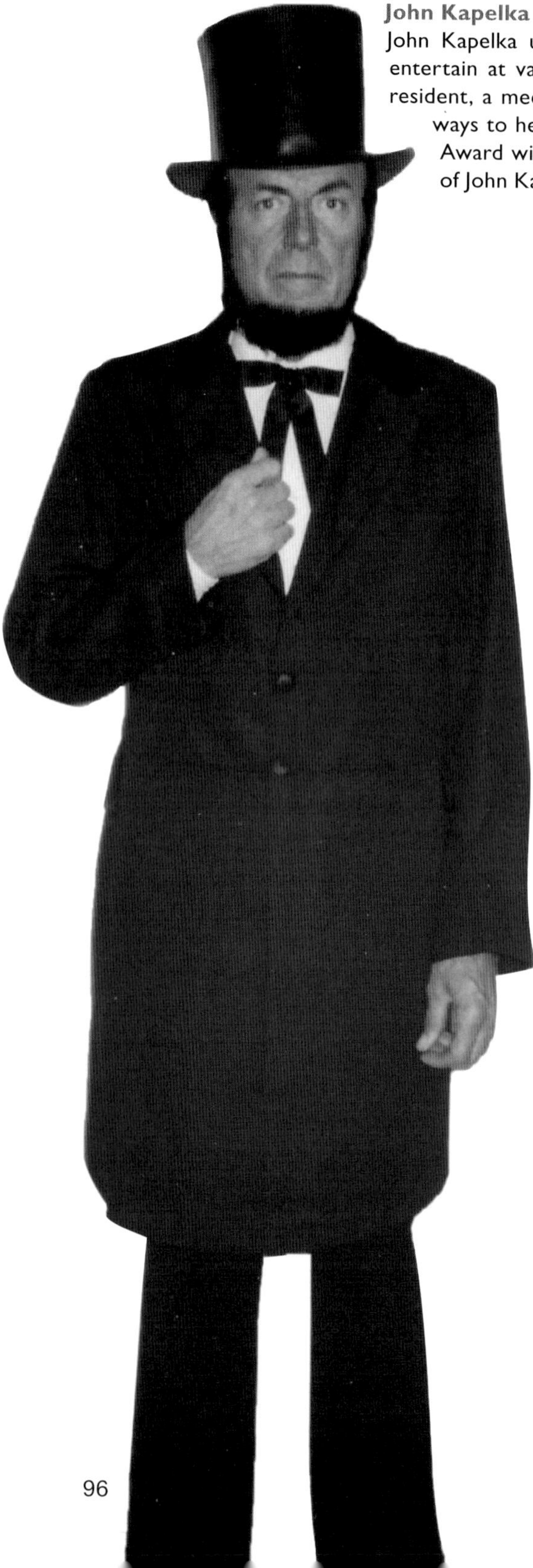

John Kapelka

John Kapelka uses his uncanny resemblance to Abraham Lincoln to entertain at various events in and around the city. The Lorain Road resident, a mechanic, owned Performance Clinic. He is always finding ways to help others. Kapelka was named the 2013 Golden Kernel Award winner, for all he has done for the community. (Courtesy of John Kapelka.)

Catherine Halagan

In 1968, the Jaycees held a contest to find "Little Miss Ridgeville." It has been so long ago, Marian Halagan does not recall the requirements. All she knows is that her little girl, five-year-old Catherine, won. The prize was a shiny new bike, which got a good workout around the neighborhood. The next year, the contest was based on a 12-point system. (Courtesy of Halagan family.)

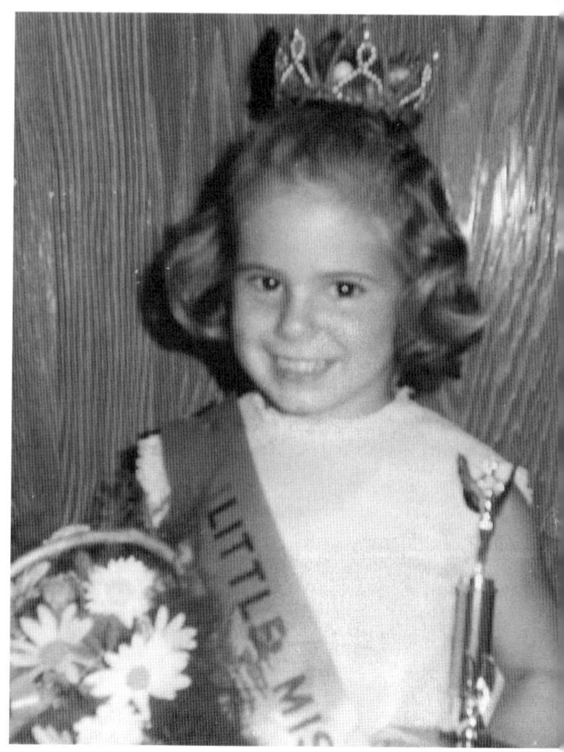

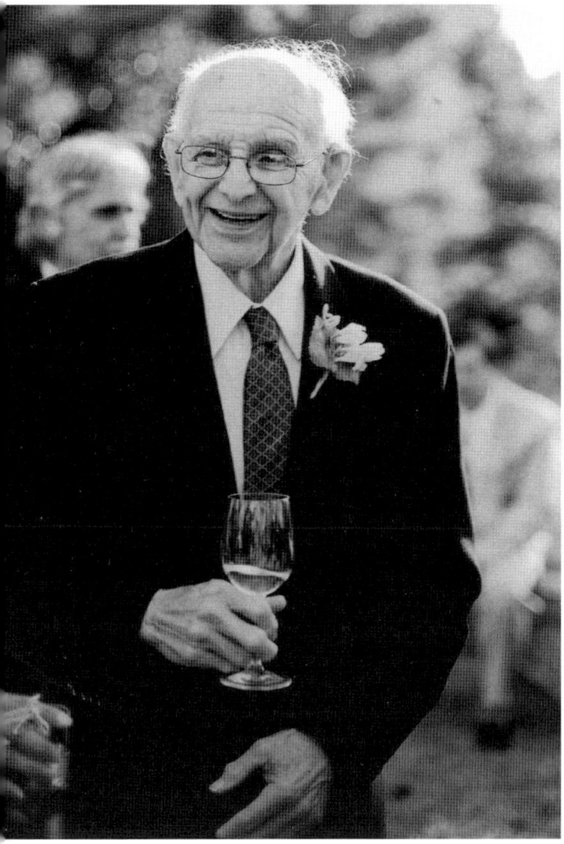

Frank Serazin

Serazin loved ships—not just traveling on them, but creating them from wood. Born in Lorain in 1923, Serazin served in the Navy in World War II on the destroyer *Norman Scott*. But his fondness for ships did not end with service; he loved working on scale models of American sailing vessels. When he left for the Navy, he had been working on a Civil War battleship. He planned on completing it when he returned. But while he was gone, his father tossed it out. Before Serazin would begin crafting a model, he studied its history thoroughly and then set to work. Building a model ship requires patience and manipulating many tiny pieces, but Serazin always had time for his ships, and his friends and relatives always took time to admire them. (Both, courtesy of Mary Ann Serazin.)

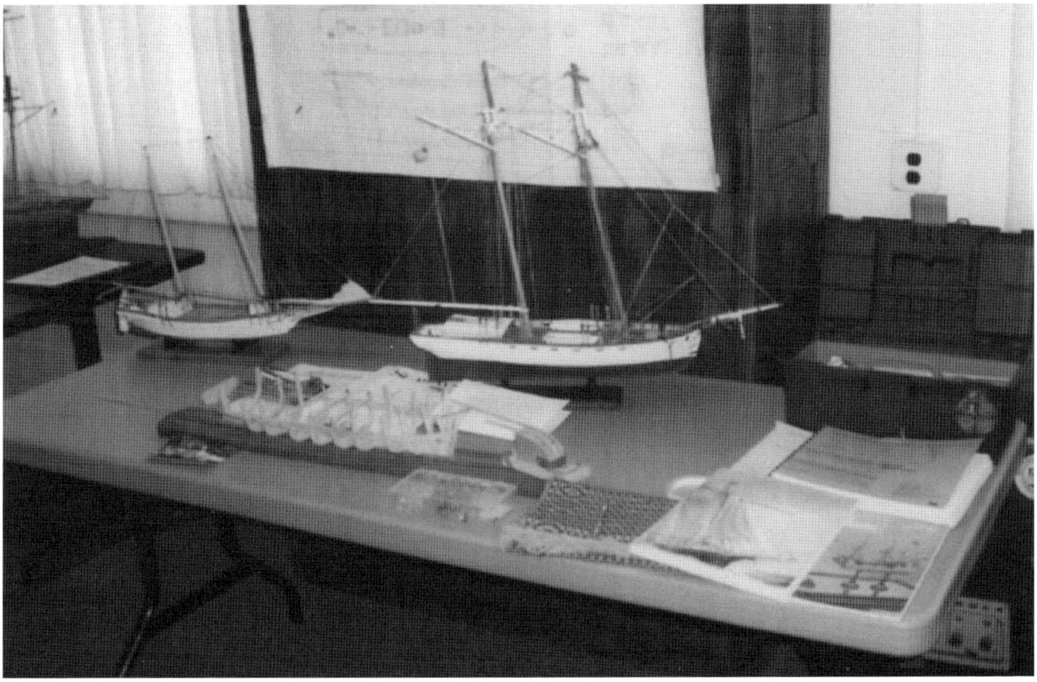

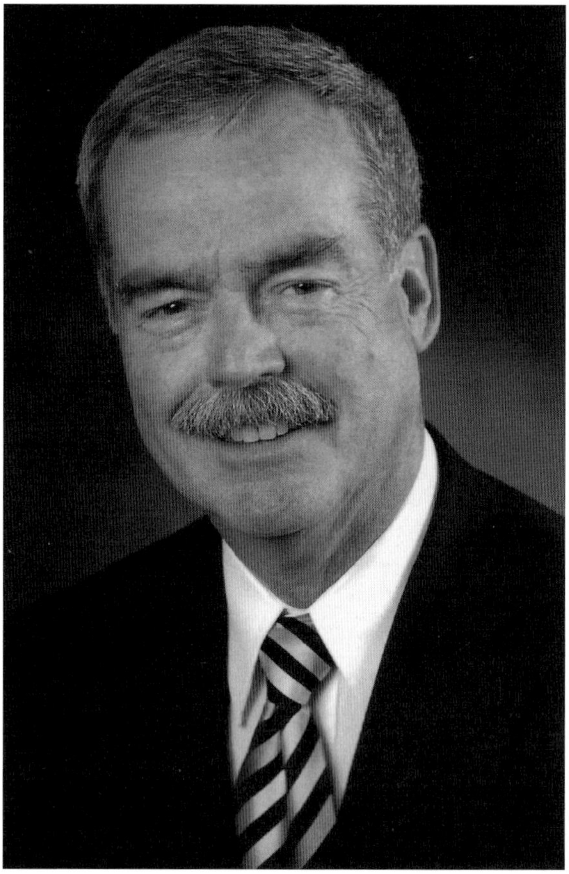

John Musson

He went from law school, to a law practice, and then to being a judge. But somewhere along the way, John Musson became a Civil War reenactor. And he thoroughly enjoys it.

Musson and Jeffrey Manning, the man who eventually became his law partner, went to Akron Law School and "hit it off," Musson said. It was 1972, and Manning went back to North Ridgeville after law school, while Musson went into the Army. He and his wife, Maureen, went to Germany for four years. Their two children were born there. He kept in touch with Manning and recalled Manning's invitation to join him in his law office: "Come to North Ridgeville to practice law and have some fun." "And we did," Musson said, adding, "it worked out well." Manning and Musson were partners for 18 years. Musson decided to run for judge, knowing that he had always been able to see both sides of a situation. He served two terms. "I always enjoyed municipal court," he said. He dealt with real people, although he admitted it was never pleasant sending people to jail. In 2010 Musson retired, but he continued to be a visiting judge.

His idea of becoming a reenactor came as a result of his fascination with the Civil War after visiting Gettysburg when he was seven years old. In 1996, Musson was in the Army Reserves and met an attorney from Elyria who was a reenactor with the 8th Ohio Volunteer Infantry Company H. Musson decided to try it and enlisted in the militia for three years. In 1964, he went to Gettysburg for the centennial and spent three days camping out. "I was living history," he said.

There were firing demonstrations, and Musson was a private in Pickett's Charge. He had the opportunity to be an extra in the movie *Gods and Generals*, and he is often called on to participate in reenactments. "I've been rained on, shot, and blown up," he said.

His wife does not participate in the reenactments, but she did purchase a Civil War dress and posed with her husband for a photograph (opposite). (Both, courtesy of John Musson.)

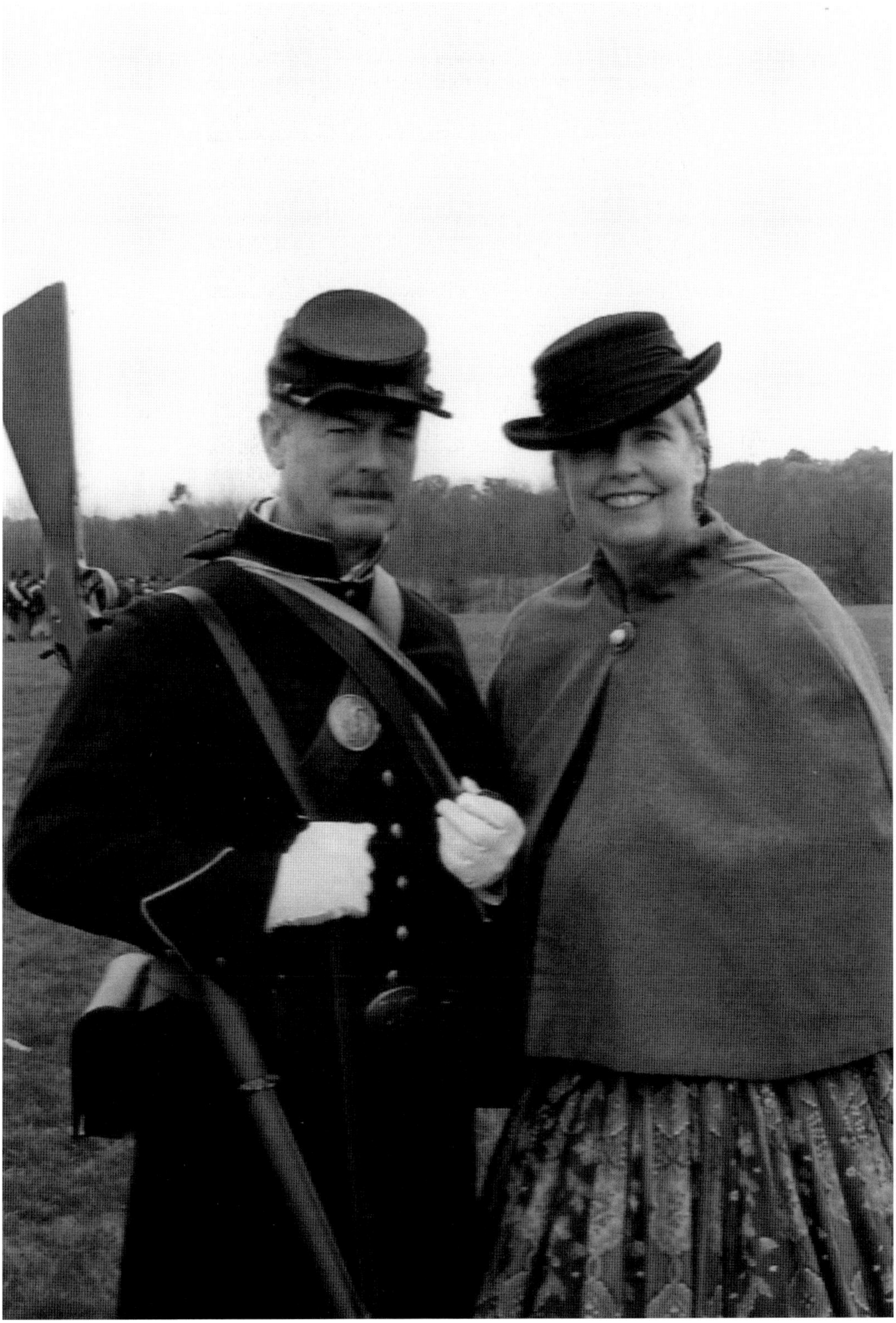

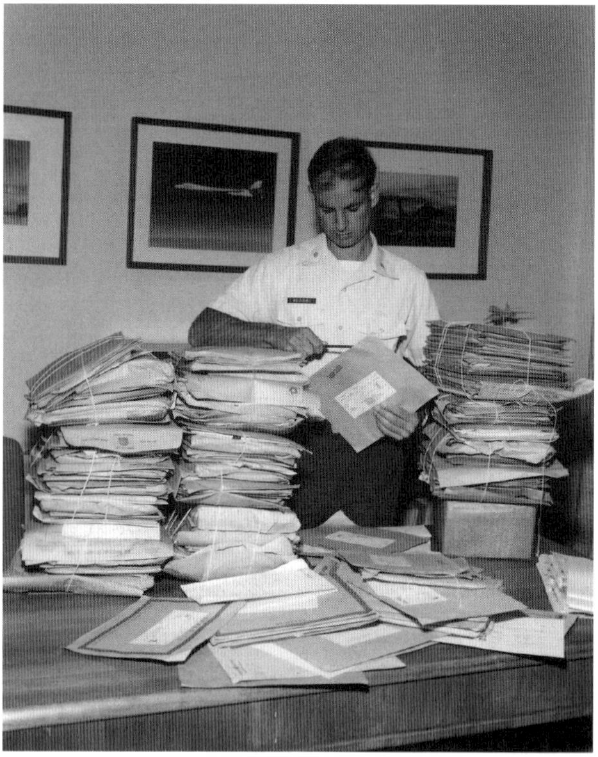

Alan J. Willoughby

Willoughby joined the US Air Force (1962–1984) as a space physicist and flew many hours aboard the KC-135 "Vomit Comet." The work his team did for NASA's Gemini program enabled in-space construction. For a decade, he fought the Cold War by designing spacecraft and electronics to perform during nuclear combat. Willoughby, a major, led the Air Force office at NASA and fostered a tenfold increase in joint USAF-NASA aerospace research. As "Asteroid Al" (1984–1995), he devised unique concepts for NASA for exploring planets, space mining, and protecting earth from asteroids, and he promoted them worldwide. Willoughby first explored history by running Massachusetts' Minuteman trails. Later, retracing Ridgeville's pioneer route from Connecticut led him to admire and portray founder David Beebe Sr. (right). His past was far in the future. His future still includes our past. (Both, courtesy of Alan Willoughby.)

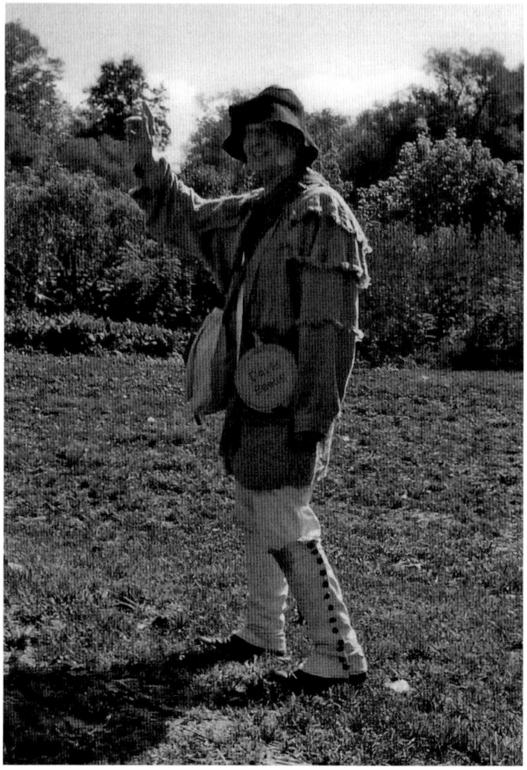

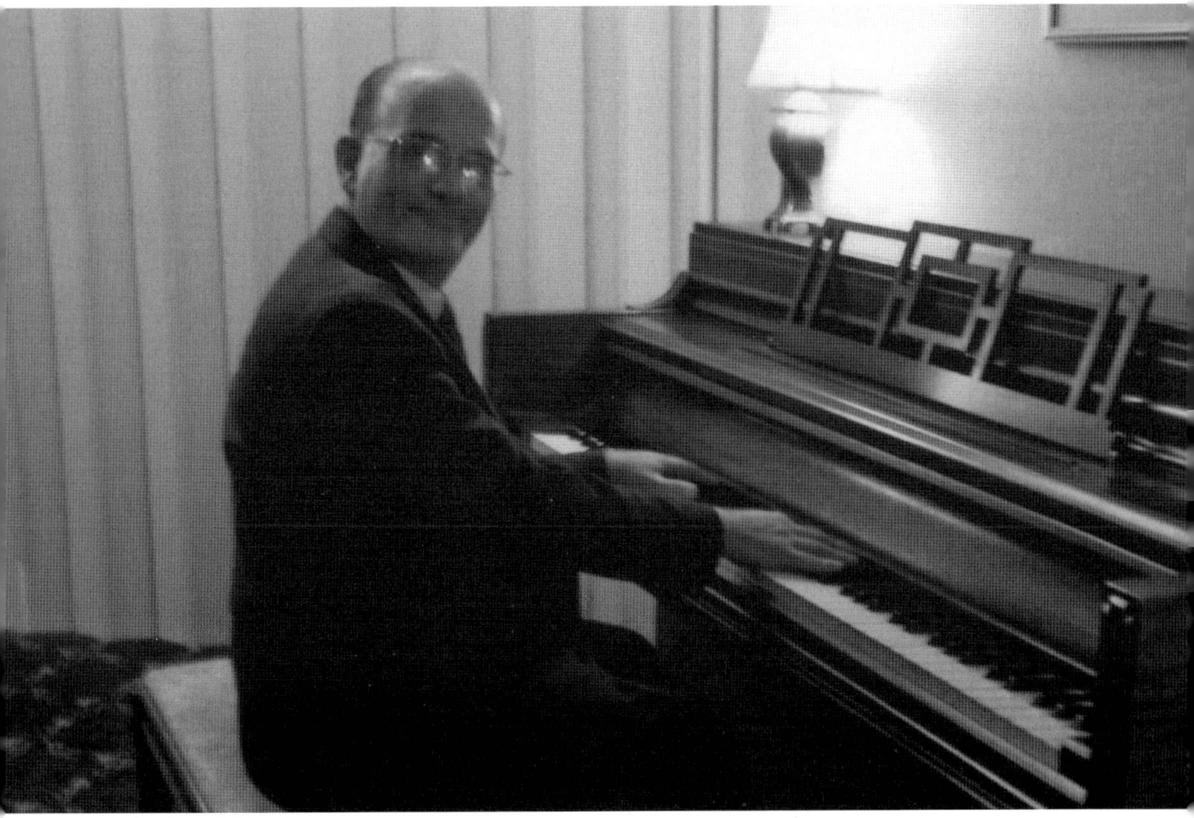

Robert Liston

Liston is the owner of the Liston Funeral Home on Center Ridge Road at Stoney Ridge. But he also is an accomplished musician, often playing the organ for friends' weddings and sometimes for the Rotary Club of North Ridgeville, as members open their meetings with song.

Liston was born in Berea and raised in Columbia Station. He went on to earn a degree in music and went to Cincinnati College of Mortuary Science, which was a one-year program. Although he could have continued in music and perhaps become a concert pianist, Liston said he had wanted to be a funeral director since his father passed away when he was 13. He couldn't exactly explain it, but "something just clicked," he said. "In high school I got an organ scholarship, but I thought maybe I should try something else," he said, adding, "everyone thought I was weird."

The funeral home owner has always been involved in church music, and he really loves it as a hobby and enjoys playing in different churches. He gave lessons in college, but students often wouldn't practice. After mortuary school, Liston went to work for a Canton funeral home, and he and his wife, Renee, got married. She was accepted to Case Western Reserve Law School, and he was trying to finish his apprenticeship. By that time, Renee was working at a large Cleveland law firm, but then she became pregnant and they did not want to use daycare after their son, Curtis, was born.

After working at a couple of other funeral homes, Liston said he went on the road to sell pre-need funeral plans, representing 37 funeral homes. Then they had a second child, Amy, and in 1994, Liston began working for the Busch Funeral Home. That firm bought the Bogner Funeral Home, and in 2001, Liston had an opportunity to purchase it. "I would never go back and work for someone [else] again," he said. "You have control over how you want things done."

Liston said that, having grown up in the area, he knew a lot of people in North Ridgeville. He also recalled always noticing the funeral home he now owns. "It is such a thrill, I still cannot believe it." Liston still plays the piano for pleasure and sometimes plays the organ on request. (Courtesy of Carol Klear.)

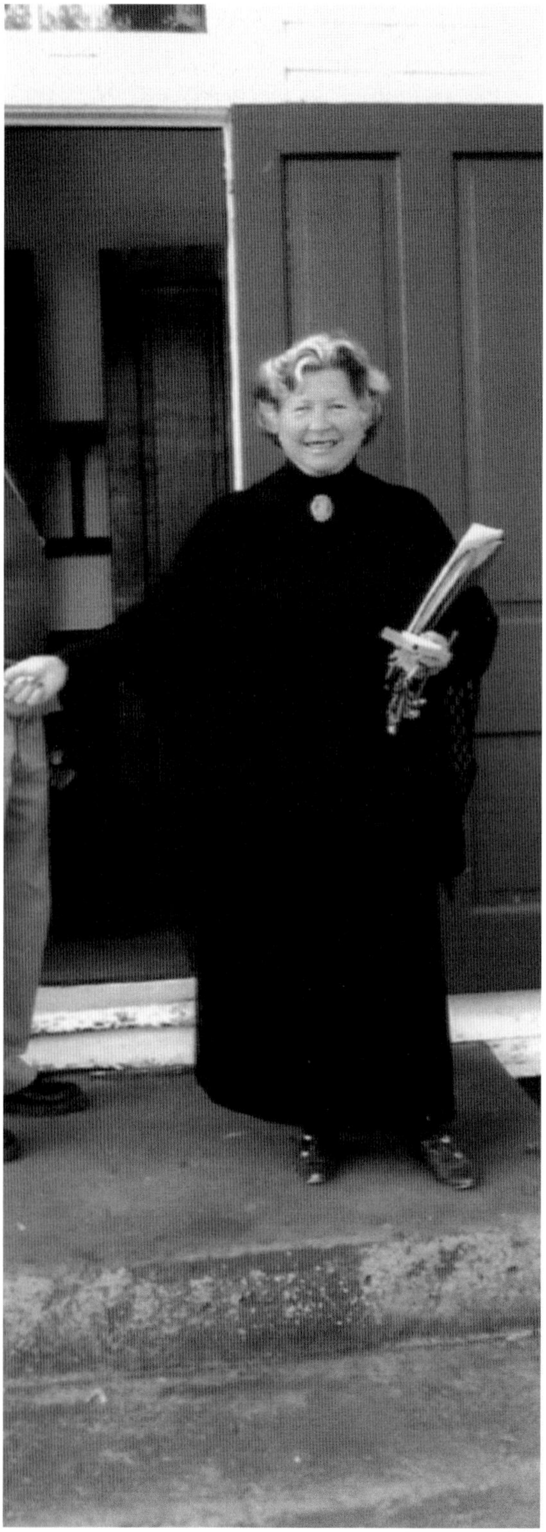

Barbara Sutton

She gets in front of an audience and she is ready to tell stories—all kinds of stories. The common denominator is that Barbara Sutton loves doing it, and her listeners cannot wait to hear her.

Sutton graduated from Kent State University with an undergraduate degree and a master's degree in health and physical education. She also earned 30 hours beyond her master's degree, in library and media services. She was a health and physical education teacher in Berea schools, and she retired as the head librarian in the North Ridgeville School System. In 1980, Sutton began telling stories professionally, and not just to children. She said, "80 percent of my audiences are adults." And there is no putting on a long skirt, sitting on a stool, and reading a book. Sutton often sets the stage for her listeners by appearing in a blazer and pants—sometimes boots—and the entire outfit is highlighted with brooches of different sizes and colors. And there are rings, several rings. As she strides to center stage, she has everyone's eye.

Sutton is a member of the Western Reserve Association for the Preservation and Perpetuation of Storytelling and several other storytelling and education associations. Her repertoire is extensive, and when Christmas or another holiday is near, her schedule fills up quickly. The clients are usually library patrons, church groups, and senior-center residents. The audiences cannot wait to hear the next yarn Sutton is ready to spin. As she talks, she walks from one place to another and back. Sutton is a bundle of energy, perhaps a result of her days as a physical education teacher. Or, maybe it is just Sutton being Sutton. Whatever it is, it is infectious.

Sutton sometimes partners with videographer Andre LeBlanc Sr. to create DVDs of special events. They did several for the North Ridgeville Historical Society when the city celebrated its bicentennial in 2010. Sutton interviewed reenactors about their roles while LeBlanc filmed.

Storytelling is an art, but Sutton has it down to just plain fun. (All, courtesy of Barbara Sutton.)

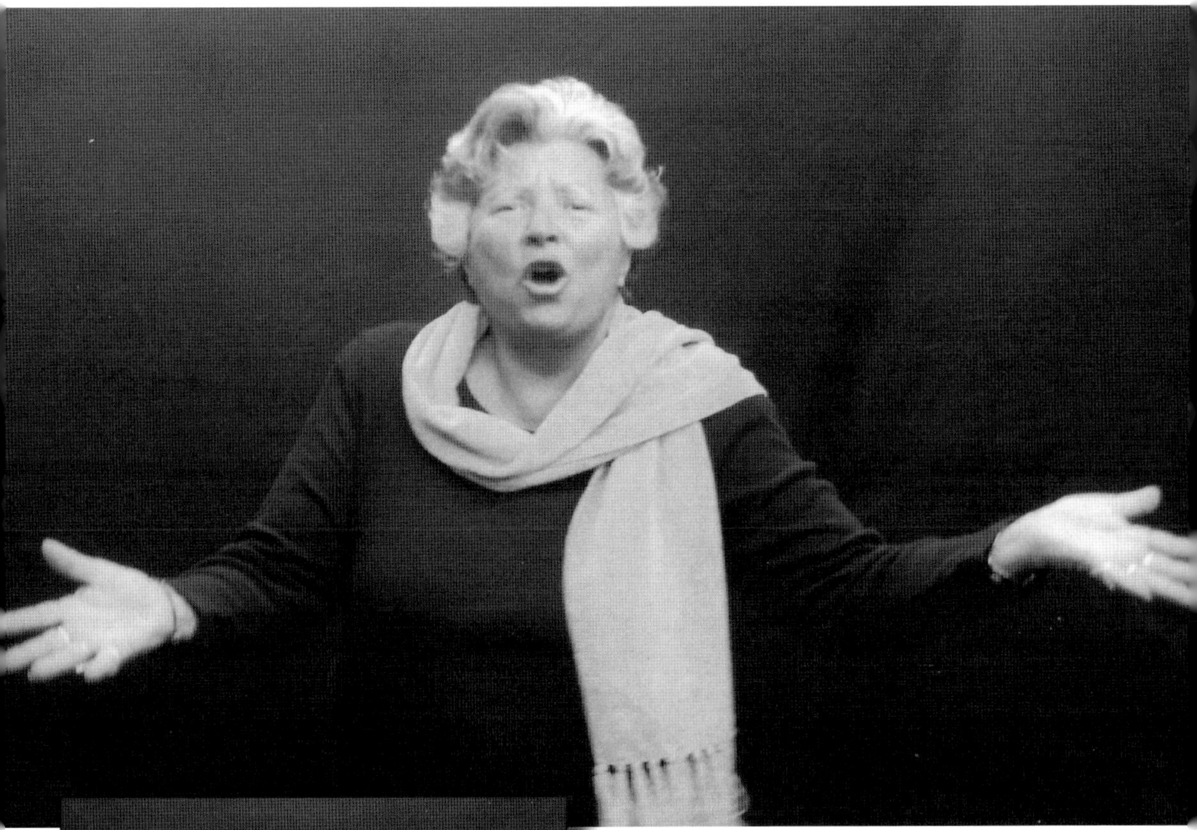

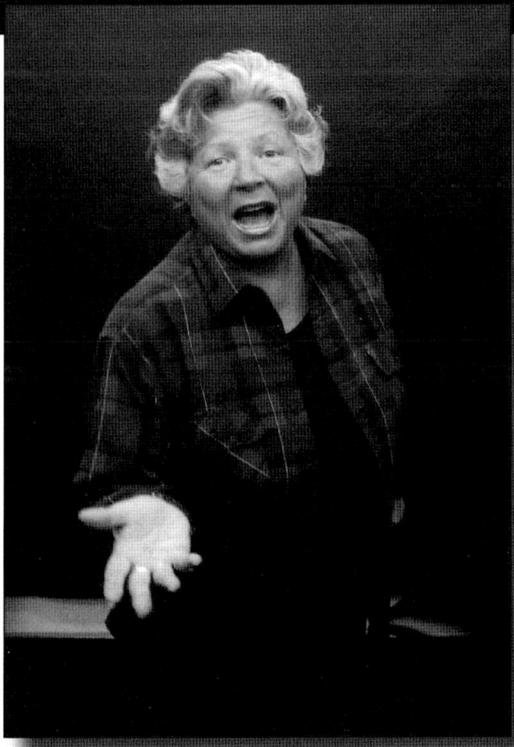

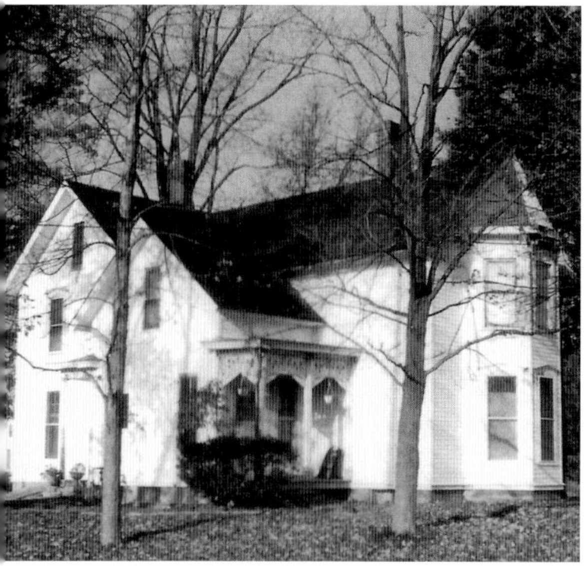

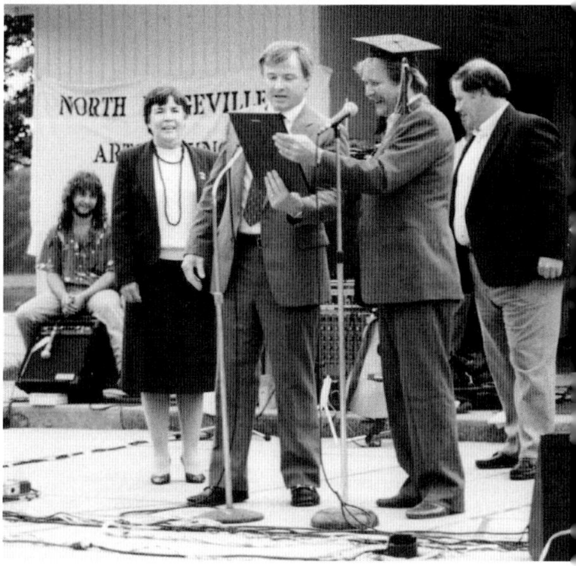

Martin Mull

Comedian and actor Martin Mull once lived in North Ridgeville. The house (above left), a large white Victorian, is on Lorain Road at State Route 83.

The humorist was in the area in 1987 to film an HBO special, *Martin Mull Live*, which was billed as a sentimental journey back to middle America, with Mull recalling his time in Ridgeville. It set the tone for a very special Corn Festival, with Mull serving as the grand marshal of the parade. One of the highlights of Mull's visit was seeing his former home. To keep that memory alive, Robert Lee, president of the North Ridgeville Arts Council, presented him with a plaque of the house.

Mull was a good sport throughout the three-day fest, even to the point of getting a good soaking in the dunking booth when a spectator with a swift arm and a few dollars hit the target. After the special guest climbed onto the back of a convertible with Corn Festival committee president Jo-Ell Jacobson to head down Center Ridge Road in the Grande Parade, he held his arms high and gave the crowd a thumbs-up of appreciation. Helen Cotterman, the leader of the Kitchen Band, loved it as Mull gave her a hug and wished her a happy 82nd birthday before the Corn Festival crowd. The 1986 Corn Festival Queen, Julie Menner, received a thrill when Mull interviewed her about her year as reigning queen. She hoped the visit with Mull would end up in the HBO production.

Mull did not graduate from North Ridgeville High School, but superintendent Paul Murphy remedied the situation by presenting him with a diploma (above right). To top off the weekend, Mayor Floyd Peaco gave him a key to the city, which represented the key to residents' hearts. (Left, courtesy of Carol Klear; right, courtesy of Floyd Peaco.)

CHAPTER EIGHT

One of a Kind

Throughout life, there are people who are referred to as "one of a kind." It could be their appearance that sets them apart, or their mental acuity that gives them an obvious edge. Or it could be a musical talent or an artistic bent that is admirable. Whatever the talent or quality, there is something about some people that others would like to emulate, if only they could.

The final chapter in this book touches on such residents. Some of them are still living and striving to do their best; others have passed on, but were special at one time or another. One such person was Norman Gerhart, a gentle, soft-spoken man. He had a big heart, especially when it came to youngsters and baseball. He wanted them to enjoy the game he loved and to have the best ballpark, even if it required some maintenance on his part.

Lois Sullivan was a woman nearly everyone knew, very much a one-of-a-kind resident. She could see things clearly and would think before she spoke. But when she had it all figured out, she said what was on her mind and moved on. Sullivan also had a great sense of humor and enjoyed a laugh, even if it was at her own expense.

Spencer Myer is a marvelous example of a piano virtuoso. His talent began to grow and flourish when he was just a little boy. By his example, perhaps Myer can instill the ambition he has into another little boy or girl, encouraging them to study and practice whatever instrument they choose.

Robert Franks has been blessed with stamina and fortitude the likes of which do not come along often. Franks's strength allowed him to withstand what he has been through and to continue to maintain a kind manner, free of complaints.

These people have been singled out, but each person, young or old, in his or her own way, is one of a kind.

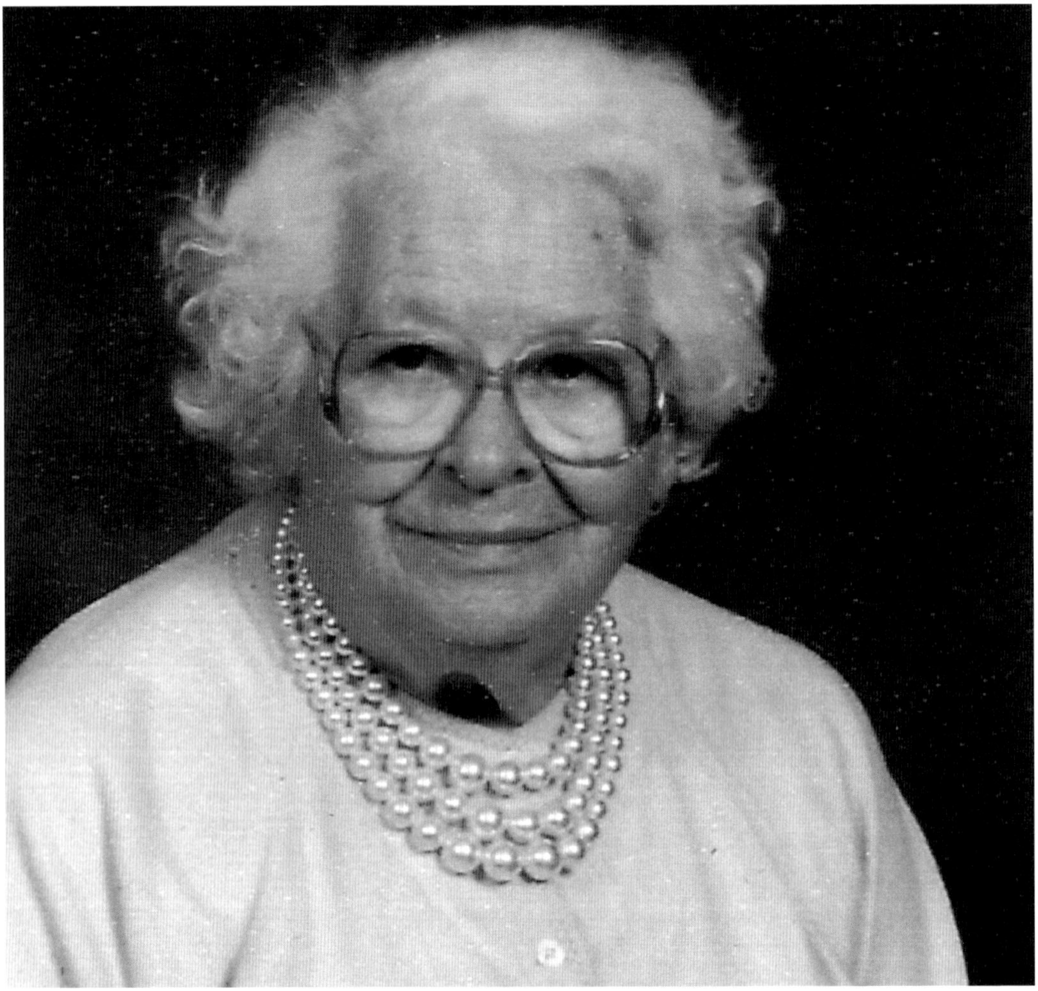

Frances Smith

Frances Smith was a 1928 graduate of Lorain High School and a 1931 graduate of the St. Joseph School of Nursing in Lorain. She also had a degree in public health from Western Reserve University.

She worked as a registered nurse and was employed by the Lorain County Health Department as a public health nurse at the Lorain City Health Department. She also worked for the Ohio State Health Department, where she inspected medical records of nursing homes. She retired in 1973.

Smith was a member of St. Peter Catholic Church in North Ridgeville, where she belonged to the Altar and Rosary Society. She also was a former member of St. Joseph Catholic Church. Smith was an active member of the North Ridgeville Historical Society, and in 1985, she wrote *The Elm Tree Talks*, a conversational book about North Ridgeville, written from the perspective of the old elm tree in her front yard. She donated the proceeds from the sale of the book to the historical society, to be used for the restoration of the one-room schoolhouse located on Jaycox Road. She was also a member of Self Help for Hard of Hearing People (SHHH) Rocky River Chapter, and she founded the Lorain County Chapter of SHHH.

In 1993, Smith received the National Award Spirit of Self Help for Hard of Hearing People. In 1996, she received an award from Hearing Impaired Services of Lorain County for raising community awareness and support. In the same year, she was recognized by the Ohio House of Representatives for her work with hearing-impaired people of Lorain County. (Courtesy of Janet Devine.)

Spencer Myer

Spencer Myer planned his career when he was just six years old, telling his mother he wanted to take piano lessons. She thought they would give it a try, and try he did. As an adult, he has become a concert pianist acclaimed the world over.

When Myer was in his early teens, he was regarded as a regular youngster. But when he began to play the piano, there was no question about his talent. By the time he was a freshman in high school, he not only studied the piano, but also had piano students of his own, was performing concerts on local stages, and was accompanying choruses in school. He enjoyed working with youngsters, but he felt that teaching adults might be more rewarding, as they took instructions because they wanted to. In a newspaper article when he was still a child, Myer was quoted as telling his piano instructor he couldn't imagine doing anything else but play the piano.

Myer is a graduate of the Julliard School. During his undergraduate studies at the Oberlin Conservatory of Music, he received numerous awards. In 2000, he was the recipient of a four-year Jacob K. Javits Memorial Fellowship from the US Department of Education. He earned his doctor of musical arts degree at Stony Brook University in 2005.

The young pianist supports educating youngsters and often is a guest artist at the workshops for students and teachers. Myer has served on the faculties of Baldwin-Wallace and Oberlin College Conservatory of Music. He has received numerous first-place awards in competitions, and was a gold medalist in the 2008 New Orleans International Piano Competition. His scheduled appearances take him across the United States and abroad. (Courtesy of Spencer Myer.)

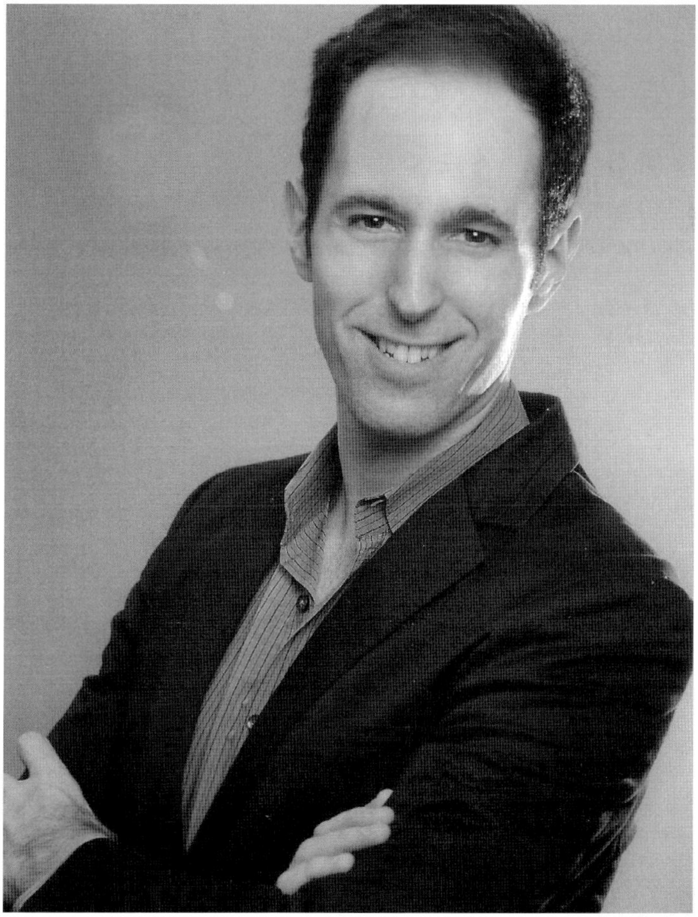

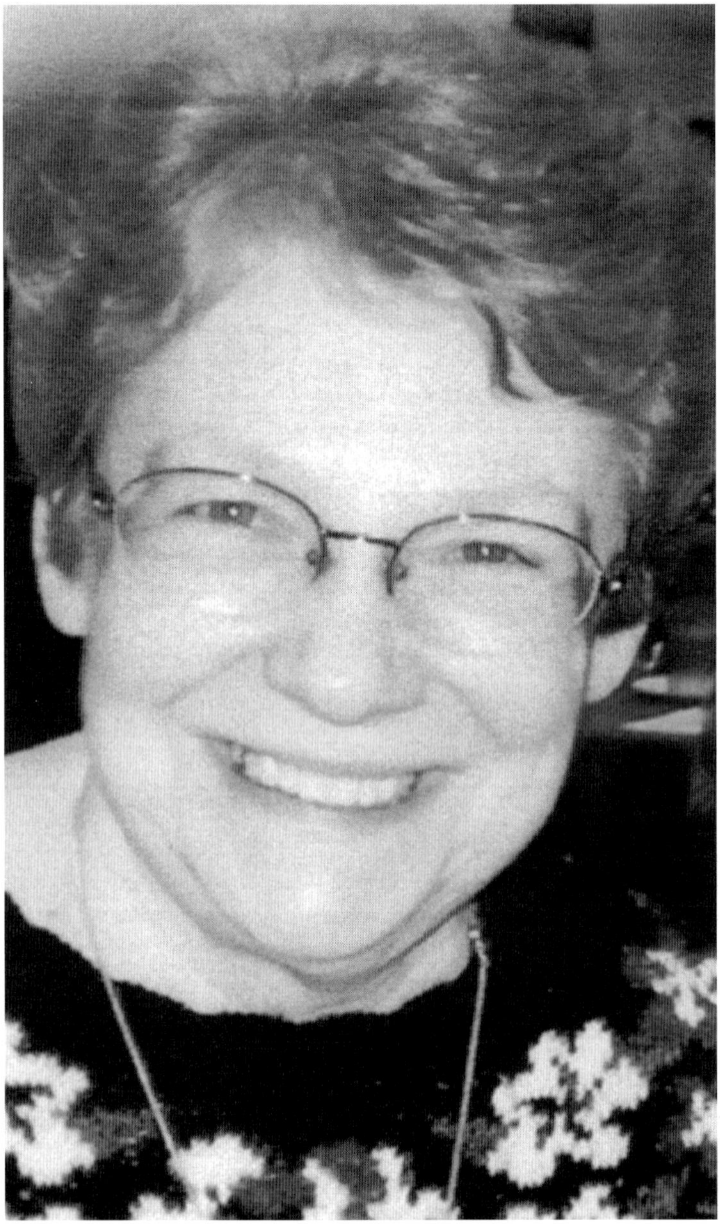

Sister Mary Patricia Vovk SND

Vovk, principal of St. Peter School, feels joy in being a Sister of Notre Dame for nearly 50 years and in working in Catholic education for 45 years. She holds bachelor's and master's degrees and has been at St. Peter for the past 15 years. In addition, she previously worked there from 1985 to 1991, calling it a "special place of ministry."

Vovk was born and raised in Lorain. While a student in her parish school, the nuns helped her realize God's call. She has been a parish director of religious education, a youth choir coordinator, and a team member for youth interventions for alcohol and drug rehabilitation, but "Catholic school is my favorite ministry," she said. In her free time, Vovk enjoys listing to music, reading, walking, and gardening. (Courtesy of Sister Mary Patricia Vovk.)

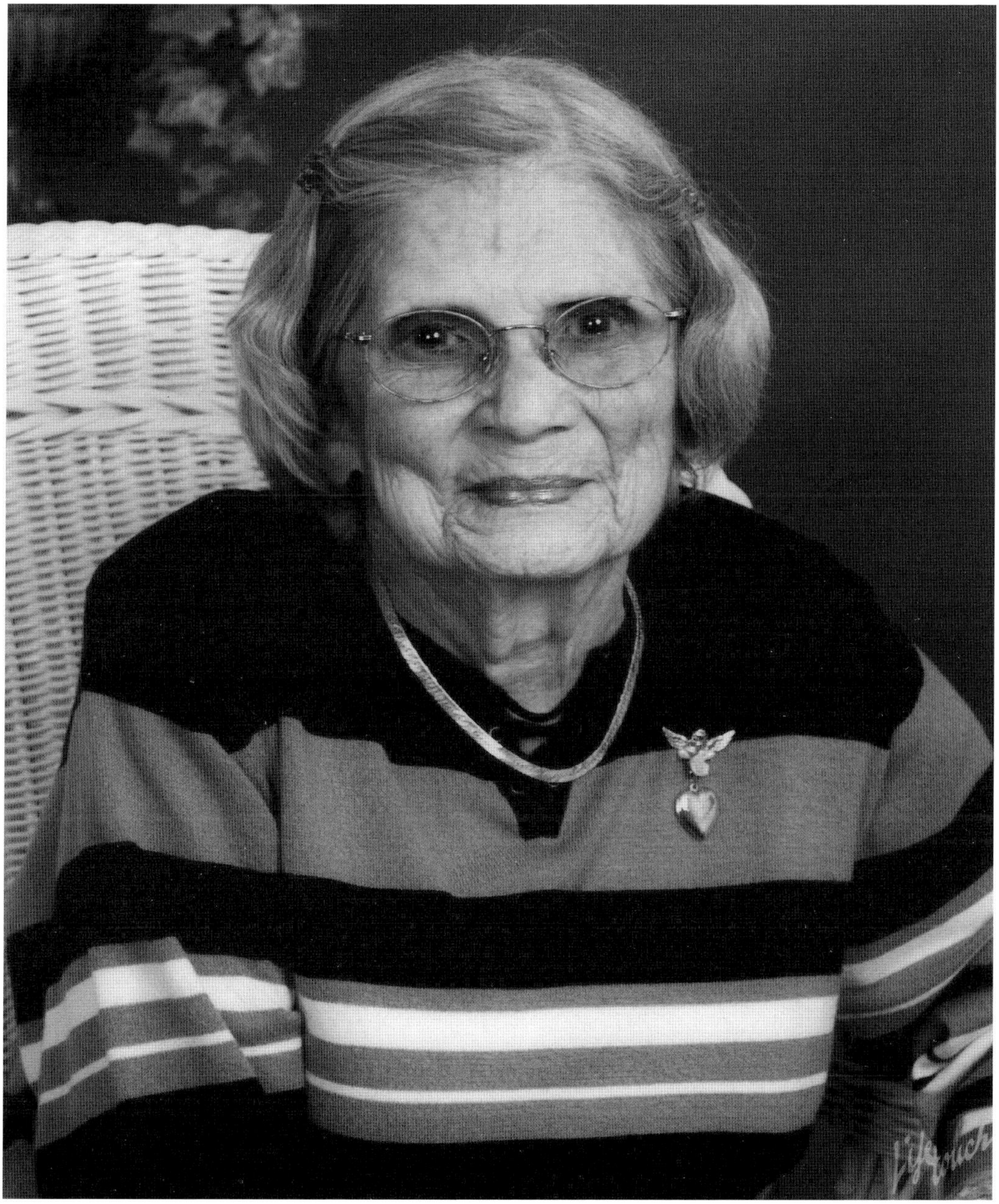

Alyce Coon
Coon was born on April 7, 1929, in Derby, Connecticut. She graduated from the Academy of St. Therese, Carnegie Institute of Practical Nursing, and the Niagara School of Speech and Psychology. A longtime resident of North Ridgeville, she worked for many years as a legal secretary for the firm of West, West and Sherman and Company. She was a member of St. Peter Catholic Church, Women of the Moose, and the Ladies Auxiliary of VFW Post 9671, where she served as president. Coon loved children and taught Parish School of Religion at St. Peter and reading classes at Wilcox Elementary School. She also mentored for Ohio Reads and was in the first class of Lorain County Speak Up for a Child. (Courtesy of Michelle Stambaugh.)

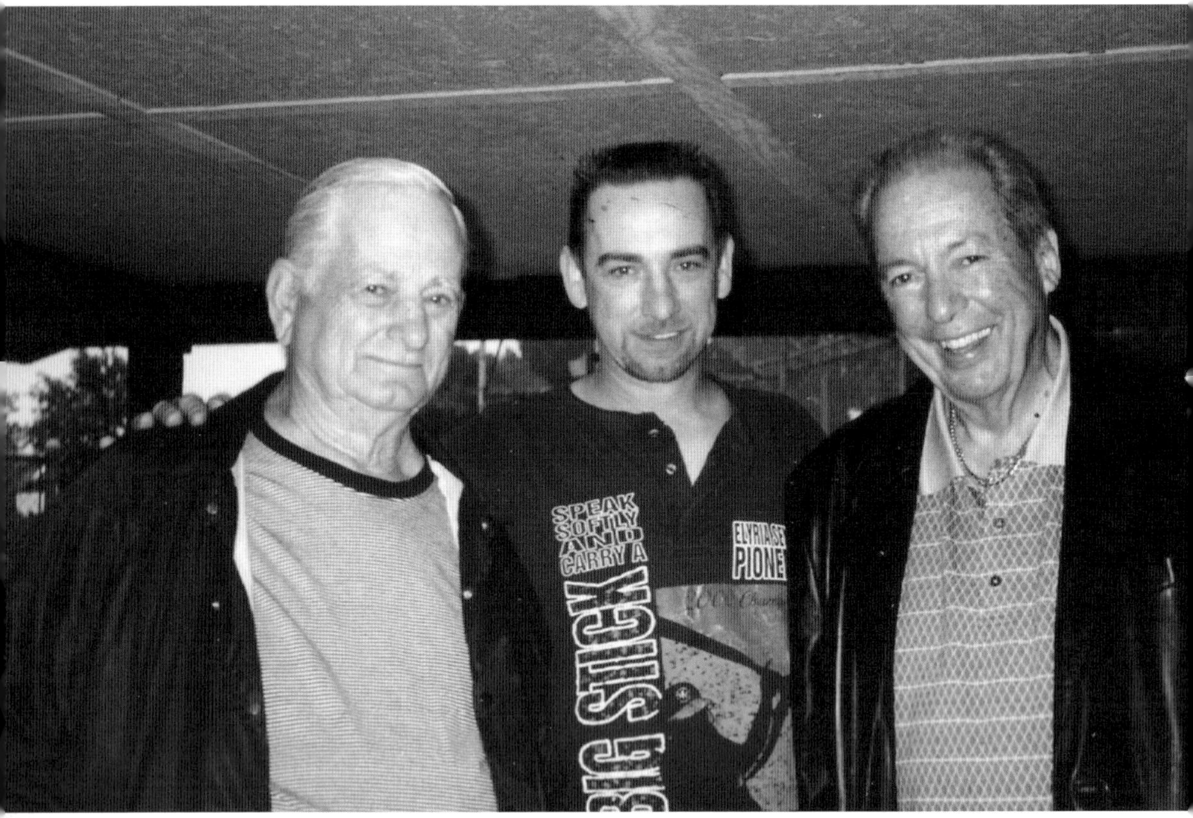

Norman Gerhart

He was a farmer with a produce stand on Lorain Road at Bagley, but the field that Norman Gerhart loved was not the one where he grew vegetables, but Palmer Field, where so many of the teams he handled played ball. He is seen here with Joseph Gerhart (center) and Del Bethel (right) at the ballfield in 2003 for the rededication of Diamond No. 2.

Gerhart got involved with Hot Stove in the 1960s. If he had a choice between baseball and farming, he would probably rather be at the ballfield. His wife, Mona, worked alongside him, whether it was tending the stand as customers purchased lettuce, carrots, or potatoes, or working at Palmer Field.

There was such a close relationship between the Gerharts and the kids that Diamond No. 2 is dedicated to them (opposite, below). Gerhart umpired (opposite, above), worked on the fields, and did just about anything else he could to make the facilities a good place to play. When he was not at Palmer Field, he watched the Cleveland Indians and Browns on television. It was all about sports.

He enjoyed going to flea markets and auctions, always by himself. And he was always certain to come home with something.

There is a small building near the Gerhart produce stand with a side wall covered with hubcaps. It was a garage at one time, but Gerhart converted it into a walk-in cooler. This was a godsend, especially in the summer, as some of the food would have spoiled if it were not for the cooler. Gerhart was president of the North Ridgeville Hot Stove League and the Lorain County Hot Stove. In 1993, he was named a Golden Kernel Award winner.

His wife died in 1996, which took a toll on Gerhart. Things just were not the same. He passed away on July 12, 2013. As the procession made its way from the funeral home to St. Julie Billiart Church, the family asked the funeral director to go past Palmer Field one last time. As the hearse traveled the road to the field, youngsters in uniforms waved a last goodbye to Norman Gerhart, a man with a heart as big as the field he cared so much about. (All, courtesy of the Gerhart family.)

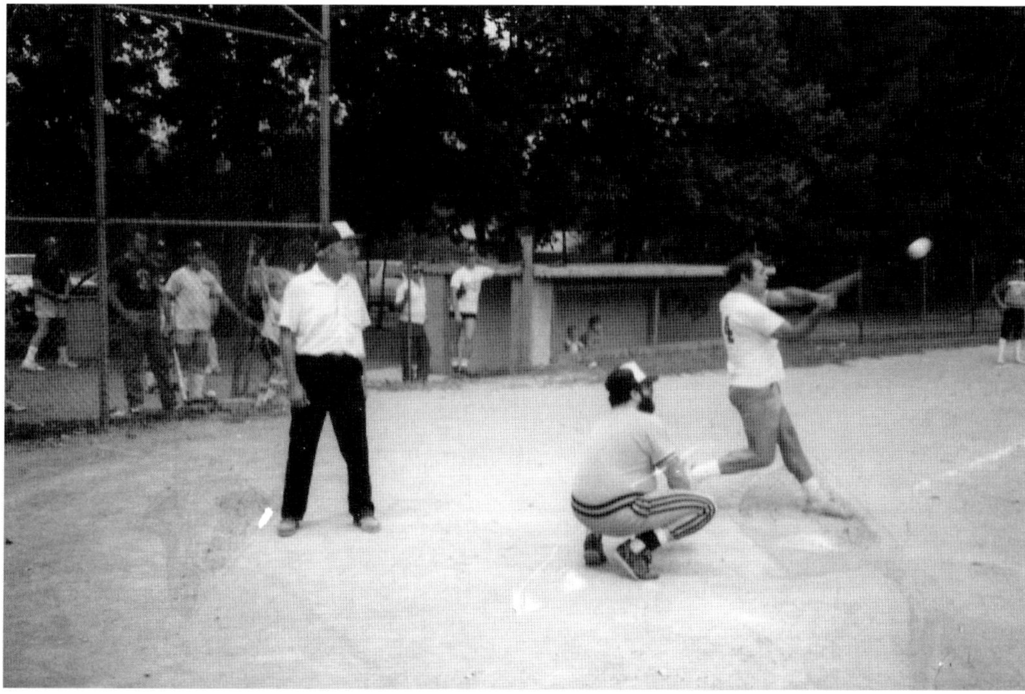

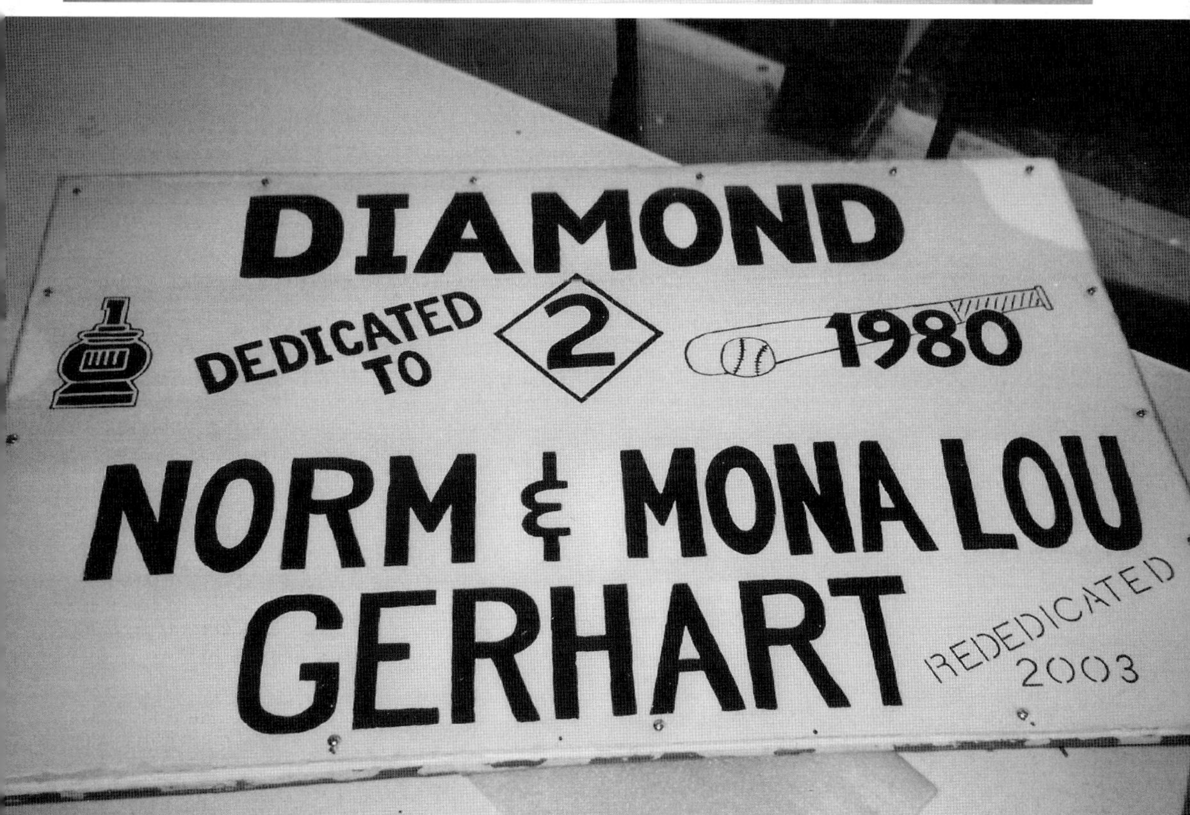
DIAMOND
DEDICATED TO
2
1980
NORM & MONA LOU
GERHART
REDEDICATED
2003

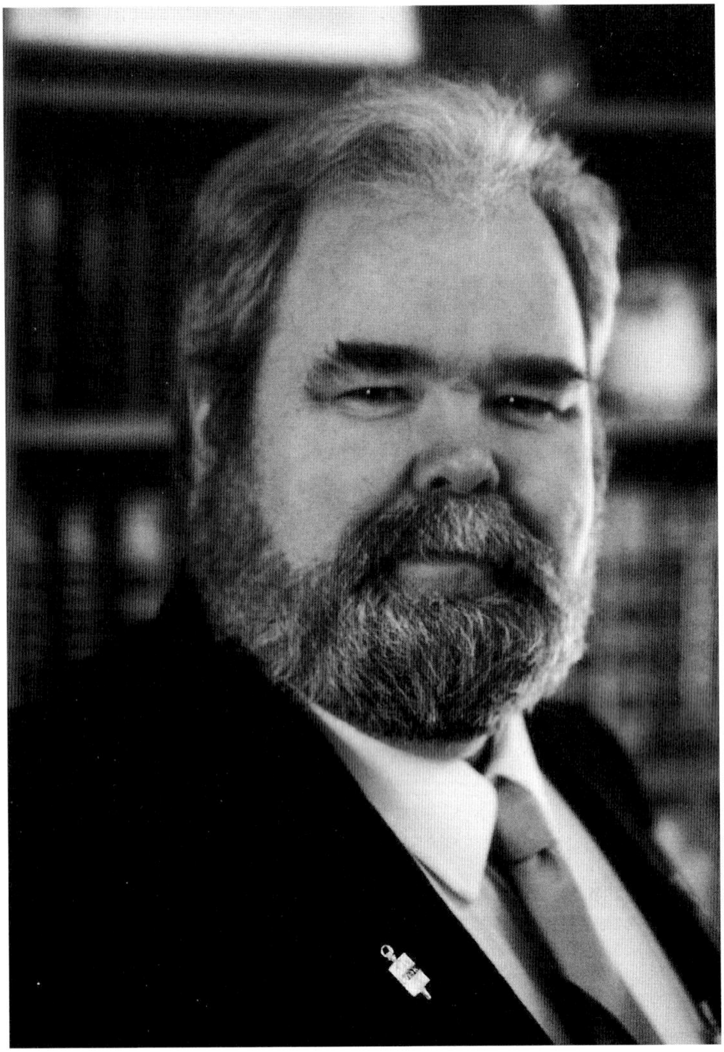

Christopher Crobaugh

Christopher Crobaugh was born in New York and moved to Medina while still in elementary school. He and his wife, Susan, attended the same school, where Susan said he was very bright, but constantly interested in people and how things worked. As an adult, Crobaugh was a giant of a man physically, with a mind to match. "He called it like he saw it, and most of the time, he was right," Susan Crobaugh said. He did not believe in political correctness.

He had a paper route as a youngster. When he completed school, he went into the military, working for four years in Army intelligence. When that stint was over, he reenlisted for two more years. Crobaugh often attended city council meetings and seemed to relish goading public officials. He boasted of being a Libertarian.

When he was 49, he decided he wanted to be an attorney and went back to school, earned a law degree, and set up his own practice. "He had a very strong personality," his wife said, "but if someone were in a bind, Chris would move heaven and earth to help." Outside of his legal work, Crobaugh enjoyed his ham radio operations and played pedal steel guitar with a band. He was a voracious reader and had a photographic memory, Susan Crobaugh said, adding, "My life was never boring."

Crobaugh died on September 18, 2007, at the age of 61. (Courtesy of Susan Crobaugh.)

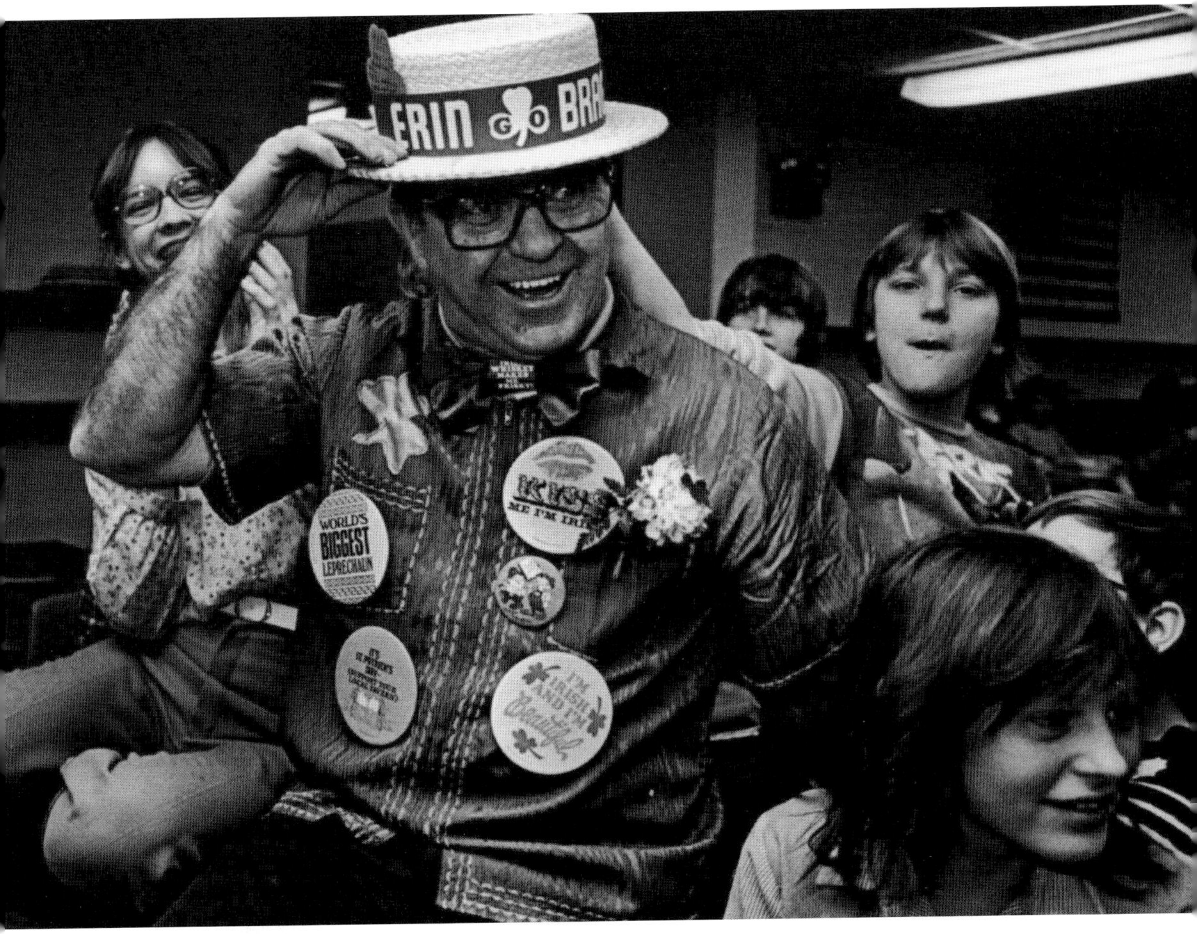

Patrick T. Ginley

Patrick T. Ginley was in the Merchant Marines for a while, then went into the Navy and served on a destroyer from 1943 to 1946. Following the military, Ginley worked as an ironworker from 1956 to 1972. He was injured in a fall on the job, and the accident left him unable to climb. He lost his job, but as the saying goes, "When God closes a door, He opens a window." After recuperating, Ginley was offered a job as custodian with the school district. He started at Wilcox and then moved to the middle school. The youngsters loved the man with the Irish brogue and the twinkling eyes. As a tribute to his Irish ancestry, each St. Patrick's Day, Ginley wore something green. Every year, the school staff added another green item to his outfit. (Courtesy of the *Chronicle Telegram*.)

Robert Franks

Franks loved his 1934 Ford Coupe (opposite, above). He could be seen tooling around the city and taking it to car shows. However, everything changed on the morning of July 14, 2009.

Franks, 69, was traveling west on Cleveland Street in Elyria when a woman driving a 1985 Buick station wagon was heading north on Olive Street. She ran a red light and crashed into Franks's vehicle, throwing him from the car and critically injuring him. The station wagon hit the coupe with such force that Franks landed on the ground and his vehicle spun around. It also hit a utility pole, causing damage to both sides of the car. His vehicle sustained a large amount of damage. The floor had to be replaced and the doors and back were compromised (opposite, below). Franks was conscious when the fire department arrived on the scene and took him to EMH Regional Medical Center. He was later flown to MetroHealth Medical Center in Cleveland. He doesn't recall where his wife, Nancy, was. All he knew was that she had gone out somewhere.

The road to recovery was long and slow. "For about two months, I lost my memory," Franks said, adding that he couldn't understand why he was in Cleveland. "I don't remember the accident," he said, but he knows he sustained nine broken ribs, used 28 pints of blood, and that his spleen and lungs filled with fluid. "I couldn't feel my legs, I thought they were gone," Franks said. But he couldn't say enough in appreciation of EMH personnel, who immediately sent him to Cleveland. "That was a godsend."

While he was in the hospital, someone set up a CaringBridge site, which connects families and friends when someone is in need. It lets people get in touch with the patient without disruption. It also helps schedule meals for the families. Franks has stacks of messages he received through CaringBridge, and he treasures every one. Franks was in therapy for over a year; some of it at home.

Just as Franks was feeling almost normal again, he fell from a ladder at church in September 2013 while trying to hang a banner for a car show. After surgery and physical therapy for a broken elbow and hip, he began once again the road to recovery. (All, courtesy of Robert Franks.)

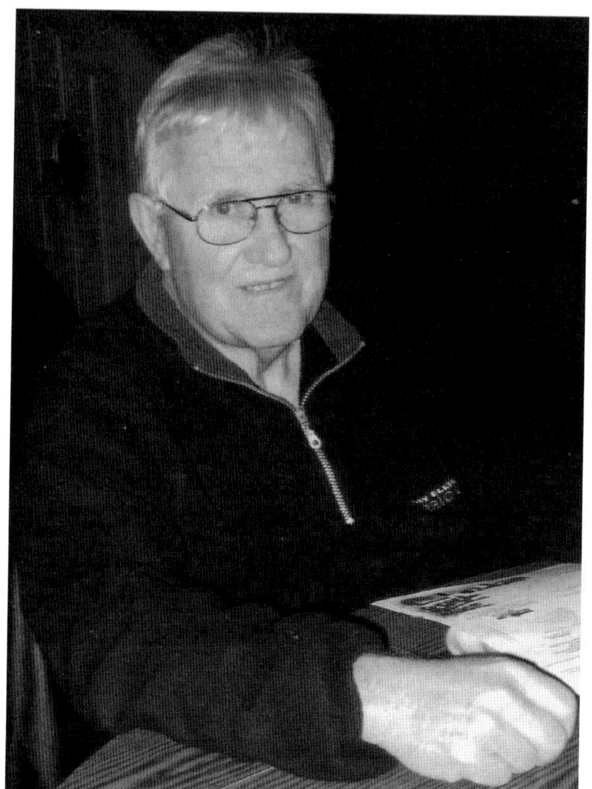

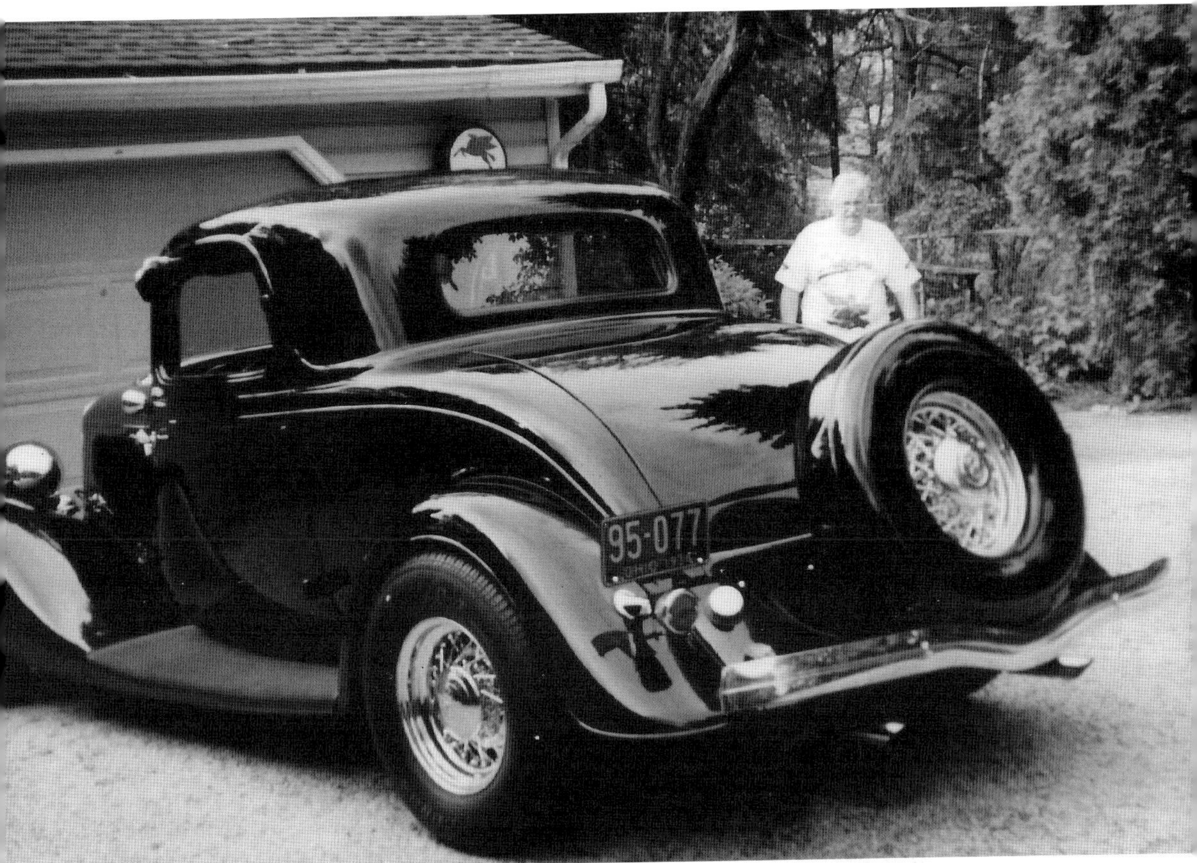
95-077

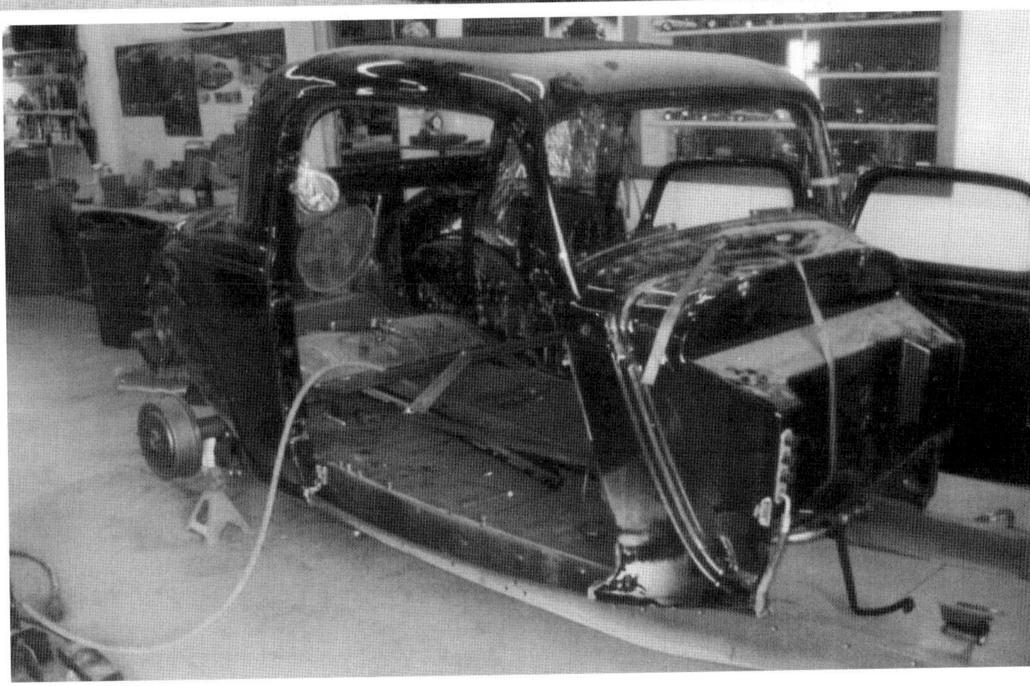

Millie Imler

Millie Imler was one of those special people who friends and strangers alike never forget. In 1997, at age 87, she was still cleaning the police station and trying to keep the men in blue in line. She would occasionally leave notes for the officers about picking up, and she could swing a mean mop across the floor. Imler was not very tall, but you knew she meant what she said. If a visitor stopped by, however, she would take a minute for a friendly chat. Imler was just as well known for singing as for cleaning. She sang with the Fields Methodist Choir and the Lorain County Banjo Band. When she took center stage with the banjo boys, people would yell, "Sing *Bill Bailey*!" And, did she ever! (Courtesy of Ronald Bauer.)

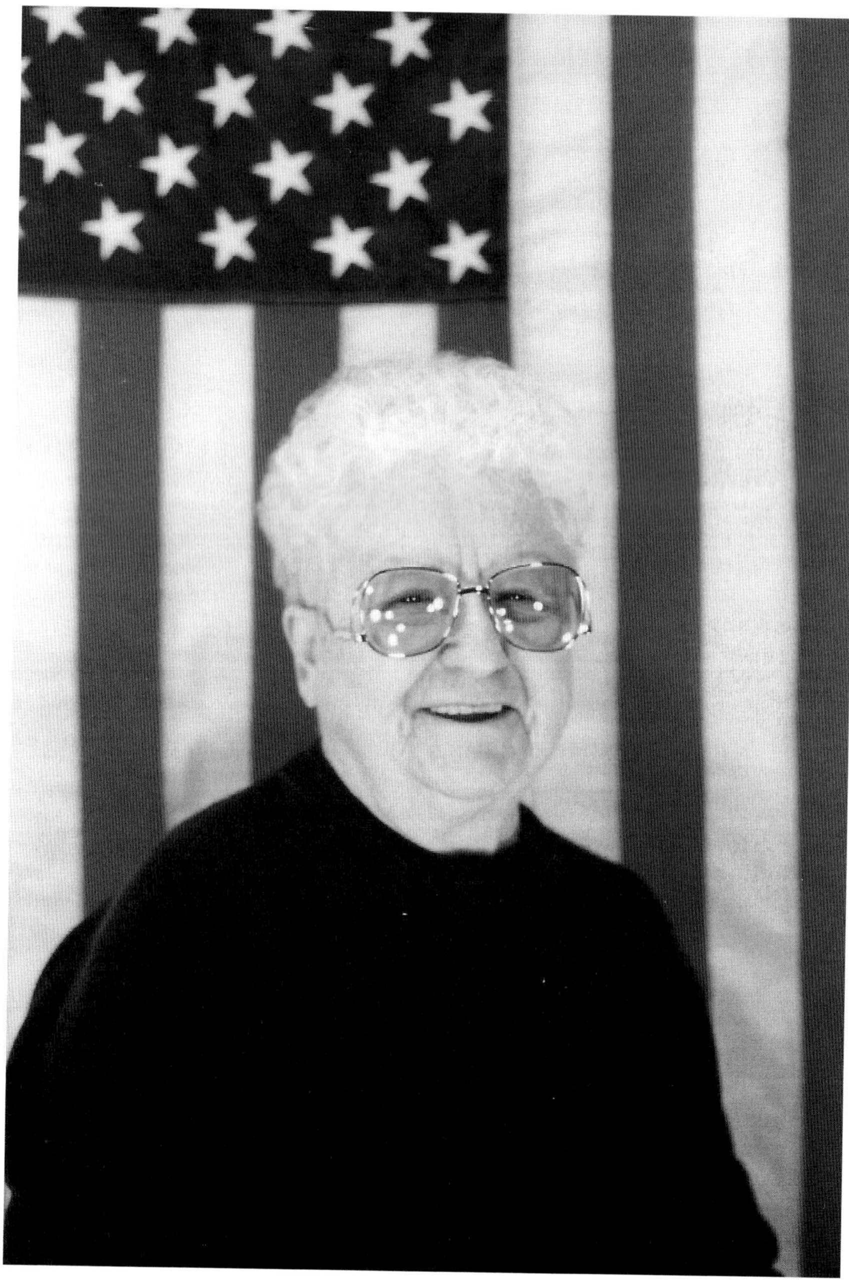

Frank Kleinholz

Kleinholz was born in Austria-Hungary on March 9, 1915, one of a set of triplets. He had a sister, Elizabeth, and a brother, Joseph, who died in infancy. Frank also had seven other siblings. He arrived in the United States through Ellis Island, and attended Berea High School and worked as a ship's chandler at the Cleveland harbor. He and his wife, Mary, moved to North Ridgeville in 1955. That was before Interstate 480 was constructed. Frank's son, Eugene, said it was like going to the country. Kleinholz worked for the New York Central Railroad for 35 years, retiring in 1975. He was a member of St. Peter Church and was a bingo volunteer for 25 years. Kleinholz was named Holy Name Man of the Year in 1983. He died on December 19, 2011. (Courtesy of Eugene Kleinholz.)

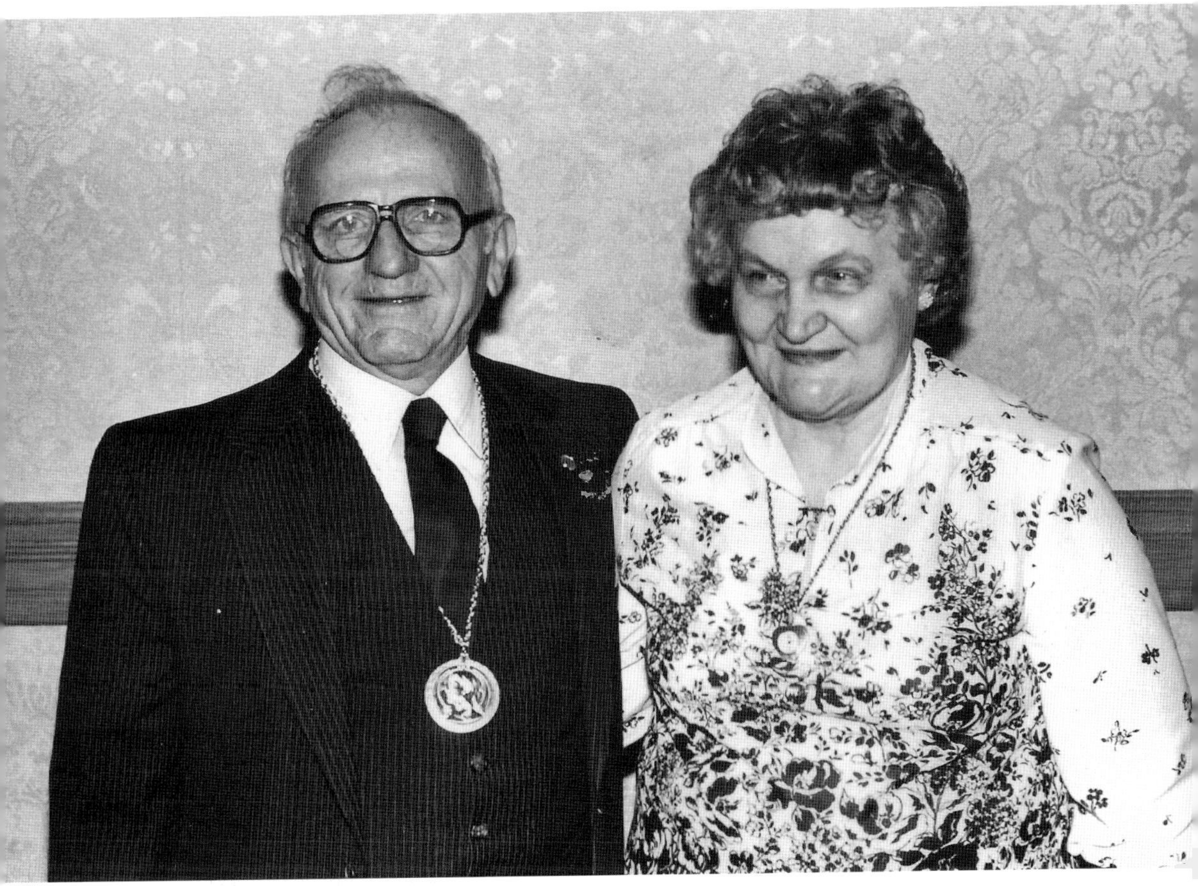

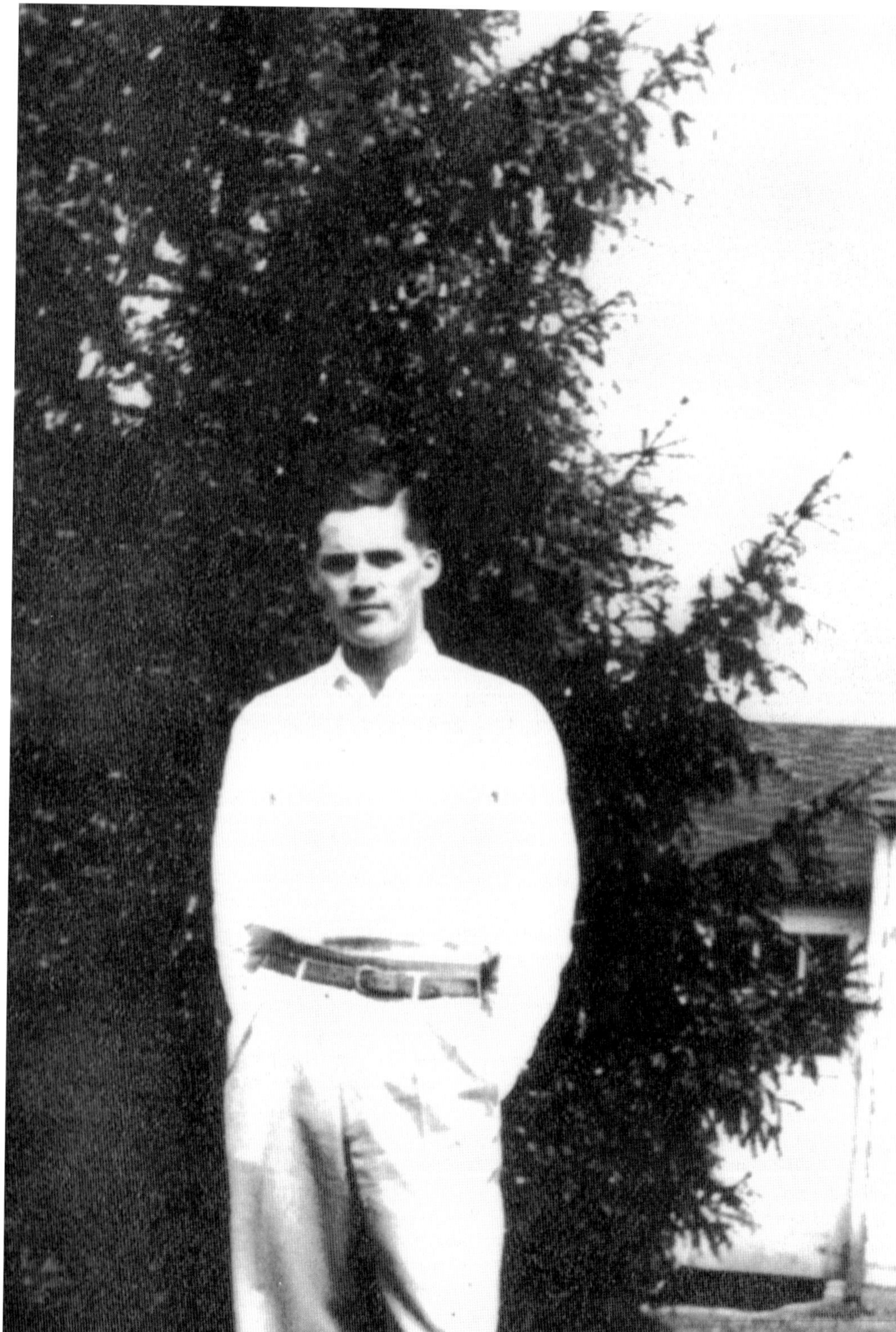

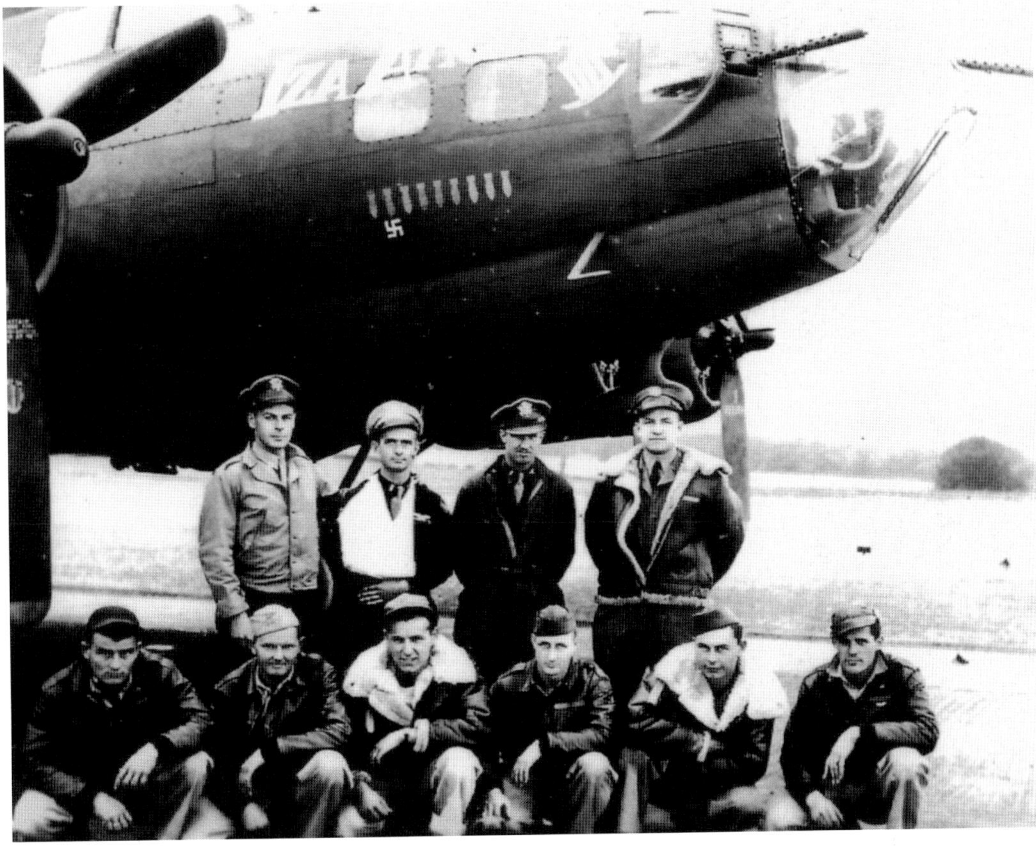

Edward Keisler

It was the 1930s and the middle of the Great Depression. Edward Keisler's stepmother told him he would have to leave school and get a job or find a family to live with. She had six children and was having a difficult time supporting them.

Elizabeth Wilcox called Keisler's mother and told her that he was a good student, a fine young man, and a good athlete. She suggested he live with the Marcellus Diederich family and earn his keep by working in Diederich's shop. Keisler shared a room with Wayne Diederich, who was just three years old at the time. Concerned that Keisler and other young men would have no outlet for their energy, Diederich started a softball team. Keisler was dubbed "Ridgeville's Joe DiMaggio."

When Pearl Harbor was attacked, Keisler tried to join the Army Air Force, but only college graduates were accepted at that time. He enlisted in the Seebees, but was drafted by the Army and assigned to the Army Air Force. After training as a top-turret gunner and flight engineer on B-17 Flying Fortresses, he was assigned to the 8th Air Force and sent to England. He could not write about what he was doing, but the Diederichs kept track of missions and the number of airplanes lost. Keisler and his plane, *Iza Angel*, undertook some historic missions, including a bombing raid in Germany in which the plane was damaged. It was repaired in Africa, and when it returned to England, the crew chief found an unexploded shell in the fuel tank.

In a raid over France, the plane was again badly damaged, but the crew had shot down four enemy aircraft, one of which was credited to Keisler (above, first row far right). During the plane's 24th mission, bombs in the plane had not been properly racked, and they fell onto the door. The mission continued, and the target flares were dropped over the seaport. The crew members had to parachute into the water; six were rescued, and three bodies, including Keisler's, were recovered. The fallen soldiers were buried in military cemeteries. (Both, courtesy of Geraldine and Wayne Diederich.)

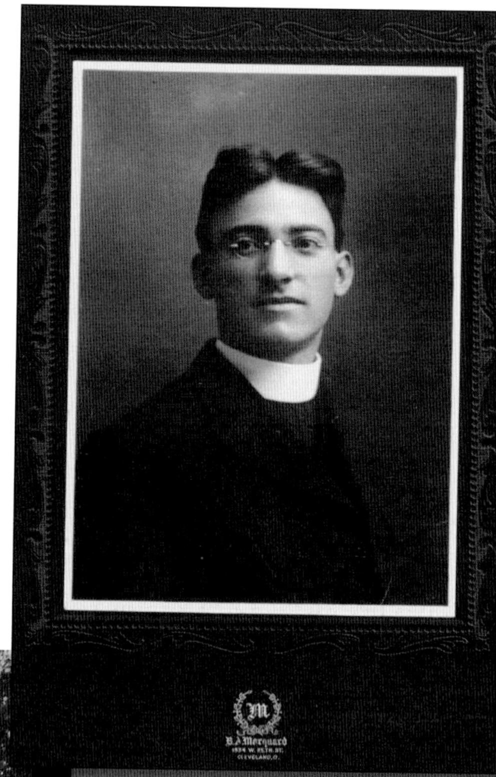
B.A. Marquard
CLEVELAND, O.

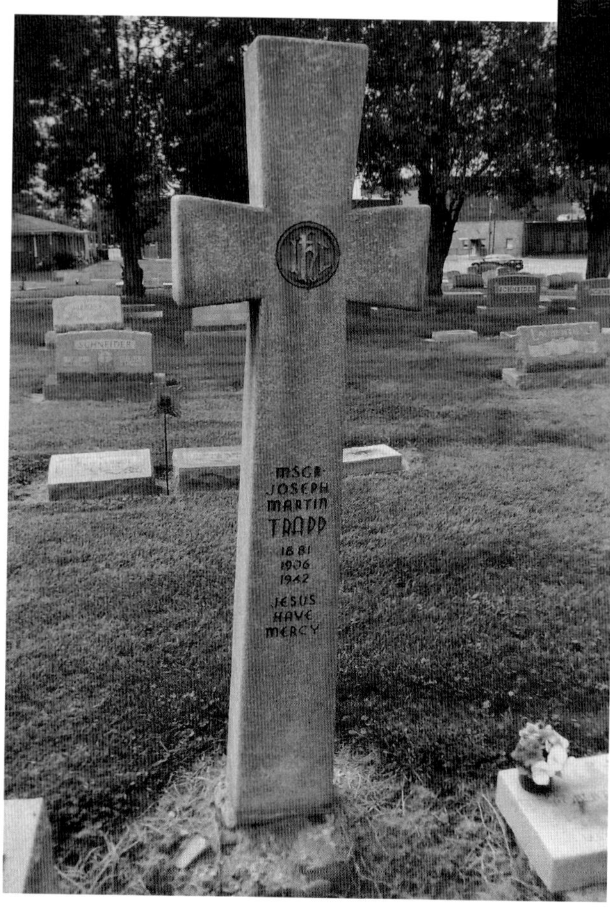
MSGR.
JOSEPH
MARTIN
TRAPP
1881
1906
1942
JESUS
HAVE
MERCY

Rev. Joseph Trapp

On June 9, 1909, the Reverend Joseph Trapp was appointed resident pastor of St. Peter Catholic Church. On June 21, Trapp and his predecessor, the Reverend Anthony Stuber, purchased 16 acres of the John Juchem farm for $6,000. The property was located off State Route 20, east of Route 83. He also bought an additional lot east of that from Nicholas Smith for $325. It had become necessary to build not only a new rectory and school, but a new church, as well.

Trapp and his councilmen asked the parish for funds to build a new school, and they collected $3,335. Paul Rissman, an architect from Lorain, was hired to draw plans. Construction would cost about $10,000. The cornerstone was laid on September 25, 1909, and more than 2,500 people, along with many clergymen, came from surrounding towns to see the parade and ceremony. Trapp engaged the Notre Dame nuns to teach, and the school opened in 1911.

Tragedy struck on January 15, 1914, at 9:30 a.m., when a fire destroyed the church within an hour's time. The pastor was not there; he was at St. Ignatius Church in Cleveland burying his brother. When he arrived, he saw nothing but burning embers. The total loss to the building and contents was $12,500. When the school was built, it included an extra-large room for a classroom-chapel combination so that the parishioners had a place to worship. There were collections and fundraisers for a new church. In the winter of 1915, the cemetery bridge collapsed due to heavy floods. Fortunately, parishioners were able to repair it.

In 1920, Trapp was transferred to Holy Trinity Parish in Avon. For more than 11 years, Trapp had run St. Peter effectively. He erected a brick school building, which was paid in full, and left his successor $34,000 in the building fund for a new church. On May 15, 1929, he ministered to many victims of a disaster at the Cleveland Clinic, and he inhaled poisonous gas, which began a long illness that eventually led to his death.

In addition to his priestly duties, Trapp enjoyed photography. His images of people and sites in Ridgeville, such as the photograph below, are today part of the city's pictorial history. (All, courtesy of the North Ridgeville Historical Society.)

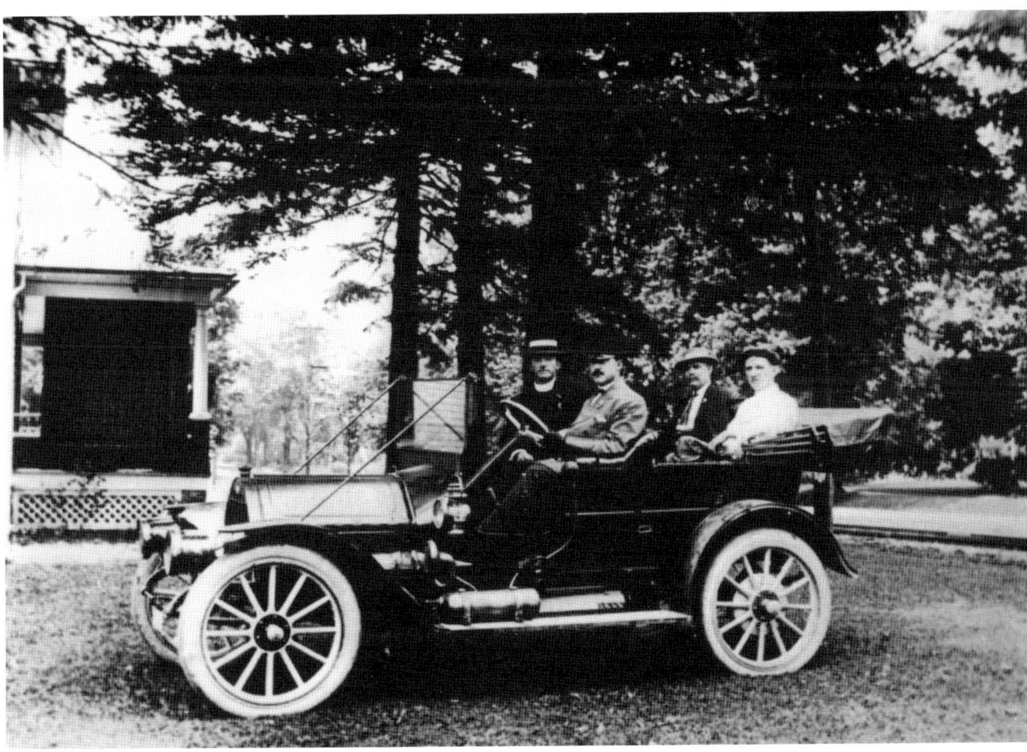

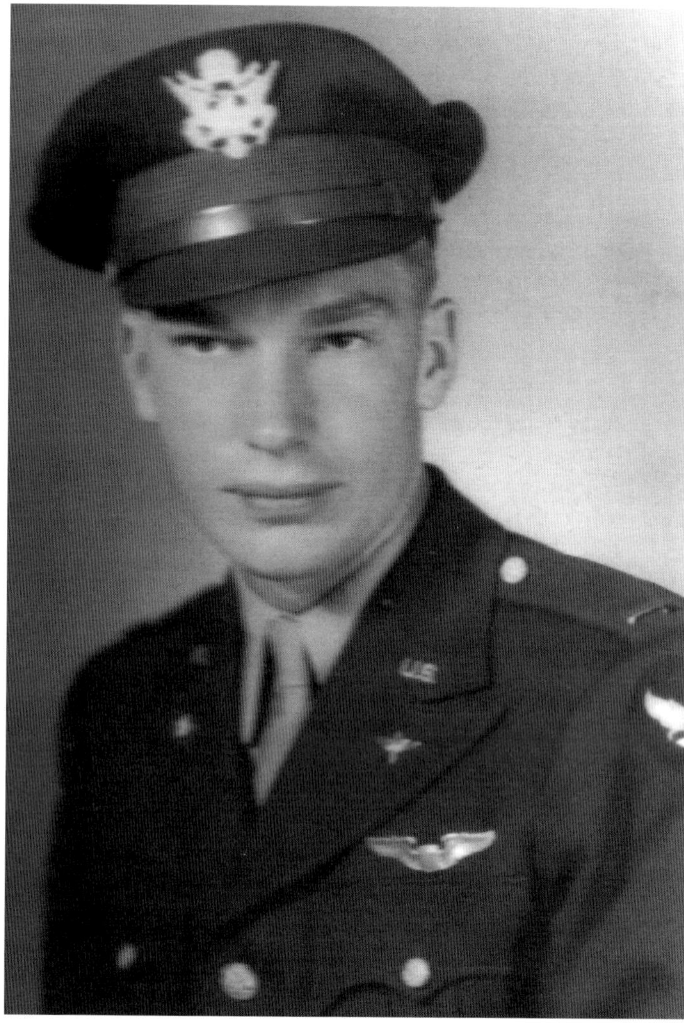

Russell Sigsworth

When he was a youngster, Sigsworth made model airplanes and hung them around his bedroom. When he was about 17, he enlisted in the Army Air Force. Following basic training, he went into the Aviation Cadet Program. By the time he was 19, he had a crew. Sigsworth enjoyed flying. When he made first lieutenant, he was flying a B-25 bomber and continued for 26 missions in the Pacific from New Guinea to Japan. He recalled flying so low that he could see the feathers on chickens.

His mother, Mabel, worked as a nurse at Elyria Memorial Hospital after graduating from M.B. Johnson School of Nursing. His brother, John Sigsworth, was also in the military. In 1944, John was shot down and taken to a Nazi prison camp for nine months. As difficult as it was for his mother, Russell said, "Mother knew we had to do it."

On August 6, 1945, the atomic bomb was dropped on Hiroshima and a second one was soon dropped on Nagasaki. On August 15, the Japanese surrendered. Sigsworth said that after the surrender, a photographer asked him to fly over the bombing sites in order to get photographs. Sigsworth also took some photographs with a small camera of his own but never had them developed.

Sigsworth was in the Air Force from 1943 to 1946, but admitted that it was good to get back home, and it was a relief that the war was over. He said that some people claimed that the Japanese were brutal, but he does not hold anything against them. (Courtesy of Russell Sigsworth.)

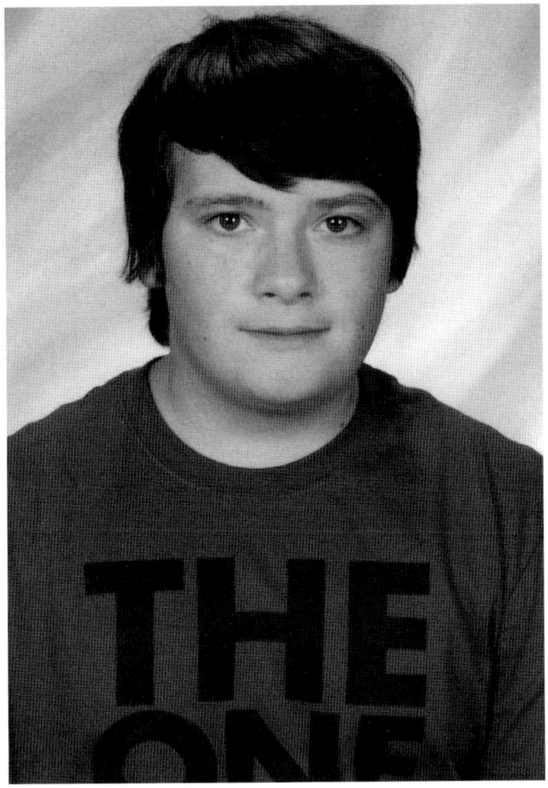

Alex Sismour

Alex Sismour had the face of a cherub and a smile that could provoke his friends into laughter. He loved sports and was always joking. His mother, Doreen Sismour, said, "He was very, very bright." But at 3:48 p.m. on September 10, 2011, at age 14, the life of the happy-go-lucky teen ended when a Dodge minivan struck his dirt bike as he crossed Route 57 at East Broad Street in Elyria.

Alex was always asking to ride his bike to wherever he was going, but "We drove him everywhere," his mother said. Alex always insisted, "Mom, I am not going to get hit by a car."

The day of the accident, Alex and his friends wanted to go down Chestnut Ridge Road to McDonald's, but there was too much traffic, and the speed limit was 45 mph. He was disappointed, but decided they could ride on Sugar Ridge Road, where the speed limit is just 35 mph. They could then get to McDonald's on the other side of Route 57.

Doreen Sismour said she was going out when the telephone rang. "Alex got hit," a voice said. She had heard no ambulance. She thought Alex had gone down Chestnut Ridge Road, so she and her husband, Brian, headed in the wrong direction. She could not think. The whole scenario was a horrible nightmare. By the time the family got to the accident scene, an ambulance was taking Alex to EMH Medical Center. He died at 4:40 p.m. When they arrived home, drained and exhausted, the family found crowds of people in the street, wishing to show the Sismours that they cared.

At the funeral home, Brian Sismour kept saying to himself, "What are we doing here?" From then on, neighbors and friends took care of everything. "The food kept coming and coming," Doreen said. Despite all the help, Doreen had just one thought, "Alex will always be 14 and a half." When the family returned home after the funeral, they were greeted by hundreds of luminaries up and down the streets of their development, glowing in Alex's honor.

Every day is a struggle for Brian, Doreen, and their older son, Andrew. Saturdays are the hardest, because that is the day Alex died. But Doreen Sismour will always remember, "Alex is the boy who brought a community together." (Courtesy of the Sismour family.)

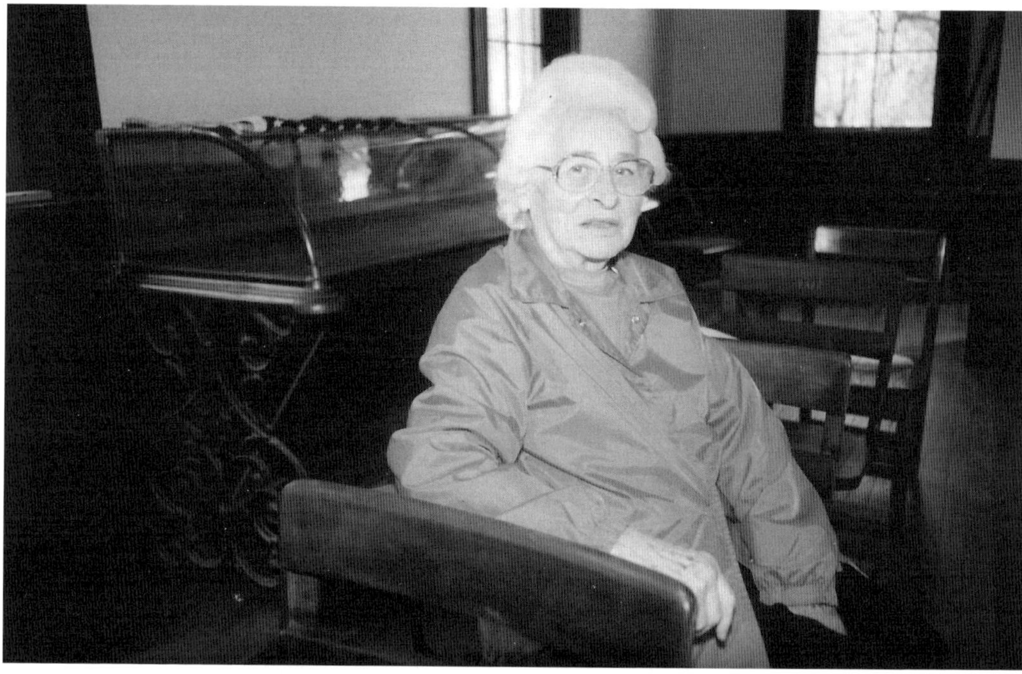

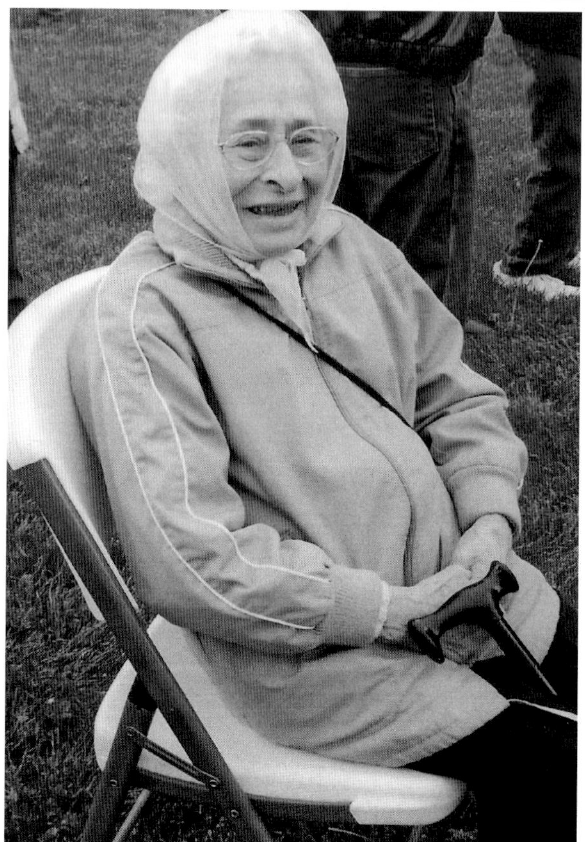

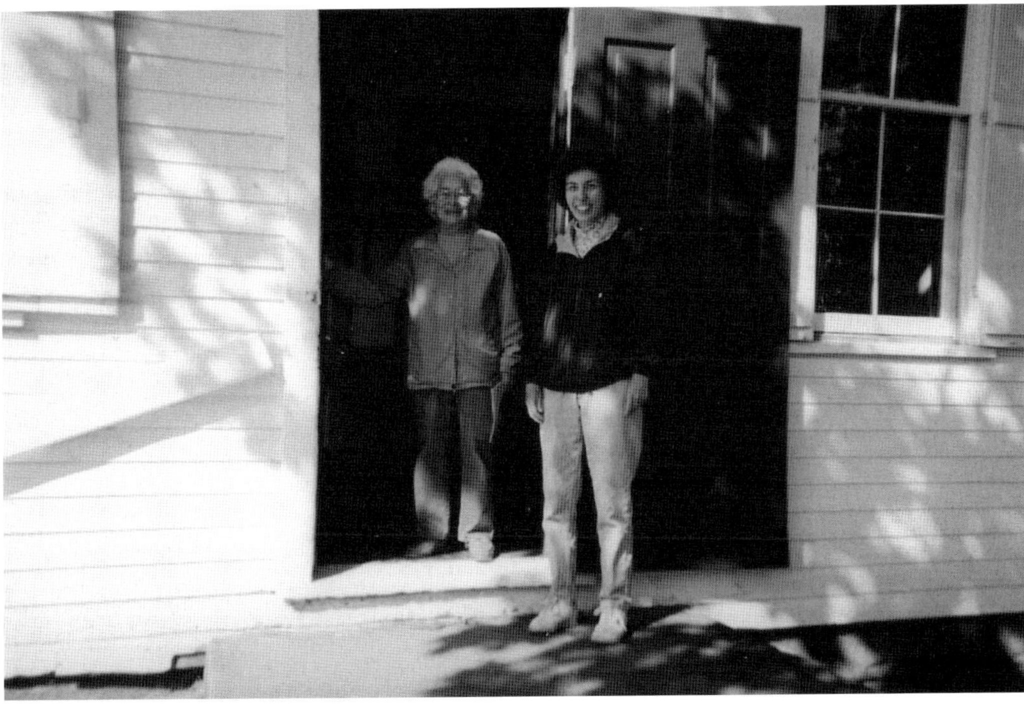

Lois Sullivan

Lois Sullivan was what some would call a legend in her own time. She was born on March 16, 1920, and graduated from Lorain High School in 1938. She moved to Ridgeville in 1941, long before it became a city. At that time, she knew just about everyone and everything about the town.

Sullivan was as active as they come, and more so than most. She was involved in the Senior Center, St. Peter Church, the Farm Bureau, and Self Help for the Hard of Hearing. One of her favorite organizations was the North Ridgeville Historical Society, of which she was a member for over 25 years. She helped with fundraisers, especially the annual Swiss steak dinners that the historical society held. She was always the top ticket seller. Sullivan enjoyed volunteering at the open houses at the museum and would often provide refreshments there and at the monthly meetings.

She was an activist and rarely missed a city council meeting. When she did attend, she often expressed an opinion or asked a question. She was thoroughly convinced that the reason there was so much flooding in the community was due to the number of houses being built. She would openly complain about "rooftops and concrete," and had no problem giving city officials a piece of her mind.

When the overpass was completed on State Route 83, she felt it should have a name. She suggested "Shawville Station Overpass." But, whatever name was chosen, she did not want it to be after a politician. Her husband's family, the Sullivans, donated the one-room schoolhouse on Jaycox Road to the historical society, and she loved to go each spring and help give the inside a good cleaning to ready it for open houses. Pictured above are Sullivan (left) and Karen Sigsworth at the schoolhouse.

Sullivan died on January 2, 2013. When she was laid out in her casket, she had a fork clutched in her hand. The reason went back to times when diners were admonished to save their forks for something better, like dessert. The clergyman said Sullivan always knew something better was coming—heaven. (All, courtesy of the North Ridgeville Historical Society.)

INDEX